Planning and Teaching Creatively Within a Required Curriculum for Adult Learners

ANNE BURNS and
HELEN DE SILVA JOYCE, EDITORS

TESOL Language Curriculum Development Series

KATHLEEN GRAVES, Series Editor

 Teachers of English to Speakers of Other Languages, Inc.

Typeset in Adobe Garamond with Frutiger Display
by Capitol Communication Systems, Inc., Crofton, Maryland USA
Printed by United Graphics, Inc., Mattoon, Illinois USA
Indexed by Pueblo Indexing and Publishing Services, Pueblo West, Colorado USA

Teachers of English to Speakers of Other Languages, Inc.
700 South Washington Street, Suite 200
Alexandria, Virginia 22314 USA
Tel 703-836-0774 • Fax 703-836-6547 • E-mail tesol@tesol.org • http://www.tesol.org/

Publishing Manager: Carol Edwards
Copy Editor: Ellen Garshick
Additional Reader: Sarah J. Duffy
Cover Design: Capitol Communication Systems, Inc.

Copyright © 2007 by Teachers of English to Speakers of Other Languages, Inc. (TESOL).

All rights reserved. No part of this publication may be reproduced or transmitted in any form or by any means, electronic or mechanical, including photocopy, or any informational storage and retrieval system, without permission from the publisher.

Every effort has been made to contact the copyright holders for permission to reprint borrowed material. TESOL regrets any oversights that may have occurred and will rectify them in future printings of this work.

All names of teachers, teacher learners, and students are pseudonyms or are used with permission. Teacher and student work samples and photos are used with permission.

"The Experiential Cycle" in chapter 6 from *An Experiential Approach to Outdoor/Social Education With EFL Students* (p. 27), by M. Davies, 1989, Cambridge: Bell Educational Trust. Reprinted with permission.

"The Teaching-Learning Cycle" in chapter 10 from *Writing a Book Review: A Unit of Work for Junior Secondary English* (Write it Right Resources for Literacy and Learning), by J. Rothery and M. Stenglin, 1994, Sydney, Australia: Metropolitan East Disadvantaged Schools Programme. Reprinted with permission.

ISBN 978-1-931185400
Library of Congress Control No. 2007900243

Contents

Series Editor's Preface v

Acknowledgments ix

1. Challenging Requirements: How Teachers Navigate to Make Changes Within Required Curricula 1
   Anne Burns and Helen de Silva Joyce

2. Sowing the Seeds: An Innovative Gardening Project 15
   Valerie Bainbridge and Janine Oldfield

3. The Transition From School to University: Learning New Behavior and Skills 43
   Janet M. D. Higgins

4. Maintaining the Learning: EFL Teacher Education in Vietnam 59
   Martyn Brogan

5. Innovations in Curriculum Development: Crossing Cultures, Crossing Generations 93
   Abigail Brown and Jennifer Wharton

6. Foreign Eyes on Thailand: An ESP Project for EFL Learners 119
   John Knox

7. No Textbook? No Problem! Reading and Writing With a Nonfiction Bestseller 143
   Sarah Dodson-Knight

8   When Writing Is *Murder:* Transforming a Composition Course With a Mystery Novel..........................161
      Todd Heyden

9   The Motive, Means, Method, and Magic of Using the Arts in a Grammar-Based Adult ESL Program......................177
      Kristin Lems

10   Responding to Learners' Language Needs in an Oral EFL Class 189
      John McAndrew

11   Not the Puppet Anymore: Infusing Critical Inquiry Into a Business Presentation Curriculum................................205
      Martin Momoda

12   Surviving a Crash Course in EAP Writing: A Cambodian Experience...221
      Stephen H. Moore

13   *Chifa:* Freewriting Within a Required Curriculum for Adults..239
      Spencer Salas and Kyra Garson

References 247

About the Editors and Contributors..259

Index...263

Series Editor's Preface

The aim of TESOL's Language Curriculum Development Series is to provide real-world examples of how a language curriculum is developed, adapted, or renewed in order to encourage readers to carry out their own curriculum innovation. Curriculum development may not be the sexiest of topics in language teaching, but it is surely one of the most vital: at its core, a curriculum is what happens among learners and teachers in classrooms.

Curriculum as a Dynamic System

In its broadest sense, a curriculum is the nexus of educational decisions, activities, and outcomes in a particular setting. As such, it is affected by explicit and implicit social expectations, educational and institutional policies and norms, teachers' beliefs and understandings, and learners' needs and goals. It is not a set of documents or a textbook, although classroom activities may be guided, governed, or hindered by such documents. Rather, it is a dynamic system. This system can be conceptualized as three interrelated processes: planning, enacting (i.e., teaching and learning), and evaluating, as depicted in the figure on p. vi.

Planning processes include

- analyzing the needs of learners, the expectations of the institution and other stakeholders, and the availability of resources
- deciding on the learning aims or goals and the steps needed to achieve them, and organizing them in a principled way
- translating the aims and steps into materials and activities

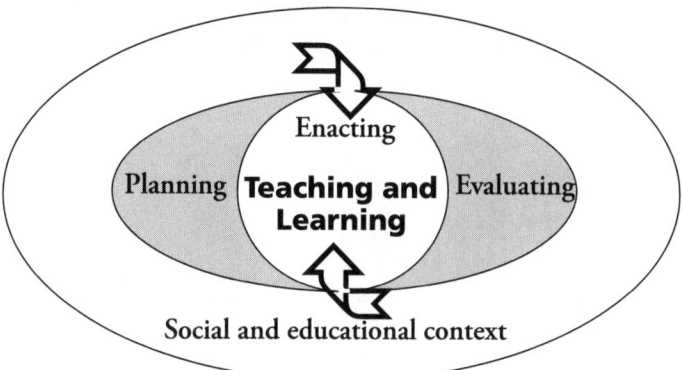

Teaching and learning processes include

- using the materials and doing the activities in the classroom
- adjusting them according to learners' needs, abilities, and interests
- learning with, about, and from each other

Evaluation processes include

- assessing learners' progress toward and achievement of the aims
- adjusting the aims in response to learners' abilities and needs
- gathering information about the effectiveness of the aims, organization, materials, and activities, and using this information in planning and teaching

These processes create a system that is at once stable, rooted in what has gone before, and evolving as it responds to change, to new ideas, and to the people involved. People plan, enact, and evaluate a curriculum.

The Series: Educators Bringing about Change

In these volumes, readers will encounter teachers, curriculum developers, and administrators from all over the world who sought to understand their learners' needs and capacities and respond to them in creative, realistic, and effective ways. The volumes focus on different ways in which curriculum is developed or renewed:

- Volume 1: Developing a new curriculum for school-age learners
- Volume 2: Planning and teaching creatively within a required curriculum for school-age learners
- Volume 3: Revitalizing a curriculum for school-age learners
- Volume 4: Developing a new course for adult learners
- Volume 5: Developing a new curriculum for adult learners
- Volume 6: Planning and teaching creatively within a required curriculum for adult learners
- Volume 7: Revitalizing an established program for adult learners

The boundaries between a program and a curriculum are blurred, as are the boundaries between a curriculum and a course. *Curriculum* is used in its broadest sense to mean planning, teaching, and evaluating a course of study (e.g., a grade two curriculum or a university writing curriculum). A *course* is a stand-alone or a specific offering within a curriculum, such as a computer literacy course for intermediate students. A *program* is all of the courses or courses of study offered in a particular institution or department, for example, the high school ESL program.

The overarching theme of these volumes is how educators bring about change. Change is rarely straightforward or simple. It requires creative thinking, collaboration, problematizing, negotiation, and reflection. It involves trial and error, setbacks and breakthroughs, and occasional tearing out of hair. It takes time. The contributors to these volumes invite you into their educational context and describe how it affects their work. They introduce you to their learners—school-age children or adults—and explain the motivation for the curriculum change. They describe what they did, how they evaluated it, and what they learned from it. They allow you to see what is, at its heart, a creative human process. In so doing, they guide the way for you as a reader to set out on the path of your own curriculum innovation and learning.

This Volume

Most language teaching practitioners work within some form of required curriculum. The contributors to this volume provide powerful, engaging accunts of how they adapted or shaped the curriculum to meet the language and learning needs of their adult learners. These living accounts of English language curricula portray the excitement of classes in which learners design a community garden, collaborate with local elementary schools, analyze discourse, write children's literature, prepare research papers, read novels and poetry, interview tourists, conduct action research and learn critical questioning techniques. The introductory chapter provides a cogent analysis of what motivates practitioners to make changes in a required curriculum, the range of models of required curricula, the types of change that are possible, teh process of change, and the central role of practitioners in bringing about change. In each of the following chapters practitioners from Australia, Cambodia, Japan, Peru, Thailand, the United States, and Vietnam describe their context, what they wanted to change and why, the principled and innovative changes they undertook, their missteps and successes, and what they learned throughout the process. These accounts aim to encourage and inspire practitioners to explore and effect change within their own curriculum.

Dedication

This series is dedicated to Marilyn Kupetz, a gifted editor, a generous mentor, and a discerning colleague. The quality of TESOL publications, including this series, is due in no small part to her vision, attention to detail, and care.

Kathleen Graves

Acknowledgments

Editing this book has given us a great deal of pleasure in a number of ways.

We have been most fortunate to work with the contributors, all dedicated and inspiring teachers, who were prepared to open up their classrooms and to show how they persisted in making changes in practice that would benefit their students, often against the odds. Their accounts should inspire other critically reflective teachers to consider how to approach curriculum problems and puzzles in adult classrooms in creative and innovative ways. We thank them for their patience in working with us and for the readiness with which they responded to our suggestions and queries. We also thank them for what we have learned about effective practices in the adult classroom.

Kathleen Graves, the series editor, provided us not only with an invitation to edit the book in the first place, but also with gracious and ready responses to our many requests for feedback on the contributions and for guidance in bringing the volume together.

We also thank Ellen Garshick for her fantastic copyediting of the manuscript and Marilyn Kupetz and Carol Edwards for their generous editorial management and insights.

As colleagues and authors who have worked together on several previous publications, it was a particular pleasure for us to be able to edit jointly a volume published by TESOL. We are conscious of the role that TESOL publications play in the professional development of English language teachers worldwide. It is our hope that this volume makes a contribution to this endeavor.

Anne Burns and Helen de Silva Joyce

Challenging Requirements: How Teachers Navigate to Make Changes Within Required Curricula

ANNE BURNS AND HELEN DE SILVA JOYCE

The contributors to this volume all teach adult English language learners and were involved in negotiating creative changes to the curriculum they were required to teach by their educational institutions. As you read their contributions, you will see that the changes they made were motivated by a variety of factors. Some teachers were motivated by a desire to meet the requirements of a prescribed curriculum in ways that better suited the learning styles of their students. Others wanted to collaborate more closely with their students in order to give greater purpose to the teaching and learning situation. Some of the teachers wanted to confront what they perceived to be ineffective curricula that limited student achievement and motivation, while some wished to experiment with new and unfamiliar approaches. Other teachers were inspired by their interests outside the classroom, such as literature and the arts, and wanted to use these with their students to creative effect in the classroom. Another underlying factor that often leads teachers to introduce change is a desire to keep themselves engaged in teaching, to avoid becoming bored teachers.

The changes the teachers describe in this volume occurred in very different teaching contexts around the world and interacted in various ways with local factors in those contexts. All the contributors taught students who were over the age of 18 years and who brought to the classroom a great variability in learning skills, motivations, and attributes. Some of the highly educated students had well-developed English language skills and were working to pursue educational aspirations. They were enrolled in *English for academic purposes* (EAP) programs, and their teachers were striving to prepare them for university study that required English as a compulsory course or for studying in a particular discipline (chapter 7, by Dodson-Knight). Some of the EAP teachers made changes to their programs because their students lacked motivation (chapter 8, by Heyden) or behaved inappropriately in academic contexts (chapter 3, by Higgins).

Other teachers were involved in *English for specific purposes* (ESP) programs, where students were developing English skills for particular vocational ends, such as tourism (chapter 6, by Knox) or business (chapter 11, by Momoda). In one account, the students were themselves preparing to be teachers of English, and their learning needed to engage with their future professional realities (chapter 4, by Brogan).

Two of the teachers worked with students who had experienced few opportunities for schooling and consequently had restricted literacy skills in their first language and in English (chapter 2, by Bainbridge & Oldfield). Two other teachers took themselves and their students into an elementary school as a way of merging educational experiences that are typically separated (chapter 5, by Brown & Wharton). They believed that the learning outcomes in both contexts were complementary and that the students in each context would gain social as well as educational benefits from working together.

Some of the curriculum changes took place in contexts where English is spoken as the dominant language, such as Australia (chapter 2, by Bainbridge & Oldfield) or the United States (chapter 9, by Lems). Programs in these contexts are typically described as *English as a second language* (ESL), *English to speakers of other languages* (ESOL), or sometimes *English as an additional language* (EAL). Other innovations occurred where students had limited exposure to English outside the classroom, in what are usually called *English as a foreign language* (EFL) contexts, such as Cambodia (chapter 12, by Moore) or Peru (chapter 13, by Salas & Garson).

However, these accounts show that teachers working within these different fields of English language education are not confined to particular types of practices and, indeed, face similar challenges and demands. These terms, commonly used to segregate the field, carry associations and assumptions that can blind educators to the similarities in teaching practice and curriculum challenges. The teacher-authors of these accounts sought to interrogate professionally and creatively what was possible within the particularities of their local teaching situations and to push the boundaries of restrictive expectations. Despite the differences in the contexts and orientations of their teaching situations, they all shared a common goal: a desire to sustain a viable and effective curriculum that reflected their values, beliefs, and ideals as language teaching professionals.

Over the past decade, there have been increasing calls to situate the teacher's voice more centrally in professional debates. It is argued that teachers' interpretations of their daily work will enrich the endeavor of the language teaching field to develop theories of teaching and to understand how curricula are enacted in classrooms. These calls make the accounts in this volume of particular interest. Each of the chapters is written from the perspective of a practicing teacher who is intimately involved in classroom processes rather than from the point of view of external researchers observing from a distance. Thus the accounts are deeply emic in nature, not only providing personal narratives of curriculum change, but also showing how the writers made sense of those changes within their own socioeducational contexts. Therefore, they provide the means for other teachers to compare and contrast the issues raised with their own classroom situations and to reflect creatively on how and why change might be initiated, even in classroom situations that can seem impossibly prescribed.

The Required Curriculum

McKay (2006) suggests that "a required curriculum is one in which learning outcomes are established by the system (e.g., the education department or the school)" (p. 2). However, aspects other than outcomes of learning can be required elements of a curriculum. The teacher could be required, for example, to adhere closely to set syllabus specifications that closely detail the activities and content for each lesson. Such syllabi are often developed by curriculum designers working in national or international organizations, or are accredited and approved according to institutional requirements through a *center-to-periphery* model. More locally, a syllabus may be produced by directors of study or educational managers catering for typical student profiles through a *generic* model. Alternatively, the institution may prescribe a textbook to follow, with little opportunity for the teacher to deviate from the activities within it. In this case, the textbook becomes a de facto curriculum, whether it is locally appropriate or not. Some organizations specify general course goals in terms of language proficiencies to be achieved by the students, and the responsibility for defining more specific objectives, learning sequences, activities, textbooks, and assessment is left to the teacher. This process-oriented approach could be defined as a *goals-objectives* model. Alternatively, teachers may be required to work to specified standards or outcomes, as McKay (2006, p. 2) suggests. These kinds of requirements are characteristic of an *outcomes* model or product-oriented approach, in which the teacher must test or assess students on specified results of learning regardless of teaching approaches or curriculum processes.

The accounts in this volume show how the teachers worked across the

Required Curriculum Models			
Model	Characteristics	Involvement of teachers	Chapters in this volume
Center to periphery	Produced in a location distant from actual teaching context and applied locally	Usually designed by those considered to be curriculum specialists; teachers may be involved	Brogan (chapter 4)
Generic	Produced locally for application to typical groups of students	Usually designed by directors or managers; teachers may be involved	Higgins (chapter 3); Dodson-Knight (chapter 7); Lems (chapter 9)
De facto	Produced implicitly by the textbook	Designed by textbook writers; teachers may be involved in trialing	Heyden (chapter 8); McAndrew (chapter 10); Salas & Garson (chapter 13)
Goals-objectives	Produced to meet generalized goals and objectives assumed to be suitable for typical groups of students	Designed by curriculum writers, teachers, or both	Momoda (chapter 11); Moore (chapter 12)
Outcomes	Produced to meet outcomes and standards identified externally to the classroom	Usually designed by curriculum writers or funding bodies	Bainbridge & Oldfield (chapter 2); Brown & Wharton (chapter 5); Knox (chapter 6)

full range of required curriculum models. Required Curriculum Models identifies these models, their major characteristics, and the extent to which teachers are generally involved in the development of these models. The right-hand column identifies the contributors to this volume who worked within these curricula.

Although curriculum models can be characterized in this way, you will realize as you read the chapters that the categories are highly variable across strong and weak interpretations of curriculum characteristics. The notion of *required,* when applied to the curriculum, shifts along a continuum. Teachers may find themselves operating at one extreme in a very rigid situation of explicitly required expectations or at the other extreme in a context where the curriculum requirements consist of unexamined assumptions about "the ways things are done here." For example, Lems describes a highly controlled situation, in which the teachers were required to follow rigidly defined content and language structures prescribed for each lesson, whereas the curriculum within which Dodson-Knight worked required her to follow a general syllabus outline and a specified textbook.

The Drive to Change

The accounts in this volume all relate to situations in which teachers were obliged to implement components of an existing curriculum that they had little or no involvement in designing. Such situations are common for language teachers worldwide, but they do not imply that there is no room for negotiation, innovation, and change. The question that this volume explores through firsthand accounts from teachers is this: What drives a teacher, working within a required curriculum, to make creative changes and innovations?

The teachers whose accounts you are about to read all identified a gap of some kind between what is required and what is desired, between their critical assessment of the situation and what they regarded as beneficial for themselves and their students. Breen and Littlejohn (2000) argue that this type of perceptual gap gives rise to an evolving curriculum, "which would include the group's aims, content, ways of working or evaluation procedures which are amalgams of what they see as prescribed or required and what they regard as their own priorities and preferences" (p. 34). Such an evolving curriculum can change from one that is fixed, reutilized, and reproductive to one that is fluid, experimental, and productive. Evolution of the curriculum becomes a way of resolving tensions between the teacher's reality, expectations, and values.

Change may be motivated by something that stimulates a teacher's professional interest or curiosity, such as new theoretical ideas that begin to influence the teacher's view of the curriculum. Brogan and Moore describe how they used the concepts of action research and genre theory, respectively, to effect change and introduce innovative approaches into their teaching. Salas and Garson's interest in the theoretical literature on freewriting led them to introduce creative modifications into their teaching of writing courses, and McAndrew's own learning about theories of discourse analysis and scaffolding led him to underpin his teaching activities with these new concepts.

In other cases, change might come primarily from a strong drive to meet realistic and authentic student needs or to merge what happens in the classroom with the students' out-of-class experiences. This is the situation Knox describes, in which his concern was to help students see how English would be used as a central aspect of their future careers. Bainbridge and Oldfield, working with Aboriginal students in Australia, understood that, if real learning was to take place, the curriculum had to be adapted to the students' lived cultural experiences and become responsive to their contextualized needs.

Another factor that might drive a teacher to seek change is a sense that the curriculum, as it stands, engenders problems of an affective or psychological nature. Momoda became sensitized to the disjuncture between his students' cultural socialization and the performance expectations implicit in the curriculum. In an academic situation where apathetic students behaved inappropriately, Higgins needed to become a change agent, overturning unproductive attitudes toward education while motivating colleagues at an institutional level. Brown and Wharton saw a way to give social, cognitive, and emotional meaning to classroom writing tasks by engaging their students in producing stories for local elementary school children.

A strong sense of student disadvantage can also be a reason for pushing against a required curriculum. Dodson-Knight believed that the prescribed textbook seriously disadvantaged her students in preparing for university study and provided them with erroneous messages about language learning. Lems was convinced that the tightly controlled grammar-based curriculum she was forced to use discriminated against her students' potential achievement and relegated them to seeing language learning as boring and unproductive.

Teaching creatively and adaptively within a required curriculum can be a high-stakes venture for a teacher. In some cases, the teachers featured in this volume had to find the persistence, and even the courage, to continue the change process in the face of opposition from managers, colleagues, and students. The desire to find optimal learning conditions and outcomes for their students was the strong motivational driver for all of these teachers. It led them to challenge the systems in which they worked and struggle with the changes they believed needed to be made.

The Extent of Change

Curriculum change is a complex process involving dynamic responses to the question "Who adopts what, where, when, why and how?" (Cooper, 1989, cited in Markee, 2001, p. 43). Markee points out that, in any attempt to promote innovation in educational contexts, the participants involved potentially play different kinds of social roles that define their relationships with others. They can be adopters (mandators of new curricula or syllabi), implementers (teachers activating the changes in the classroom), clients (students receiving the innovation), suppliers (curriculum and materials writers), change agents (initiating the changes), or resisters (apart from change agents, any of the people in the roles described). These roles are not mutually exclusive, and within the scope of curriculum activity, teachers may take up more than one role. The teachers in this volume were all expected to be implementers of an existing curriculum but made the decision also to become

- change agents who perceived a pressing need for change
- suppliers who produced new curriculum methodologies, tasks, processes, or products

For some contributors, these roles became cyclical as they reentered the cycle of change to initiate new tasks or processes or to implement them in the classroom.

Change processes can also result in very different kinds of outcomes that interact with the ongoing sustainability of the innovation. The sociocultural context of the educational organization, and its openness to change initiated by teachers, will have a strong impact on the extent to which change influences others in the educational context, is diffused into the curriculum, and is sustained.

The Scale of Change Through Curriculum Innovation shows how the impact of change might vary, as illustrated by the chapters in this volume. In some instances, broad change became possible across a whole institution

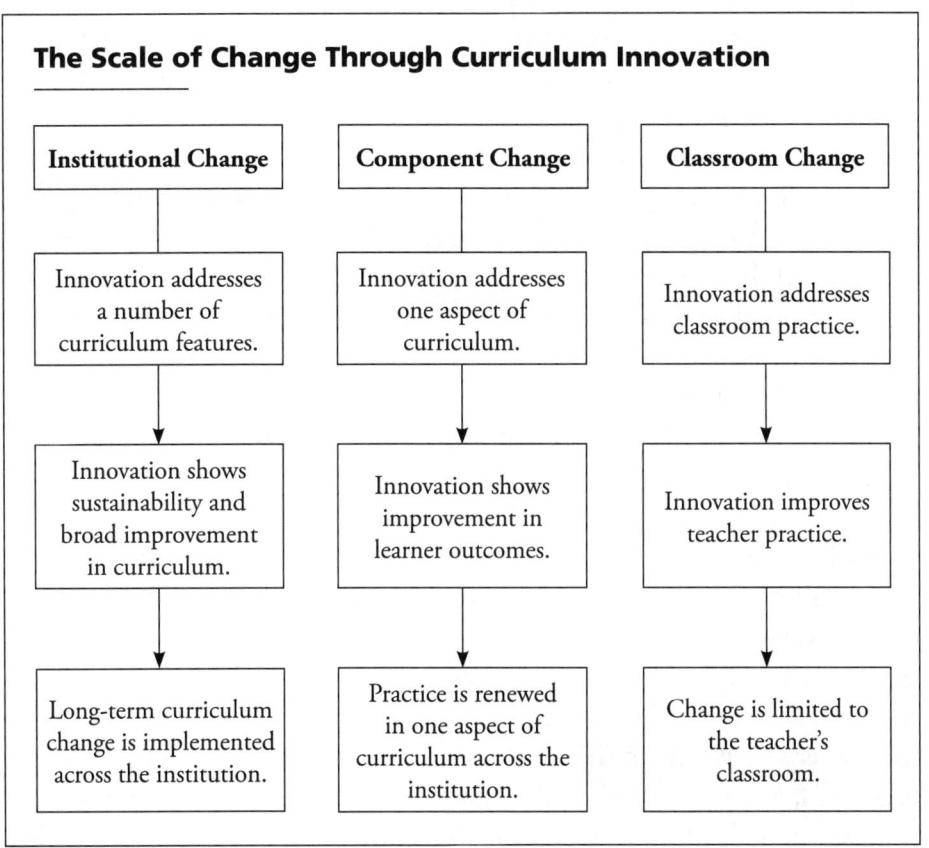

and motivated continuing curriculum improvement. In other instances, the impact of change was limited to specific classrooms but was nevertheless significant for teacher professionalization and student learning.

The chapters by Bainbridge and Oldfield and by Higgins illustrate *institutional change,* which eventually permeated the whole organization. Bainbridge and Oldfield were able to align two existing curriculum frameworks to introduce methodological changes that met required curriculum outcomes. With some modifications, their changes continued into future curriculum delivery. Higgins was able to develop a study skills course for first-year students in a Japanese university that began as a short orientation course and is now a compulsory seminar delivered across the academic year.

Component change involves innovation in certain elements of the curriculum that might be taken up more broadly across the institution. Brogan describes how he introduced action research tasks into a teacher training program in Vietnam to encourage teachers to maintain a reflective and exploratory approach in their current and future teaching contexts. This change has continued in the teacher training institution. Brown and Wharton brought together teachers from two institutions—an elementary school and a college in Hawaiʻi—to develop new writing methodologies that would meet the outcomes of two diverse curricula. These changes are continuing through materials made available to future teachers in these programs. Knox developed a learner-centered, learner-generated project within an English for tourism course at a university in Thailand. He needed the university's support to engage the airport authorities in the project, which involved students interviewing outbound tourists at Bangkok Airport. The project was maintained in subsequent courses, but students had more flexibility in terms of where they could interview tourists.

Seven of the chapters provide examples of *classroom change,* which is perhaps more typical of what teachers can achieve within the constraints of most institutions. Changing from a required set of readings to a nonfiction bestseller allowed Dodson-Knight to unify the approach to academic writing in a U.S. university. Not only did her own teaching practices change, but she continues to develop ways of using a single book to model writing skills. Heyden believed that a single text, a mystery novel, would provide contextualized content for U.S. ESL university students in New York and improve their writing. Although his students were successful and he attempted to convince the institution to make an overall change in curriculum, he experienced resistance to wider changes that he is still attempting to overcome. Lems integrated music and artistic activities into an EAP course at a Midwestern university in the United States to offset the effects of a highly prescribed, grammar-based curriculum and a high-stakes examination. In her institutional context, she was forced to turn her innovations into a hidden curriculum, although the responses of her students convinced her that her approach brings rewards for both teachers and students.

McAndrew's dissatisfaction with a set textbook led him to use learner-generated spoken discourse as the starting point to develop conversation skills in an EFL course in Japan. Although he still needed to confront the institution's and his students' traditional beliefs about language teaching, the project was successful for a particular group of learners at a particular time and in a particular context. Momoda embarked on a cycle of observation, reflection, and revision as he introduced a new approach to teaching business students how to give effective spoken presentations in English. The change helped the students modify cultural attitudes and behavior and develop more engaging presentations.

In Cambodia, Moore, who felt relatively inexperienced in his teaching context, sought a way to help students improve their academic writing. Discarding the textbook, he developed scaffolded sequences of activities that enabled the students to develop skills in writing genres fundamental to academic discourse. Salas and Garson, working in Peru, found that free-writing, used in short phases within a tightly prescribed curriculum, helped students express their thoughts and perceptions about authentic, relevant, and contemporary issues and encouraged them to search independently for new vocabulary and structures.

Graves (1996) comments, "Effecting change requires both recognizing what can be changed and accepting what cannot" (p. 35). If teachers are to be change agents in their given contexts, the constraints and opportunities operating through the *who, what, why, where,* and *when* of the context cannot be overlooked. It is the extent to which the teacher is able to, and enabled to, challenge each of these variables and to problematize the specifics of the context that will result in different kinds of change processes and outcomes.

Learning From Change

The notion of professional learning through pedagogic reconceptualization is strong in each of the illustrations that the chapters provide. The practical experiences, and the act of writing about them, enable the contributors to make sense of the creative changes they explored. Burns (1996) refers to such sense making on the part of teachers as developing *theories for practice,* in contrast to the theories *of* practice put forward in the professional literature. Theories *for* practice are the implicit or explicit theories by which the teacher mediates classroom practices through the values, beliefs, and attitudes that underlie professional action.

Curriculum sustainability, as exemplified in this volume, is also the product of a strong appetite for experimentation. Although the term *action research* is not specifically used in the majority of the chapters, the mind-sets and processes of exploratory teaching (Allwright, 1993) and action-research-based approaches (Burns, 1999) toward teaching are present in all. The chapters reflect processes in the enactment of change that are commonly associated with action research: planning, acting, observing, and reflecting (Kemmis & McTaggart, 1988). Describing action-research-oriented processes and what was learned from them is valuable not only for the teachers concerned but as a professional act of sharing insights with other teachers (Burns & de Silva Joyce, 2001).

The chapters also illustrate how creative teaching involves continuous decision making in which teachers must learn to problematize and evaluate future action at each stage of the change process. The sociocultural nature of the educational environment in which change must take place means that each new step along pathways of change responds to new developments and involves new learning. The Process of Change provides a general illustration of the various points in these chapters at which teachers make decisions about implementing change.

The impetus for the types of changes described in this volume comes from teachers' dissatisfaction with the constraints of curriculum or teachers' motivation to improve their students' learning experiences. If teachers believe change is necessary, they need to decide whether they will restrict change to their own classrooms, involve colleagues, or try to stimulate change in the broader institution. Restricting change to the classroom minimizes the need to seek institutional permission to experiment, but in very closely monitored contexts, even when change is limited to the classroom, permission may still need to be sought. Broader curriculum change brings change into the open, and teachers will need to seek permission to modify approaches or materials. Involving colleagues can provide support in the change process, as different aspects of the experimentation can be discussed and different perspectives can bring new insights to the change process. This involvement can be informal or formal, through mechanisms such as committees.

Whether change is driven by individual teachers or through collaborative processes, the final decision at the end of the process is whether the effectiveness of the change warrants its continuation in subsequent courses. Individual teachers may continue to apply new approaches or methodologies because the change brought about the results they were seeking or the change process may influence institutions to implement curriculum modifications across programs. The scale of change and the lasting effects of change might vary, but all effective change in educational contexts is brought about

The Process of Change

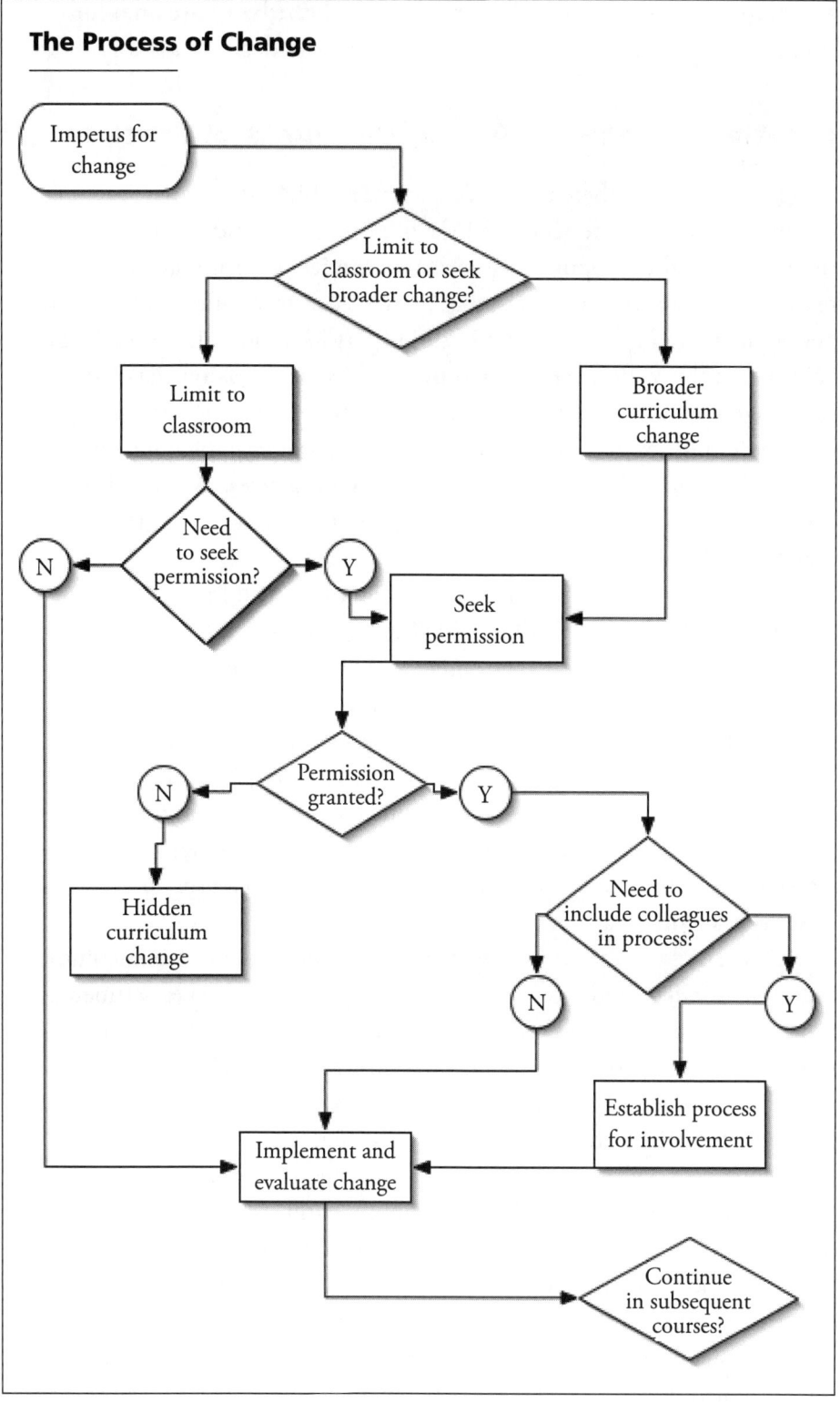

by reflective practitioners, who continue to seek the best outcomes for their students through a continuous process of reflective decision making.

Creative Changes in Action: Accounts of Practice

In most classrooms, there is only one teacher, which means that teaching can be an isolating experience and the increasing demands on teachers' time can limit their opportunity to share experiences or thoughts about teaching. Reading accounts by other teachers can be a source of professional development and a way to bring fresh insights into these classrooms. The accounts in this volume are written by teachers who took on the challenge of changing aspects of practice within prescribed curricula. These accounts describe a range of experimentation and lasting results, which may prompt you to effect change within your own teaching practices. The motivations for change will be familiar to all language teachers even though the contexts may be less familiar.

The first two chapters in the volume describe broad institutional changes. Bainbridge and Oldfield, in "Sowing the Seeds: An Innovative Gardening Project," describe a program, delivered to remote Aboriginal communities in Central Australia, in which collaboration between language teachers and content teachers provided a purpose and context for language, literacy, and numeracy learning and an impetus to implement broad curriculum change with institutional support. Higgins describes the development of a study skills program for first-year university students in Japan, which grew from a short course in orientation week to a program integrated into the academic year.

Chapters 4–6 focus on change within one component of curriculum that was sustained in delivery across institutions after initial experimentation. Brogan provides an example of how the integration of action research tasks into a teacher training course can encourage creativity in teaching and develop reflective teachers. Brown and Wharton were inspired by Frank McCourt to make learning tasks more meaningful and to provide social engagement for college students by bringing them together with elementary school students. In a private university in Thailand, Knox developed and implemented a learner-centered, learner-generated project in response to the expectations of the students that the course would enable them to use language in work situations relevant to their chosen career.

The remaining chapters focus on change limited to the teachers' classrooms, which most closely reflects the experience of most teachers. In "No Textbook? No Problem! Reading and Writing With a Nonfiction Bestseller," Dodson-Knight describes how she moved away from a prescribed academic writing textbook to a nonfiction bestseller to integrate, rather than separate, reading and writing tasks. Heyden relates a similar change with his introduction of a crime novel into a university curriculum to motivate the reluctant writers in his classroom.

Integrating the arts into the curriculum was the way Lems attempted to meet the needs of her students, especially those with less academic preparation. McAndrew's dissatisfaction with a syllabus and textbook for university students in Japan led him to design a course that used the language the students were producing as a starting point for increasing their awareness of the social nature of texts and assisting them to produce discourse appropriate to social contexts.

The discomfort of Momoda's Japanese students as they undertook spoken presentations led him to critically question the puppetlike performances of his students and to question his role as a puppetmaster. He set out to provide incentives that would change student behavior and to introduce effective communication techniques. His chapter highlights the need to base educational change on principles and constant reflection in order to sustain new developments. "Surviving a Crash Course in EAP Writing: A Cambodian Experience" describes how Moore and his students survived the course he developed on a genre-based approach to writing, delivered through scaffolded teaching sequences. Moore's experience shows how curriculum constraints can be less forbidding if the teacher and learners can work together through the change process. In the final chapter in the volume, Salas and Garson show how they introduced freewriting into the curriculum as a way of engaging students in sustained writing to increase their confidence. They draw attention to the small changes teachers can make within a broader curriculum and the advantages these can bring.

Conclusion

The chapters in this volume, like others in the Language Curriculum Development Series, offer living accounts of English language curricula as they actually occur in real classrooms for adult learners. They offer a collective contribution to the strand of research emerging in the field of second language teaching that focuses on the practical knowledge and reasoning of teachers (e.g., Freeman & Johnson, 1998). They highlight the complexity of authentic classroom situations and the way classroom practice is inevitably embedded within particular cultural contexts and animated by particular participants in socioeducational settings. The accounts also emphasize the central role the teacher plays in determining what *affordances* (van Lier, 1996) for learning are ultimately made available to students. The perspectives of creative teachers are very important, as they offer insights into how and why change is motivated in educational practice. Zeichner and Liston

(1996) explain why teachers' voices, such as those highlighted here, are critical: "Because of teachers' direct involvement in the classroom, they bring a perspective to understanding the complexities of teaching that cannot be matched by external researchers, no matter what methods of study they employ" (p. 5).

We trust that this volume offers an opportunity for teachers' perspectives to be more fully heard.

Sowing the Seeds: An Innovative Gardening Project

2

VALERIE BAINBRIDGE AND JANINE OLDFIELD

Batchelor Institute of Indigenous Tertiary Education (BIITE) and the Centre for Appropriate Technology (CAT) are two Central Australian educational institutions. We are employed by BIITE, and we worked as a program manager (Valerie) and an ESL teacher (Janine) on the project described in this chapter. Both institutions have campuses based in the Alice Springs region that provide rural and remote delivery to Indigenous communities. In 2004, the institutions collaboratively delivered two courses that they had previously delivered separately. We delivered the BIITE courses, which were the Preliminary Course in Spoken and Written English and the Certificate I in Spoken and Written English (New South Wales Adult Migrant English Service [NSW AMES], 2003).

The Certificates in Spoken and Written English (CSWE) are a five-level, nationally accredited ESL curriculum framework. The curriculum proposes 300 nominal hours to complete each level, depending on the students' learning skills. The first level of the curriculum framework is the Preliminary Course in Spoken and Written English, which addresses the needs of preliterate students. This course deals with alphabet and number recognition, form filling, basic social interaction, and social-sight words and signs. The course delivered by the building construction trainer, Robin Ellis, from CAT, was a nationally accredited construction course, Certificate I in Applied Design and Technology (CADT). The collaboration involved concurrent delivery of the two courses through a construction project, which would meet the skill development outcomes of CADT and provide a context for developing the English language and numeracy skills required in the Preliminary Course in Spoken and Written English.

The remote Central Australian community of Utopia was identified as the best place in which to deliver the courses because the women there were students of BIITE and had been involved in previous pilot collaborations between the two institutions. The recently constructed Batchelor Institute Study Centre at Utopia still needed a landscaped garden to complete the development, and, in consultation with the students, it was decided that the construction project would be to design and construct a garden. The project involved designing the garden, concreting the pathways and design features, making barbecues, and selecting and planting native species that incorporated natural bush medicine plants utilized by the women in their everyday cultural practices (see Students Making Garden Feature). These tasks directly reflected the outcomes defined in the CADT course. The CSWE literacy and numeracy tasks were based around the design and construction tasks associated with the garden project and other intersecting activities of cultural interest, such as bush medicine.

In this chapter, we describe how and why we chose to go beyond the outcomes-based CSWE curriculum in generating literacy and numeracy resources that were based around the garden project and the students' language needs and interests. In doing so, we maintained the integrity of the curriculum so as not to compromise accreditation opportunities for the students.

Students Making Garden Feature

The Motivation for the Adaptation

BIITE has taught Certificate I in Spoken and Written English and Certificate II in Spoken and Written English since 1999 to students from rural and remote Indigenous communities across the Northern Territory. English is usually the third or fourth language for these students.

The first two levels of this curriculum have been adapted for Indigenous ESL learners by BIITE. This adaptation provides opportunities to increase students' understanding of and fluency in English and provides a pathway into other tertiary courses offered by BIITE. The courses are delivered under license from NSW AMES. The curriculum defines a number of learning outcomes that take as their point of departure particular English texts, for example, descriptions and recounts. Students are expected to achieve a number of learning outcomes within different modules.

Collaborations between CAT and BIITE had begun in 2002 and had involved short, 2-week courses each semester that combined language and vocational competencies. These initial collaborations involved a group of women from a range of Central Australian communities and focused on discrete, well-defined construction tasks, such as making a picture frame and making a tucker-box (a food box). The courses combined language competencies from CSWE I, such as *Can read social sight signs and words,* and vocational CADT competencies, such as occupational health and safety procedures. In this way, literacy and numeracy had been contextualized in construction activities and knowledge.

The students had shown enthusiasm in these pilots and had been successful in terms of learning outcomes. This success led the teacher from CAT and us to consider a yearlong project that would give students the opportunity to complete the CADT and CSWE courses. We decided to conduct the project at Utopia, as previous students had above-average participation rates, and strong relationships had already been established between teaching staff and students. The fact that the students came from one region meant that delivery could be on-site and the end product of the project would be of use to the community.

The Curriculum Context

THE PARTICIPANTS AND THE COMMUNITY

The 19 women participating in the 2004 Batchelor Institute and Centre for Appropriate Technology ESL-CADT program were a strong and united group. They spoke the local Indigenous languages of Eastern Anmatyerr and Alywarr but had limited literacy in them. The women ranged in age from early 20s to early 80s and were culturally strong in that they actively maintained and participated in cultural ceremonies. The majority of the group had had limited access, if any, to formal Western schooling, given that Western primary schooling became firmly established in the district only in the mid- to late 1980s (Kral & Schwab, 2003). The 6 women who had had any significant schooling attended the Yirara College in Alice Springs, which provides the only secondary schooling in the district. Despite having left school at Year 9, they could operate in literacy and numeracy only at a Year 3 or Year 4 level. The women who had had some secondary schooling were assessed at Level I in the CSWE curriculum framework for placement and teaching purposes. The remainder of the group were assessed at the preliminary CSWE course level.

The women at Utopia had been involved in a Certificate I in Spoken and Written English program for approximately 4 years and, although highly motivated, had made minimal progress toward achieving the learning outcomes. We decided that a contextualized approach, building on the previous collaborative pilot model, might provide a higher degree of success. The CAT lecturer also saw possibilities in having the support of an ESL specialist in delivering the competencies relevant to the CADT program. The region known as Utopia is approximately 240 kilometers northeast of Alice Springs, with approximately 1,000 people living on 17 outstations (Kral & Schwab, 2003, p. 7). The people in this area still engage in traditional ceremonies and hunting activities and predominantly speak Indigenous languages, largely Eastern Anmatyerr and Alywarr, with a smattering of English (Richardson, 2001, p. 56). English can be a second, third, fourth, or even a fifth language for these students. One of the primary reasons for the level of illiteracy and innumeracy in the community is the economic and educational marginalization experienced by people at Utopia, with only one primary school servicing the community since 1969 (Kral & Schwab, 2003; Richardson, 2001).

SHARED INSTITUTIONAL PHILOSOPHIES

The low literacy and numeracy levels in the Utopia community, as well as other communities within and around Central Australia, were the initial prompt that led to the development of the CAT-BIITE collaborations. It was thought that hands-on construction tasks would better illustrate the principles of English literacy and numeracy and the inherent Western concepts, which are largely absent in the knowledge framework of remote Central Australian Indigenous students. The teachers in both institutions regard knowledge as socially constructed and language as the medium through which social meaning and knowledge are created (Cole & Wertsch, n.d.). This task-based approach was an attempt to make literacy and numeracy tasks experiential, social, and meaningful so that students could draw on their prior experience and understandings to develop English language skills.

Another important consideration was the pedagogical philosophy of Both Ways Education, which both CAT and BIITE adhere to. Loosely defined, this philosophy has come to include using the students' cultural artifacts and tools where possible, drawing on their prior knowledge and previous experiences. This approach allows shared meanings to develop between cultures and allows Indigenous and shared discourses to emerge as it provides access to dominant discourses (Jordon, 2002).

These shared institutional philosophies were evident in the project in a number of ways. In the language component, we derived model texts from the students' experiences of completing the construction tasks and, where possible, these texts were created from the students' oral discourse. Texts were also created from the students' lived experience and their knowledge of the bush, for example, plant descriptions. A number of the construction and design tasks used the students' traditional knowledge. For example, the design of the garden was based on a traditional Tjurkupa design owned by an Elder participating in the course (see Garden Model). *Ownership* in this context means inherited traditional songs, stories, and designs passed down over many generations. The design, directed by the students, also

Garden Model

incorporated the students' lifestyle preferences, which included sleeping and cooking areas. Student language and protocols were also incorporated into classroom practice. These factors transformed a generic curriculum into a curriculum that focused on processes and outcomes that were suitable for the students in terms of interest, experience, and English language usage.

The Process of Adapting the Curriculum

The teachers collaborated intensely and supported each other in the classroom. This collaboration informed teaching preparation and practice on a daily basis and resulted in an extremely fluid program that changed according to the students' needs.

COLLECTIVELY DESIGNING THE GARDEN

In the initial few weeks of the project, both the language instructor and the design instructor engaged the students in many off-site excursions in order to identify the features that they wanted to incorporate into the garden design, including trees, shrubs, flowers, herbs, bridges, seats, and barbeques. These trips conformed to the Both Ways philosophy and gave the students a sense of ownership. We took photographs of the excursions to provide a basis for language activities associated with planning the garden, and the students later used their ideas to design the garden individually and then collectively. This collective garden design helped determine the construction and language content of the curriculum.

The two distinct areas of the course, literacy and numeracy and construction, developed after these preparation activities. The Preliminary CSWE students lacked foundational skills, including letter formation, alphabet and number recognition, and knowledge of alphabetical order, and they could not undertake simple calculations. To address these students' needs, the ESL teacher, using the support of tutors, developed literacy and numeracy activities focusing on generic skills. These activities were not necessarily associated with the project but used the project as a context, when possible.

The CSWE I students lacked skills in grammar, spelling, the construction of texts, and complex calculations, such as those associated with calculating quantities of building supplies. To address these areas of need, activities were developed that related directly to the construction tasks, for example, reading sets of instructions. Groups of CSWE I students would rotate between literacy and numeracy tasks and construction tasks, with one group involved in construction while the other group was involved in literacy and numeracy tasks. At times, all students were required to participate in some construction tasks related to the collective design and consultation. However, the students were not always grouped according to level, and sometimes students with a low level of literacy worked with higher-level students in the construction and literacy classes.

Because of some problems in coordinating the written texts with the construction tasks, we reversed the process of having the students work on literacy tasks and then on construction tasks. Instead, we decided to film the construction tasks, review the experience orally using film and photographs, and then embark on the written activities. The need to film the construction activities meant that all students participated in these tasks at the same time, which enhanced the sense of collective ownership. As a result, students engaged with the material more confidently and successfully, as the process better reflected the intended pedagogies of the program. Initially, literacy and numeracy activities were taught for 4 hours a day, and construction tasks were taught for 2 hours in the afternoon. With the change in approach, literacy and numeracy were taught for 2 hours in the morning, and construction tasks were conducted for 2 hours in the afternoon, but this was reversed in the hotter months.

INTEGRATING CURRICULUM OUTCOMES INTO THE PROJECT

The teachers were determined to integrate the requirements of the language and design curricula into the course. For example, the construction tasks, which were determined by the needs of the project, such as reticulation and the making of pavers, related to information and instructional texts within the CSWE and CADT construction competencies, such as *plan and organize work, carry out measurements and calculations,* and *use hand and power tools* (see Matching Project Activities and Learning Outcomes on page 22).

Because of the construction requirements for the CADT course and the gardening requirements of the project, the instructors of both programs often asked students to do similar tasks. This meant that verbs and nouns were often repeated. We reinforced these words with worksheets around information texts and instructional texts, which also contributed to familiarization with lexis. As we noted language difficulties, we taught them as explicit elements, for example, question forms. Project Activities on page 23 outlines the types of activities the students undertook over the life of the project.

Some written texts in the CSWE curriculum did not relate directly to the construction of the garden. These largely description and information texts related to the students' broader interests. For example, descriptions of bush medicines (traditional herbal ointments and potions for various illnesses and disorders) arose out of the production and sale of these medicines to community-based and noncommunity individuals as well as the

Matching Project Activities and Learning Outcomes

Garden Construction Activities	Preliminary CSWE Outcomes	CADT Outcomes
Ordering goods	Can recognize alphabet and numbers Can use an alphabetical index Can participate in a short conversational exchange Can provide basic personal information Can complete a formatted text	Occupational health and safety Tools and equipment Communication skills
Making a garden model	Can recognize alphabet and numbers Can respond to simple instructions Can participate in a short conversational exchange	Occupational health and safety Tools and equipment Measurements and calculations Construction design
Making pavers	Can recognize alphabet and numbers Can respond to simple instructions Can participate in a short conversational exchange	Occupational health and safety Tools and equipment Measurements and calculations

local health clinic. These texts gave us an opportunity to assist the students in producing packaged bush medicines, and the labels included descriptive texts about bush medicine that reflected the students' oral English language use. Other descriptive texts involved the garden itself and were therefore based on the students' experience of language generated through the project. The information texts, which were a component of the external curriculum, were based on advertising literature for garden supplies and hence reinforced important lexical terms and numerical skills that recurred and were recycled through the project (see the Appendix for classroom activities).

WORKING WITH THE PRELITERATE STUDENTS

As we have noted, many students were at a preliterate stage of development, so it was important to establish and reinforce foundation skills for at least one session per day. These sessions largely involved learning by rote and repetition, dealing with forming letters, recognizing letters, learning alphabetical order, learning numbers and number recognition, filling

	Project Activities	
Weeks	Language and Literacy Activities	Design and Technology Activities
1–5	Using the alphabet Doing arithmetic Understanding place value Understanding occupational health and safety instructions Making pavers—names of tools and instructions Using indexes (e.g., the phone book) Asking for information	Making a garden model Making pavers
6–10	Practicing alphabet, numeracy, phonics Writing an invitation (e.g., to garden design opening) Writing and reading faxes about ordering Writing postcards (e.g., about events at the workshop) Describing a garden Inquiring and ordering by phone Writing bush medicine descriptions Completing forms Listening to and reading personal descriptions	Making pavers Doing mosaic tiling Painting concrete painting
10–17	Practicing alphabet and phonics Practicing numeracy around place value, number recognition, addition, subtraction Filling out forms Recognizing dates Using a postcode index of place names Practicing question forms Listening to and reading personal descriptions Writing bush medicine descriptions Going on a nursery excursion Doing bush medicine research Doing food and nutrition research Asking for help and greeting Working with garden reticulation information texts Using maps Completing take-off sheets Fixing taps—names of tools and equipment and instructions Listening to personal descriptions Describing bush foods Describing a garden	Doing garden reticulation Fixing taps Creating the garden

Simple Form to Fill In

Title: ☐ Mr.   ☐ Mrs.   ☐ Ms.   ☐ Miss

First name: _____

Surname: _____

Skin name: _____

Date of birth: _____

Address: _____

_____

Postcode: _____

Language spoken at home: _____

Telephone number: _____

Date: _____

Signature: _____

in simple forms such as the one shown above, and providing personal information.

We taught the reading of social-sight signs, which repeated material covered in earlier programs, within the occupational health and safety component of the construction course. To teach the alphabet, the construction teacher created 26 A4 lowercase and 26 A4 uppercase letter cards and created a clothesline in the classroom. Each morning, the preliterate students were given alphabet cards, which they had to peg on the clothesline in alphabetical order (see Alphabet Activity in Class). During the process, the teaching staff and students sang the alphabet to reinforce sound and letter recognition. In fact, the tutor and literacy teacher had to go to great lengths to introduce different versions of the alphabet song, including country-and-western and blues versions, to keep the students interested in the process.

Students received complete and incomplete alphabet sheets to complete. These worksheets proved useful in developing letter-writing skills. Alphabet exercises were then rounded off by putting names printed on cards in order. Initially, we used the names of class members for this activity, but the students found this practice problematic, and we reverted to Northern Territory place names, which proved more effective because the students were more familiar with the look of these names.

For numbers and number recognition, students used the same

Alphabet Activity in Class

worksheet over a number of days. The worksheet included the numeral, the value of the number in dots, the number in words, and a variety of activities requiring the students to work with these different formulations. For example, the students were asked to write a word in numbers, match numerals to dot values, color in dot values to identify numbers, count the dots and write the numeral, match the numeral to the number-word and complete number patterns, complete clozes, and write dictations. In addition, the students undertook place-value exercises in which they were given a number and, with the assistance of multibase arithmetic blocks (base 10), had to put the numerals in the correct place-value columns.

For form-filling practice, students received the same form every morning. Because this activity was repeated, they became familiar with the text and the requirements and, consequently, needed less assistance with each attempt at the task. The language instructor often rounded off this activity by asking for personal information from a few senior members of the class. In this way, the whole class could answer without individuals being targeted. The students then played the game Snakes and Ladders using personal information.

WORKING WITH THE HIGHER-LEVEL STUDENTS

Relative to the preliterate students, the higher-level students were able to engage more with project activities related to creating a garden. Tasks included ringing suppliers (see Students Role-Playing Telephone Calls to Suppliers), reading and writing faxes, and completing take-off sheets, which depicted the type, quantity, and prices of construction materials. These activities were still highly scaffolded with worksheets and prerecordings; for example, cloze exercises and vocabulary activities were used to build up the field. Communicative language teaching techniques were used for listening and speaking tasks. Written tasks, such as reading and writing a fax, concentrated on structure, language functions, lexis, and simple grammar (see the Appendix for fax exercises).

Because two courses were being delivered concurrently, the ratio of teaching staff to students was high. At times, there were 2 teachers to 15 students, and on some occasions a ratio of 2 teachers to 5 students. This high teacher-student ratio, and the repetition of activities combined with *situated learning* (Lave & Wenger, 1990), in which the literacy and numeracy tasks related to authentic task-based activities, enhanced the achievement of the higher-level students.

Students Role-Playing Telephone Calls to Suppliers

Evaluating the Innovation

Certificate I in Spoken and Written English and Certificate I in Applied Design and Technology are both nationally accredited courses with nationally standardized learning outcomes. Both were created by industry, and the registered training organizations (RTOs) that deliver them must meet agreed standards for the skill levels and for assessment of students. Assessments must be regularly moderated, and CSWE moderation sessions are held internally within BIITE and across RTOs annually at a national conference. Teachers of these accredited courses must meet qualification requirements, including the Certificate IV in Workplace Training and Assessment. Completion of the courses leads to nationally recognized awards.

Students were assessed formatively against the CSWE outcomes through the ongoing production of oral and written texts. Summative assessment took place when the students had a reasonable chance of successfully passing the assessment tasks determined by the curriculum.

The garden project provided a context and purpose for doing particular numeracy and literacy activities, and the needs and stages of the project, as well as the students' interests, dictated the development of the course. Continual collaboration between the language instructors and the construction trainer in planning course content was needed, and the curriculum was realized through a fluid, evolving, and dynamic process of course delivery. The students' positive and negative reactions to tasks as well as their successes were noted. Simple nondescriptive oral questioning was used because of the students' literacy level. Simple yes/no responses to questions (e.g., *Did you like doing things on bush medicine?*) were noted and combined with teacher reflections on student performance, motivation, and perceived enjoyment to make changes to the curricula. This resulted in repetition of some activities, the exclusion of others, and the creation of additional ones.

STUDENT OUTCOMES

As a result of these adaptations, we noted the following outcomes for the lower-level students' English language and numeracy performance:

- enhanced number recognition and understanding of place value
- enhanced knowledge of many consonant and some vowel sounds in the context of simple words
- improved cluster and diagraphic recognition and pronunciation in whole-class drilling and eliciting activities

However, constant review was required, and there were often lapses in student progress. Even higher level students exhibited a heavy dependence on teacher assistance, and the adaptations did not enhance independence in learning. Generally, all the students progressed slowly, but the lower-level students progressed particularly slowly. Factors contributing to this slow progress included irregular student attendance as a result of the pressures of community living, such as child care and cultural and social obligations; the context in which the students lived; and the lexical overload of the construction tasks.

The construction competencies require the identification of tools and equipment, a heavy load of vocabulary learning that was beyond the students' level. The oral communication and numeracy demands of these competencies were also quite high (Oldfield, 2002, p. 163). The knowledge underpinning some of the construction competencies involved abstract Western concepts, which required a higher standard of language and numeracy competence to unpack. These concepts were obviously above the capabilities of the preliterate students, who had a restricted lexical and numerical range and limited theoretical understanding. As such, even though the students made small gains in terms of literacy and numeracy, they made virtually no gains in the CADT course, with the exception of manual skills such as using hand and power tools (see Student Learning to Use a Power Tool).

Student Learning to Use a Power Tool

Social behaviors also influenced the outcomes of the garden project. The students tended to copy from those whom they perceived as having superior skills and knowledge, despite attempts to persuade them to work on their own. The obvious result was a lack of progress for some students. One strategy used to overcome this behavior was to group similarly skilled students together so that they had to rely on their own resources.

Partly because of cultural factors, the students did not recognize that the oral activities were designed to enhance the literacy activities. For example, the great reluctance, particularly among the less senior members of the group, to participate in conversations could be attributable to the custom in Indigenous communities for senior women to be designated as speakers for a group (S. Darcy, BIITE lecturer, personal communication, May 8, 2004). It is also culturally appropriate for students to adopt roles within the group. For example, students with particular skills are often called on to give answers on behalf of the whole group, which effectively impedes individual progress. Dividing the class into smaller groups of women with similar group roles for oral exercises was one strategy used to overcome this reluctance to speak, and younger speakers were not singled out in whole-class activities.

SUCCESSFUL TEACHING STRATEGIES

In achieving the learning outcomes specified in the curriculum, the project identified the following successful strategies for teaching the students.

Physical Involvement

- Physical application of knowledge, such as standing up and physically organizing the group into alphabetical order, helps develop understanding.
- Cutting and gluing exercises are useful when instructors draw students' attention to the detail in a practical application.

Contextualizing Language

- Discussing and teaching grammar in context supports understanding and application.
- Bush plant activities hold attention because the topic is of high interest and draws on the students' cultural knowledge.

Scaffolded Teaching

- Scaffolded teaching sequences, which gradually withdraw support, work well.

- Students need work at the sentence level before tackling full texts such as narratives.
- It is beneficial to use models and to increase the difficulty of tasks incrementally.

Working at the Word Level

- Alliteration and word-shape activities work well.
- In phonics practice, students need to practice consonants as well as vowel sounds.
- Transfer of knowledge seems to take place for individuals who demonstrate more phonic awareness and word recognition.

Group Work

- A combination of group work and individual activities works best, with collaborative sessions working well for more complex tasks.
- Grouping students at the same language level for some tasks forces students to rely on their own resources rather than copying from more advanced-level students.

Variety in Tasks

- Activities need to be varied across the day to avoid boredom.

Repetition

- Students like reading and writing activities that use the same text repeatedly.
- Constant repetition of items is necessary to promote retention.

Use of Computers

- Computer exercises are good for alphabet practice and facilitate individual progress, as learners work against themselves rather than copying from or passively watching others.
- Typing practice needs to focus on spacing and capital letters.

ISSUES AFFECTING SUCCESS

A number of problematic issues affected the success of the project. The 3-month break over the summer months before the onset of the project was too long and reduced the retention of previously learned knowledge and skills around grammar and vocabulary. This meant, of course, that students had to relearn the skills during the project. Using cloze exercises for grammatical items proved problematic, as the beginning-level learners could identify the missing word in a cloze exercise only when the word was first pronounced for them, with words such as *this* proving difficult to retain even after extensive use in formulaic sentences. Word shapes continued to be problematic as the students could not distinguish between long, short, and tall letters.

In evaluating the project innovation, we decided that the workshop schedule had not incorporated enough planning time. As a result, there was insufficient time to link the language activities closely enough to the construction activities. The content of the Certificate I in Applied Design and Technology was far beyond the learners' language level, with concepts embedded within a highly technical register of language. Students used an everyday, commonsense vocabulary, and it was difficult to explain technical terms to them. All the content needed to be broken down into vocabulary-building activities and phonics practice. The low level of the class meant that the students would cover only one task each week, and this task needed to be broken down into small, defined tasks rather than broad, open-ended ones.

The skills expected in the course were culturally bound, and we needed to teach abstract concepts and symbols explicitly. In their first languages, students get straight to the point and tend to use one word to bring about action. Some students seemed to refuse to take English on, which could be an ongoing effect of colonization. Some students left the room during oral activities and did not seem to see spoken language as part of their learning.

The students were not oriented to the school culture, as most had never gone to school. The ones who did well in the language learning component of the course had gone to Yirara Secondary College, but for others the language learning process was slow, with any progress remarkable. Some students did have a commitment to learning, and they liked the idea of having access to learning. These students had a high work ethic and showed gradual improvement in their language and numeracy skills and learning strategies.

Conclusions

What can we draw from this experience? First, the students' progress was perceptibly improving, as the language instructor (Janine) noted in reflections on the course:

> *The intensity of the workshop delivery has been highly beneficial to learning outcomes. The increased delivery has meant that there are, of course, far more opportunities for learning skills and reinforcement of skills. The consequence of such workshop delivery is that students are retaining more knowledge than the previous year.*

A range of strategies appeared to assist learning, such as constant repetition, collaborative group work, and focused individualized activities, which drew the students away from overdependence on peers and the teacher. It is worth noting that many of these findings and the context of the learning mirror the situation described by Barber (2002) in relation to work with students recently arrived in Australia from the Horn of Africa.

THE CHALLENGE OF TECHNICAL LANGUAGE AND CONTENT

Developing basic, commonsense language and then moving on to the technical language embedded in the design and construction course proved to be a challenge. It was a lengthy process that required time and constant reinforcement. Not surprisingly, students at the preliminary course level, who were still learning alphabetical order and building their preliteracy skills, had more pronounced difficulties. Even though the students were fully engaged in developing the skills, knowledge, and understanding associated with the landscape gardening design and were able to apply their bush foods and bush medicine knowledge to the project, progress continued to be slow.

Because the language learning in the course concentrated on the content knowledge of the Certificate I in Applied Design and Technology, the students could have missed out on learning more fundamental language. However, Janine noted,

> *Even so, there are huge gains by having a project of this type. Virtually all the students are highly engaged in literacy, numeracy, design and construction activities. Although their numeracy and literacy mean that they can't hope to complete all construction competencies [in the time available] and are still unable to complete some CSWE I competencies, they do have a purpose for learning literacy and numeracy and this is shown in the participation in classroom and outdoor learning.*

The garden project's literacy and oracy end products, such as giving instructions, ordering goods over the phone, or writing a fax, appear to be the most important aspect of learning for the students, as opposed to understanding the application of literacy and oracy skills. Many students in the group were quite reluctant to take risks and make mistakes. This group of students did not necessarily value the elements that constitute Western learning strategies and that are exhibited by good language learners (Rubin, 1975, cited in Lynch, 2003). Group cohesion and dependency, which are important to Indigenous learners, have an adverse effect on the creation of the "autonomous Western language learner—an independent learner who manages and monitors their own learning as opposed to valuing the 'sociability and cooperation' and identification with a group" (Lamb, 2002, p. 38).

THE IMPACT OF THE CONTEXT

The context in which the students live also had a profound effect on the outcome of the curriculum. The students live in a non-English-speaking environment, and any English they use at the school, the clinic, the store, or the council office is limited. The few opportunities the students have to engage in English outside the classroom are not enough for them to acquire oral proficiency. As oral English proficiency and vocabulary are predictive of English reading proficiency, this limitation affects their chances of enhancing their reading skills (Slavin & Cheung, 2003).

Literacy practices in a particular social context also determine reading proficiency, and residents of Utopia have little exposure to print. The few books, newspapers, or magazines found there are not generally circulated. The students themselves live in substandard and crowded conditions and cannot store reading materials. The students therefore lack exposure to, and acquaintance with, Western literacy practices. Moreover, due to this lack of exposure, the students do not see literacy activities as everyday tasks (Kral & Schwab, 2003). "The linguistic ecosystem in which to acquire [English] literacy is impoverished" (Lamb, 2002, p. 46). Consequently, the students often perceive their own language abilities as being higher than they actually are and may not see the need to develop their language skills further. They may lack the motivation to seek learning opportunities, so language development is arrested or slowed (Lamb, 2002). Because of the lack of employment and infrastructure, there is no apparent evidence in Utopia that Western education can result in rewards, which limits motivation as well.

A QUALIFIED SUCCESS, AND ROOM FOR MODIFICATION

Although the construction competencies were not completed, the project was a success on many levels, considering the social and cultural context in which the students live. Not only were the students highly motivated and engaged in design, literacy, numeracy, and construction tasks, but many were able to complete the language learning outcomes of the Preliminary Course in Spoken and Written English and the Certificate I in Spoken and Written English. This demonstrates that the project was able to engender a purpose and context for learning in an environment that offers few such opportunities. Part of the success can also be attributed to the instructors' flexibility in creating and delivering resources for activities that often cropped up from the project design or the students' interests.

For a program such as this to continue, a number of modifications are required. Both instructors noted that the lexical load could be managed better if the curriculum included fewer tasks. In class, students could then deal with the tasks more thoroughly and could repeat them. Because of the pressure to achieve the construction competencies, the students could not review all the construction activities orally through video and photographs (see, e.g., Students Pouring Concrete), or explore them through written activities such as instruction sheets, recounts, or numeracy activities. The project simply ran out of time to go through a full cycle of activities for each construction task. A better model would be to enroll the students in a number of short construction courses throughout the year, similar to earlier

Students Pouring Concrete

collaborative efforts. This would provide more time to spend on foundational literacy and numeracy skills and the literacy and numeracy activities associated with the construction tasks.

The time pressures meant that the students could not explore further any of the construction activities, such as those focusing on bush foods and bush medicine. The students expressed an interest in writing a book about bush foods, in both English and Indigenous languages, with other BIITE students. However, the pressures to complete the construction competencies meant that there was no time to pursue this interest, which could be a valuable future project.

We observed relatively early that the group's literacy and numeracy levels, largely due to the social context in which the students lived, were too low for any great gains to be observed in a curriculum project of this type. Future collaborative efforts of this type would need to engage students with higher literacy and numeracy levels.

Appendix: Language and Literacy Activities

ACTIVITY TYPE 1: READING A SHORT INFORMATION TEXT

Exercise 1

Read the information on the previous page and answer these questions.

1. What is the **shop name**? _____
2. **How long** is the **sale** for? _____
3. What is the **address**? _____
4. What is the **Internet address**? _____
5. What costs **$50.00**? _____
6. **How much** is the **helmet**? _____
7. What costs **$15.95**? _____
8. **How much** are the **overalls**? _____
9. What is the **cheapest** thing? _____

ACTIVITY TYPE 2: VOCABULARY AND SPELLING

Exercise 1

Write these words under the correct boxes:

shrub   nursery   list   ground cover   prices   tree

			$ 2.60 $0.90 $7.50
		Mulga tree Wattle shrub Pine tree Saltbush shrub Verbena	

Exercise 2

Look, say, cover, write, and check.

ground cover		tree		bush	

list		nursery		prices	

Exercise 3

a. Read this list of plants.

> Mulga
> Wattle
> Pine
> Saltbush
> Verbena

- Which plants are trees? _____
- Which plants are shrubs? _____
- Which plants are ground covers? _____

b. Put the names of the plants in alphabetical order below. Look at the alphabet to help you.

_____
_____

Aa	Bb	Cc	Dd	Ee	Ff	Gg
Hh	Ii	Jj	Kk	Ll	Mm	Nn
Oo	Pp	Qq	Rr	Ss	Tt	
Uu	Vv	Ww	Xx	Yy	Zz	

ACTIVITY TYPE 3: READING A FAX

Exercise 1

Read this fax and answer the questions.

BATCHELOR INSTITUTE OF INDIGENOUS TERTIARY EDUCATION

CENTRAL AUSTRALIAN CAMPUS

PO Box 9170 Alice Springs
Northern Territory 0871
Telephone: (08) 8951 8300
Facsimile: (08) 8951 8311

FACSIMILE

TO: Tangentyere Nursery
FROM: Janine Oldfield
RE: Plants and prices
DATE: 22/01/04

Your fax no: (08) 8952 3185
Our phone no: (08) 8951 8302
Our fax no: (08) 8951 8311
Number of pages (including this one): **1**

To whom it may concern

Could you please send me a list of shrubs, trees and ground cover plants in the nursery **as well as** their prices. Thank you for your help.

Cheers

Janine Oldfield

---

1. **What** kind of letter is it? _____
2. **Who** is the fax from? _____
3. **Where** does the sender work? _____
4. **What** is their fax number? _____
5. **What** is their phone number? _____
6. **What** is their address? _____
7. **Who** is the fax to? _____
8. **What** is their fax number? _____
9. **When** was the fax sent? _____
10. **How** many pages are in the fax? _____
11. **What** is the fax about? _____
12. **What** does the fax sender want? _____

Exercise 2

Read this fax. Match the labels below with the numbers on the fax.

BATCHELOR INSTITUTE OF INDIGENOUS TERTIARY EDUCATION (1)	CENTRAL AUSTRALIAN CAMPUS PO Box 9170 Alice Springs Northern Territory 0871 Telephone: (08) 8951 8300 Facsimile: (08) 8951 8311 (2)
	FACSIMILE (3)
TO: Tangentyere Nursery (4)	**Your fax no:** (08) 8952 3185 (8)
FROM: Janine Oldfield (5)	**Our phone no:** (08) 8951 8302 (9)
RE: Plants and prices (6)	**Our fax no:** (08) 8951 8311 (10)
DATE: 22/01/04 (7)	Number of pages (including this one): 1 (11)

To whom it may concern (12)

Could you please send me a list of shrubs, trees and ground cover plants in the nursery **as well as** their prices. Thank you for your help. (13)

Cheers (14)

Janine Oldfield (15)

	Sender		Sender's address, phone, and fax
	Sender's work		Receiver
	Sender's phone number		Receiver's fax number
	Sender's fax number		Number of pages in fax
	Date fax was sent		Letter introduction
	What the fax is about		Letter body (middle)
	Letter end		Signature

Exercise 3

a. The sender is asking for something in the fax. What three words show that the sender is asking for something?

b. Look at these ways of asking for things. Which ones are questions?

_____

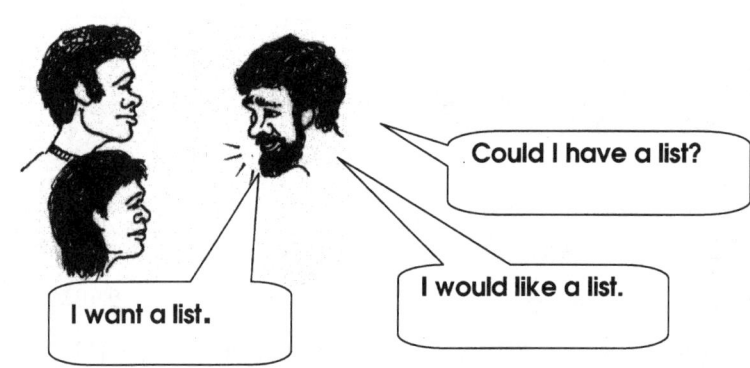

c. Fill in the gaps in the conversation below with *would* or *could*.

You: _____ I have a list of shrubs and trees please?
Nursery: Certainly. Do you want local plants?
You: Yes, I _____ like plants from Utopia.
Nursery: I'm sorry, but we haven't got any. _____ plants from Alice Springs be OK?
You: Yes.
Nursery: OK then, here is the list.

d. Listen to the conversation and check your answers.

e. Now have the conversation with your partner.

Exercise 4

a. In the fax:
  • What are the two things the sender asks for?

   _____
   _____

  • How does the writer join these two words in the letter? What words does she use?

b. Make up sentences asking for two things using ***and*** and ***as well as***. The first one has been done.

  • **shrubs/trees**

    Could I have a list of shrubs **and** trees.
    Could I have a list of shrubs **as well as** trees.

- **trees/ground cover plants**

  _____

  _____

- **paints/brushes**

  _____

  _____

- **wattles/saltbushes**

  _____

  _____

- **trees/ground cover plants**

  _____

  _____

- **grasses/gums**

  _____

  _____

ACTIVITY TYPE 4: VOCABULARY AND SPELLING EXTENSION

Plurals—talking about more than one thing

Single	**Plural**
tree	trees
bush	bushes

RULES for making plurals: Words ending in an *s* or *sh* sound—add *es*

a. Write the singular and plural words in this table.

Single	Plural
tree	
	bushes
	plants
shrub	

	brushes
grass	
	wattles
saltbush	
	paints

b. Can you think of any other words ending in **sh**? Write these here.

   _____

   _____

c. Can you think of any other words ending in **s**? Write these here.

   _____

   _____

The Transition From School to University: Learning New Behavior and Skills

3

JANET M. D. HIGGINS

This chapter describes the development of a very short study skills program (SSP) that was introduced in April 2000, during the orientation week of the first semester, in the International Communication Division of the Faculty of Humanities at Okinawa University. April 1999 marked the inauguration of the Faculty of Humanities, with its two divisions of International Communication and Welfare Culture. The 1999–2000 academic year was a trial period, and as the second semester drew to a close, the faculty began evaluating course organization, curricula, courses, and students, and began planning changes. The SSP continued for first-year students until April 2003, when study skills became a core element in a compulsory, first-year basic introductory seminar.

The Motivation for the Innovation

During the evaluation at the end of the second semester, many of the discussions about students focused on problems stemming from inappropriate behavior in a university environment. Faculty members teaching a variety of academic courses across the curriculum, as well as professors in the Law and Economics Faculty, shared concerns about a variety of behavior problems, such as lack of concentration, poor attendance and lateness, failure to complete study assignments, and lack of motivation. They were also concerned about some students' poor skills in note-taking, dictionary use, report writing, material gathering, preparation for class tests and final examinations, and out-of-class use of learning resources such as the library, language lab, and computers.

These problems were largely due to a lack of preparation for university life. They were, and continue to be, shared by graduates from a large number of senior high schools throughout Japan. Many of the students experienced a major cultural change in moving from a highly guided, uniform secondary school system to the university environment, where they were expected to take responsibility for their own learning and where they met a range of new expectations. Most students were dependent and not self-directed, with no training at high school in the skills they needed to succeed at university. The multiple-choice form of high school assessment did not provide practice in argumentative essay writing based on evidence, and students had little experience in discussion and debate or in giving their opinions. They found it difficult to transfer to a system in which those skills were expected and valued.

Many students had received no training in learning strategies and probably had never been asked to think about their individual learning styles. A further problem was poor self-confidence, leading to an anticipation of failure or a lack of perseverance, when faced with difficulties. Very few students had received training in how to organize their study time and how to plan their schedules for a balance among study, club activities, and part-time work. Furthermore, many students had not considered what their real objectives were in coming to university, what specializations they wanted to follow, or how best to choose their courses. Compounding these problems was an institutionalized belief that university is a reward for high school cramming and a place to develop social skills in society at large through part-time work. Raising awareness of what being a responsible university student involves was a key issue in helping the students make the best of their study opportunities and enjoy their university social life.

The place to train children in learning strategies and study skills, in my opinion, should be the school system, but if university entrants do not have these skills, then the universities have a responsibility to undertake this training. While teaching in the United Kingdom, I had been involved in a variety of short-term and long-term study skills courses for undergraduate and postgraduate students entering UK universities from abroad. The courses were designed to introduce students to the British university environment as well as develop their English confidence and skills. I felt that a study skills program could address a number of the problems experienced by undergraduates at Okinawa University.

I made the SSP proposal in February 2000, but it was clear that there could be no radical curriculum change for the coming academic year, beginning in April. Individual courses and course schedules had been discussed and agreed on during the previous semester, and any initiative would have to fit into the existing scheme of things. I proposed holding a very short introductory program before the commencement of academic courses. My proposal was accepted by the faculty, and I headed up a team to develop a short study skills course to take place during the university orientation week. This was not an ideal time, as it was a period of intense readjustment for the students and was filled with administrative sessions. However, in discussions with Academic Affairs, four sessions of 90 minutes over a 2-day period were allocated to the SSP.

My colleagues and I recognized from the start of this teaching and learning initiative that an introductory study skills course could not deal effectively with the study problems we had identified. Changing behavior, attitudes, and skills requires systematic exposure to new ideas and lengthy practical training. However, it was a starting point in raising awareness of the skills required, pointing to the difference in the learning environment and providing experience with tasks that students would subsequently have to handle. After the course, the division would need to strongly encourage all professors to continue raising awareness and training students in study skills throughout the academic year.

The Curriculum Context

Okinawa University is a small, 4-year private university. In 2000, it was one of five 4-year universities in Okinawa Prefecture. The university has two faculties, Humanities and Law and Economics, and three divisions, International Communication, Welfare Culture and Law, and Economics. All divisions offer a day course and an evening course.

The SSP was designed for the students in the International Communication division, which in 2000 included approximately 150 first-year students and 21 faculty members ranging from lecturer to professor, specializing in Japanese, Okinawan, Chinese, and English language and literature; communication studies; comparative economics; comparative ethnography; tourism; Okinawan studies; international exchange studies; communication studies; and international exchange. Courses are offered within three profiles—language studies, communication studies, and international exchange—but there is great flexibility, and students can easily switch between profiles. Students are offered short-term and long-term programs of study in China, Taiwan, the United States, and Australia, and seminar teachers can take their students on short, 3- to 5-day study trips abroad.

Students come primarily from within the prefecture, but the division also enrolls students (other than first-year students) from other Japanese universities, who study at Okinawa University for 1 year. Foreign students at the university are predominantly from China and Taiwan, with some from Indonesia, Vietnam, and Korea. These students have studied Japanese for 1–3 years before they enter, either in a specialized language school or on a special Japanese language program at university.

All faculty members have a master's degree in their fields, and many have PhDs and publish actively in their respective fields. When the SSP started, there were three foreign faculty members. The SSP initiative was supported by the International Communication Division of the Humanities Faculty. My team consisted of faculty members specializing in English, Japanese, and communication studies.

The Process of Designing the Program

DEVELOPING THE INITIAL 2000 PROPOSAL

The initial development took place within a very short time frame, from February to April 2000, with the whole program designed by the beginning of April and sessions held on April 6 and 7.

The initial proposal included a rationale and a draft plan of the format, content, length, and methodology. I presented this to the staff for discussion and revision. I thought that a concrete syllabus and examples of activities would be helpful to faculty members for whom the concept of study skills was unfamiliar and that it would be much easier and faster to work from a draft than to begin from scratch. In this original proposal, I identified the following aims for the program:

- to raise awareness of the differences between school and university study by identifying student responsibilities and university expectations
- to make students aware of the need to examine their purposes for studying and to set clear long-term to short-term personal study objectives
- to introduce basic study strategies in a simple, practical way
- to present the content of the program in ways that exemplify, through task-based sessions, the different study skills being discussed

The proposal received the support of the faculty, and I became chair of a committee of seven. The committee assumed a heavy burden in developing the ideas and being responsible for organization and teaching. The members were core organizers and session leaders, and were responsible for major revisions of the syllabus during the 3-year life of the SSP. The division supported the committee's decision that all faculty members should be involved in the program. In practice, this meant that all members attended all SSP sessions and worked with groups of students during the sessions to help them in the brainstorming and practical tasks. The rationale was that all division members should be familiar with the principles and goals of study skills training so that they would be able to carry on the process in their own classrooms.

As in all Japanese universities, part-time faculty members are responsible for a large part of the teaching at Okinawa University. We wanted the part-time staff to be aware of the SSP principles and goals. We encouraged part-time teachers to attend, and several did. However, we felt the response was not good enough, and in subsequent years, we paid all part-time teachers the equivalent of one teaching period to attend at least one session. They helped in the student groups and got to know students more informally. A valuable spin-off was that the part-time staff who attended felt more involved with the students than they had in previous years.

Structure, Content, and Methodology

The original draft of the SSP in 2000 envisaged four sessions of 60–90 minutes each. Ninety minutes is the usual lecture period. In collaboration with the Academic Affairs Department, I found time slots within the orientation week. A serious problem in 2000 was the additional burden the SSP placed on division staff during an already busy period. The division offers orientation sessions to both day and evening students. In addition, in 2000 the SSP was compulsory for second-year day and evening students. Hence each session was delivered four times. Without the cooperation of the committee members and the whole division, plus the support from Academic Affairs, carrying out the program would have been impossible.

In drawing up the draft syllabus for SSP 2000, I was guided by the following set of principles around different aspects of the course.

Content

The SSP would cover

- the differences between high school and university life: expectations of students, what teaching staff would and would not do for students, and student responsibilities
- study methods: learning styles, study materials, revision methods, concentration levels
- time scheduling: balancing study, leisure, and part-time work
- learning strategies: concrete examples using the example of language learning, covered in detail

Students would also be given some idea of how fortunate they were to have the opportunity to pursue higher education by looking at worldwide statistics on higher education.

Sessions

Sessions 1 and 2 would focus on the transition from school to university and general approaches to study. Sessions 3 and 4 would focus on language learning.

Facilities

The SSP would be supported later in the orientation period by an introduction to the university library and an introduction to the computer facilities, given by a member of the Multi-Media Center.

Methodology

Methodology would

- be task based to give the students brief experiences of a variety of learning tasks, some of which they had probably not previously encountered, such as brainstorming in small groups; doing assisted note-taking; filling in charts, mind maps, and diagrams; and solving simple problems
- involve sessions that would be more like workshops than lectures
- keep students active as they completed the various tasks

I wrote the draft content for the SSP in English, and the committee members then made changes and refined the learning tasks. Leaders assigned to each section or subsection further refined the material and translated it into Japanese (see Content and Tasks in the 2000 Study Skills Program for the final framework). The final worksheets were prepared in the form of a booklet. This contained evaluation sheets, which acted as attendance forms submitted after each session. Nine faculty members were directly involved in the sessions, and their role was to coordinate the preparation of the content and to be responsible for the overall timing and smooth running of the sessions. I acted as overall manager.

Students were divided into groups of around eight, which were mixed according to gender, high school origin, and nationality. In this way, we created groups whose members needed to talk in order to get to know each other and to work together. The sessions took place in a large, galleried lecture hall that had excellent facilities for overhead projection, computer slide presentations, and video, but the environment made it difficult for groups to work together. Attending faculty members were allocated groups and sat with them, helping them in the activities.

Evaluation

There were two sources of evaluation: formal feedback from students and informal feedback from faculty members. Students evaluated each session

Content and Tasks in the 2000 Study Skills Program

Components	Tasks
Session 1: School and University Study—Same or Different? **Time: 90 min.; Lecturers 1 and 2 (3, 4)**	
A. Introduction to the program • Welcome • Contents of the four SSP sessions • Video introduction to the university • Computer slide presentation: higher education in the world	Tasks 1–2 • Guided note-taking
B. The change from school to university • Motivation: Why go to university? • Your privileges; your responsibilities • The choosing of your courses, the setting of long-term and short-term objectives • Worries about student life • Expectations about university life	Tasks 3–7 • Brainstorming ideas • Summarizing • Note-taking
C. Your responsibilities • Attendance, lateness criteria, classroom behavior	
Session 2: The Study Process **Time: 110 min.; Lecturers 5, 6**	
A. Organizing your time • Planning your time: weekly, by semester • Balancing study, relaxation, part-time work	Tasks 8–12 • Guided note-taking • Completion of a timetable (in students' own time)
B. In class and outside class • Classroom-concentration levels; being an active learner • Learning in lectures; asking questions • Preparing for classes • Recognizing the value of reviewing as a study strategy • Knowing your course requirements • Doing independent study—planning and resources	Tasks 13–16 • Filling in charts • Completing statements • Reading a graph • Brainstorming ideas

continued on p. 50

Content and Tasks in the 2000 Study Skills Program (cont.)	
Components	Tasks
Session 3: How Can I Learn a Language? **Time: 60 min.; Lecturers 7 (8) (6, 9)**	
A. What is language learning? • Why learn languages? Examples of language learning strategies (Japanese/Chinese) • Factors affecting your learning	Tasks 17–21 • Making a summary • Activating own experience • Taking notes and summarizing
B. Facilitating your language learning • Being a good learner • Learning nonverbal communication—gestures • Learning nonverbal communication—personal space	Tasks 20–21 • Using a checklist • Taking quizzes
Session 4: Language Skills Strategy Training **Time: 140 min.; Lecturers 7 (8)**	
A. Vocabulary-learning strategies • What does knowing a word mean?—form, meaning, use • Personal strategies of second language learners	Tasks 22–26 • Brainstorming • Taking notes • Reading examples
B. Grammar-learning strategy training • Accuracy and fluency • Form and function • Recognition of patterns • Personal strategies of second language learners	Tasks 27–30 • Summarizing/taking notes • Completing statements • Reading examples
C. Speaking skills strategy training	Tasks 31–32 • Completing a chart
D. Reading skills strategy training	Task 33 • Writing ideas and follow-up reading assignment

for interest and usefulness through two questions, which they rated from 4 (high) to 1 (low):

1. How interesting was this session for you?
2. How useful was this session for you?

Results of the 2000 Evaluation (page 52) shows responses to each question by first-year day and evening students in each session. All four sessions of the program generally received high ratings from both day and evening students. In general, students valued the sessions more highly in terms of usefulness than interest. However, the difference was rather small, showing a positive pragmatism.

Faculty members gave informal feedback in the form of comments. In addition, Academic Affairs requested feedback on the entire orientation process, including the SSP. Based on this feedback and the results of student evaluations, the division decided to run the SSP again during the orientation week of 2001, with changes based on the evaluations and the recommendations of the SSP committee.

DEVELOPING THE 2001 PROGRAM

The basic organizational framework for SSP 2001 remained the same, but the four sessions were slightly longer. Eleven teachers were involved in presenting the sessions, which showed a high level of commitment to the program. The changes focused mainly on session content, as the committee considered that there had been too much emphasis on English language learning. As a language specialist, I had intended using language learning as a means for dealing with study skills, but my materials and those subsequently developed were perceived to be too specific. We agreed to refocus from foreign language to first language skills, an area where we felt many students were weak. We retained a small language learning section dealing with Chinese. In my own evaluation of SSP 2000, I had noted a lack of input from languages other than English. Seven other languages were taught at the university, and I felt that using examples from these other languages would have more appeal.

A second main area of change in 2001 was the inclusion of career issues. In Session 1, a 30-minute section dealt with new careers in the international communication field. This change reflected the ongoing discussions in the division about the lack of motivation of some students and the lack of clear guidelines about potential career paths for students.

Another area of change was the inclusion of concepts and issues connected with international communication, the heart of our division. In my report on SSP 2000, I stated that "over this past academic year there has been increasing awareness among faculty members of the lack in our students of understanding what meanings this term might have and what action and attitudes are involved." Session 4 of SSP 2001, renamed Cross-Cultural Intercultural Communication Skills, dealt with intercultural exchanges, during part of which three second-year and third-year students talked about their experiences abroad.

Results of the 2000 Evaluation

Score	Session 1				Session 2				Session 3				Session 4			
	Interest		Usefulness		Interest		Usefulness		Interest		Usefulness		Interest		Usefulness	
	D	E	D	E	D	E	D	E	D	E	D	E	D	E	D	E
4	35	3	65	11	29	8	51	11	64	10	69	12	47	12	53	14
3	76	18	60	10	65	14	51	12	39	12	36	11	53	10	43	7
2	16	3	2	3	24	3	16	2	4	1	2	0	3	0	5	1
1	2	0	2	0	2	0	2	0	0	0	0	0	0	0	1	0
Total	129	24	129	24	120	25	120	25	107	23	107	23	103	22	103	22

Note: D = daytime students, E = evening students. Students rated each session from 4 (high) to 1 (low).

Results of the 2001 Evaluation

Score	Session 1				Session 2				Session 3				Session 4			
	Interest		Usefulness		Interest		Usefulness		Interest		Usefulness		Interest		Usefulness	
	D	E	D	E	D	E	D	E	D	E	D	E	D	E	D	E
4	41	10	56	16	67	11	58	8	60	12	78	18	95	15	98	15
3	102	10	96	8	72	10	76	10	80	10	65	4	51	7	49	7
2	16	5	0	2	14	5	18	5	12	2	7	2	1	1	0	1
1	1	1	1	0	4	0	4	1	3	0	1	0	1	0	1	0
Total	160	26	153	26	157	24	156	24	155	24	151	24	148	23	148	23

Note: D = daytime students, E = evening students. Students rated each session from 4 (high) to 1 (low).

Evaluation

Like the evaluation of SSP 2000, the evaluation of the 2001 program involved asking the students to rate its interest and usefulness and asking faculty members to comment. Their evaluations were again very positive for all sessions, with ratings rising through the sessions, as Results of the 2001 Evaluation shows.

Evaluation from faculty members demonstrated concern about the same issues that the SSP Committee was grappling with. For instance, when referring to the changing emphasis of the program, staff made the following comments:

Don't lose the focus on study skills.

The focus should be more on study skills than attitudes.

The program had indeed changed from its initial firm focus on study skills, and some faculty members questioned whether a focus on journalism was necessary. The practical section of Session 2 was generally well received, but some faculty members called for more detailed assessments of student presentations, as this would lead to a greater understanding of what makes for good communication. The quizzes in Session 4 were well liked and considered very motivating, but several staff members felt that we had gone too far in reducing the language component and would have liked to see more time devoted to English. One staff member commented, "English classes contribute the greater part of the freshmen's curriculum. Thus we should have given [this presenter] much more time."

DEVELOPING THE 2002 PROGRAM

Once again, the division supported holding an SSP during the 2002 orientation week. The four-session format was maintained, though the length of the sessions was considerably reduced. The division and the committee felt it was important to reduce the load, and only eight faculty members and seven students were involved in presentations. There were fewer major changes in content, and any rewriting aimed to achieve greater clarity in the tasks with the goal of increasing active participation by students. English was allocated more time than Chinese even though the overall time devoted to foreign language remained the same. There were some minor changes in content arrangement, as shown in Content and Tasks in the 2002 Study Skills Program (pages 54–56).

The biggest changes were made in organization, and the top priority was the organization of the groups. The galleried lecture hall had not been a huge success, so the program was moved to a large hall with small tables arranged for groups of six to seven students. Technical resources were

Content and Tasks in the 2002 Study Skills Program

Component and Time	Content	Activities/Tasks
Introduction (10 min.)		
Presenters 1–3 (10 min. maximum)	Brief welcome to SSP 2002 Brief introduction to purpose and goals Brief introduction to methods, evaluation, registration of attendance, etc. Introduction of the faculty by name only	Look at booklet/evaluation form
Session 1: The Transition From School to University (60 min.) **All full-time faculty will be present as either presenters or group advisers.**		
Presenter 5 (10 min.)	Brief getting-to-know-you time for the groups	Task 1: Groups and advisees find out about each other and start working together cooperatively
Presenter 4 and students (50 min.)	From school to university: a change of life The past is the past! Here starts the future! New skills are needed; what skills, how to develop them How life is different at university—student perspectives (two students, 5 min. each) How to balance study, leisure, and part-time work Goals and responsibilities Brief reference to career planning, to chart, and to off-campus seminar	Task 2: Group brainstorming Task 3: Note-taking Task 4: Group brainstorming Tasks 5–6: Rating; chart in the booklet
Session 2: Communication Skills for Study and Life (75 min.) **All full-time faculty will be present as either presenters or group advisers.**		
Presenter 4 Presenters 1–3	Welcome to session (Japanese, English and Chinese)	
Presenter 5 (60 min.)	Need for good native language communication skills Reasons skills are necessary (persuade others, talk to others outside peer group, basis for foreign language study) and ways to acquire them Speaking/writing/listening examples Strategies for developing these skills (reading, exchanging opinions, discussing)	Tasks 7–10: Practical tasks (students write and speak to show skills); group tasks

continued on p. 55

Content and Tasks in the 2002 Study Skills Program (cont.)

Component and Time	Content	Activities/Tasks
Presenter 4 (10 min.)	Communication in the real world Communication resources (e.g., media, Internet, computer skills; positive and negative features of technology; need to become a skilled user—basic skills you need)	Task 11: Self-assessment of computer and Internet skills Task 12: Self-assessment of regular use of a variety of media resources
Session 3: Study Strategies (70 min.) **All full-time faculty will be present as either presenters or group advisers.**		
Presenters 1–3 (5 min.)	Welcome (Japanese, English, Chinese) and introduction to session topics	
Presenter 6 (20 min.)	What is learning? Being an active learner → taking action; goals; revision, notes	Tasks 13–15: Group work Task 16: Using a graph
Presenter 7 (15 min.)	Note-taking skills—minitalk	Task 17: Note-taking
Presenter 8 (10 min.)	Tools needed for studying Things to bring; importance of dictionaries Reference → library (mention of the library orientation in Week 1)	Task 18: Brainstorm four essential items required for studying and several other important ones
Presenter 4 (20 min.)	Have something to say Need contents/knowledge to be able to communicate—how to get this; systematic reading of newspapers, watching news, etc. Know your own culture: brief description of university courses	Task 19: Two quizzes to demonstrate knowledge of the situation in Southeast Asia and the world; examples of our courses—read information
Session 4: Cross-Cultural Intercultural Communication Skills (70 min.) **All full-time faculty will be present as either presenters or group advisers.**		
Presenters 1–3	Welcome (Japanese, English, Chinese) and introduction to the session topics	
Students (35 min.)	Cross-cultural experiences (verbal/nonverbal) Panel of five students from Bali, Taiwan, Australia, and the United States	Tasks 20–21: Guided note-taking

continued on p. 56

Content and Tasks in the 2002 Study Skills Program (cont.)

Component and Time	Content	Activities/Tasks
Presenter 2 (10 min.) Presenter 1 (20 min.)	Foreign language study New experiences: focus on phonology—Chinese New challenges: English—focus on vocabulary learning, stress, and rhythm through chants	Watch DVD Identify tones Tasks 22–28: Follow-up reading
Presenters 1–3	Goodbye from SSP 2002	

brought in as required. The disadvantage was the time taken to set up the room and return it to its former state for a different orientation session. Another organizational change was that staff members were allocated to groups based on the division's new adviser system. This change proved a valuable spin-off, as both students and advisers got to know each other over the 2-day period.

Evaluation

Everyone in the faculty continued to think creatively about study skills training at the university through discussions at divisional and committee meetings and evaluation of the SSP. As the Division of International Communication developed, the SSP changed to reflect changes in our thinking about studying and the learning process. For instance, over the 3 years, the program maintained the original four-session format, with each session running 60–90 minutes. However, as the program developed, the content changed to incorporate ideas that reflected the maturing of the division. As debates and discussions about career profiling and international communication took place, and as the needs and problems of the learners became more apparent, the content of the SSP changed. The division developed a structure of three specializations, and the focus of discussion turned to career paths. Session 1 in SSP 2001 reflected those discussions with the introduction of a focus on career planning, for example, journalism as a career. In 2002, the focus on careers decreased, but the focus on international and intercultural experiences and learning increased. The place of language training in the core curriculum was a topic of ongoing discussion within the division.

We saw the student evaluation process as part of the debate about the course. However, it was the feedback from staff and the shifting priorities of the division that most radically affected the evolution of the SSP. In addition to characterizing the SSP positively as a developing creative process in which all faculty members were catalysts, I would highlight a number of positive outcomes. The first is the commitment to teaching and learning excellence. The program showed students from the very beginning that lecturers were serious about helping them develop good study strategies and get the most out of university life. We also presented some hard truths about responsibilities and privilege in a semiformal setting. In my own experience, the first-year students had a very positive attitude to study at the beginning of the semester, which I saw as a direct benefit of the program. The students were able to meet all the staff as presenters or facilitators in the program, which seems to have been a much more effective way to introduce ourselves to students than giving a prepared speech. The students saw the staff interacting with each other through team teaching and facilitating, and a positive outcome for staff development was that the faculty members were committed to working together to make the sessions a success.

A very powerful outcome for me personally, and one that other colleagues shared, was the interaction with students in a semiformal learning environment. I had quite a different relationship with students as a result of this program, and they were more willing to speak to me when they saw me outside the classroom. Some students whom I did not see subsequently in class continued to speak to me on campus.

Conclusion

The program clearly had its limitations, which had to be addressed in discussions about future developments. Operationally, each SSP required large time and work commitments at an extremely busy time of the academic year. It also took up a significant part of the time available for general freshman orientation. In terms of provision of training, the program was very short and relied on staff members to maintain and develop the momentum in their own classes. However, the committee provided neither follow-up materials nor guidelines. Teachers could refer to the concepts introduced during SSP, but there had not been time for students to develop new skills. Some of the language teachers commented that the students seemed to have acquired a heightened awareness of study strategies, but other staff continued to express dissatisfaction with the preparedness of students for university study.

At the divisional level, it was decided that from April 2003 the SSP would no longer run. It its place, study skills were incorporated into a compulsory first-year seminar run concurrently by a large number of full-time staff. The seminar was traditionally a brief introduction to the lecturer's specialization for the students. In 2003, the first-semester seminar had a study skills focus, and the second-semester seminar focused on content. However, as a result of discussions among the faculty, during 2003, the division decided that this setup was insufficient and that from April 2004 the study skills focus would be extended over the whole year and incorporated into the content. Through this development, the university acknowledged the importance of assisting the students in making a successful transition from high school to university. The first-year seminar is now a compulsory, universitywide class, which means that systematic study skills training has passed into university practice, a huge step forward. (For resources on basic study skills, see the Appendix.)

My initial concern with the new system was whether the concept of study skills training could be implemented without a common core syllabus. However, since 2004, a committee for the first-year seminar has developed such a syllabus and has issued guidelines on content and methodology. Members of this committee are now drawn from all university divisions.

The SSP demonstrated, in a small way, that a training program could address the problems faced by students in the transition from school to university and could raise students' awareness. To this extent, the program was a success, but it also demonstrated that changing the attitudes and behavior of incoming students and helping them develop new skills required a systematic and long-term training program. The positive outcome is that this is exactly what has happened on a universitywide basis. There had been discussion and awareness of the need for study skills training before 2000, but the SSP served as a catalyst for systematic and systemic change.

Appendix: Resources

Teachers interested in tertiary study skills development will find plenty of study guides for university-level study dealing with a range of topics, including note-taking, seminar skills, and report and essay writing. However, for the students addressed by our SSP, the level of those resources was inappropriate, and we focused on basic skills that many professionals might expect secondary students to have developed. The following are resources I have found useful.

Bligh, D. A. (1972). *What's the use of lectures?* Harmondsworth, England: Penguin Books.

Wallace, M. J. (1980). *Study skills in English tutor's book.* Cambridge: Cambridge University Press.

Wallace, M. J. (1980). *Study skills in English workbook.* Cambridge: Cambridge University Press.

Maintaining the Learning: EFL Teacher Education in Vietnam

4

MARTYN BROGAN

This chapter explores the use of postcourse action research (AR) tasks for continuing professional development, especially in relation to the development of pedagogical decision-making skills within controlled teaching contexts. The chapter also investigates the value of these AR tasks as an assessment mechanism in postgraduate degree programs for EFL teachers in Vietnam.

The tasks were designed to maintain, sustain, and develop the learning outcomes of the degree programs and were used in TESOL postgraduate certificate and diploma level in-service programs awarded by Victoria University (VU), Australia, but taught in Vietnam. The Vietnamese course participants responded positively when they incorporated AR approaches into their language teaching. I argue that these approaches made the outcomes of the teacher education programs more relevant and sustainable for teachers attempting to teach EFL creatively. Teachers can use the skills gained during the completion of the required AR tasks to ameliorate the constraints of mandated curricula.

The Hanoi University of Foreign Studies (HANU) and VU in Australia have conducted TESOL programs as partners in Hanoi and Ho Chi Minh City since 1999. The Australian teacher trainers teaching on these programs have used a weak version of AR as the main assessment method for the course participants, who are all Vietnamese teachers of English.

This analysis of the completed postcourse AR tasks from two groups of graduate participants (see the Appendix) indicates that most of these teachers continued to develop their teaching skills autonomously after completion of each program. It also demonstrates that such tasks assisted in developing reflective teachers who were able to continue enhancing their teaching skills independently. This is an important aspect of any teacher education program in the Vietnamese context, given the mandated curricula. These imposed curricula often work against the use of exploratory or innovative methodologies. The major thematic concerns addressed by the participants of the program fall into five broad categories: motivating students; introducing new methods or changing methods; increasing learner-to-learner interaction; designing syllabi; and teaching large, mixed-ability classes.

Throughout the chapter, I use the terms *sustaining* or *sustainability* to describe the improvement in teaching skills continuously developed by the program participants after the completion of the programs. Perhaps the word *synergetic* could also be used, as the methodologies used in the training programs, the assessment tasks incorporated into the programs, and the expected professional behaviors of the program participants after the conclusion of the programs were interwoven.

English Language Teaching in Vietnam: Context and Problems

Economic conditions have changed radically in the past 15 years in Vietnam, but educational changes have not been as rapid or as dramatic. The economic changes have demanded that more Vietnamese citizens become proficient in English as used in the English language domains of Vietnam. The type, number, and size of these domains are increasing and include intergovernmental forums, aid projects, trade, academic studies, tourism, and joint ventures. Workers employed in Vietnamese government agencies are now required to reach prescribed English proficiency levels to access promotions and, in some cases, to maintain their current employment. In Vietnam, students may also be studying English to obtain advanced degrees in English-speaking countries.

To date, published and accessible research about the outcomes of English language teaching and learning and about English language teacher education and training in Vietnam is not readily available. For example, no studies detail the number of learners who become successful users of English after they have finished courses or the extent to which teacher education has contributed to any such success. This lack of research reflects a need to develop a culture of research in Vietnam in general and as part of any pedagogical activity among teachers in particular. Positional papers and educational histories have been written (e.g., Do, 1999; Le, 1999; T. H. A. Nguyen, 2002; X. T. Nguyen, 1993). Primary research is still scarce but is beginning to increase.

MANY MANDATED CURRICULA

Two important issues related to English language teaching and English language teacher education in Vietnam are the teaching methods used in both intensive (e.g., private English language classes to prepare for the International English Language Testing System examination) and extensive (e.g., Years 7–12 in secondary schools) English language courses and the increased popularity and importance of English.

The Vietnamese Ministry of Education and Training, English departments (e.g., at the Ho Chi Minh City University of Economics), and private English language centers have all attempted to develop effective curricula. These prescribed, mandated curricula have been developed in an ad hoc manner, and, as a result, many different approved curricula for English courses exist. These curricula are problematic for many reasons, including lack of coordination, issues of learner articulation, and the expectations of institutional administrators that teachers will implement these curricula unquestioningly. Teachers are required to implement teaching programs without conducting needs analyses of prospective learners, and the outcomes expected of the learners, such as high grades in final examinations, are often unachievable.

AR usually begins with the gathering of data about the current state of affairs, for example, what is known about learner needs, in order to plan curriculum changes. A preliminary needs analysis in AR would normally include ascertaining the learners' present proficiency levels, the skills or proficiency levels they need in future workplaces and other domains, the learners' language learning goals, their prior learning experiences, and their preferred learning styles. Unfortunately, in the current Vietnamese context, policy makers, course designers, and teachers frequently assume knowledge about the language needs and purposes of both the learners and the English-speaking foreign employers or others who may employ the students. A vague and often haphazard evaluation of the learners' proficiency level is currently the extent of any precourse needs analysis. This analysis is often the precursor to the selection of an available course book, usually from Britain, Australasia, or North America (one of the *BANA* [Holliday, 1994] countries). The content pages of these books become the core course content and de facto syllabi, and, as a result, many courses do not help learners develop their English language proficiency. Learners of English can find themselves studying *Headway Intermediate* (Soars & Soars, 1986) at their university, in their English for engineers program, at their private evening classes, and in specialized examination cram programs.

Program evaluations of English language courses and the introduction of any subsequent changes are rare. Courses are usually designed once, materials are usually selected and developed once, and a methodology is usually chosen once. Although English language teachers are aware of problems in the courses they teach, they are reluctant, or unable, to analyze what can be done to alleviate these problems. Often, those who wish to make changes are discouraged or dissuaded from doing so.

OBSTACLES TO CHANGE

There are many reasons for this discouragement or reluctance to analyze and address classroom problems or questions. English language teachers in Vietnam may teach all day for 6 days a week, as well as in the evening, and have little or no time to reflect on what could be improved. They may not have access to human or physical resources to assist with AR or program evaluation. Further, many Vietnamese English language teachers and their learners believe that teachers who are nonnative speakers of English cannot produce useful and meaningful activities and tasks. They may not recognize that the English language is a form of communication and not simply a content subject in the curriculum. In addition, teachers may not have the necessary power or access to power to influence courses or make changes.

English language teachers in Vietnam have told me that they accept that the grammar-translation method is not effective in enabling learners to communicate in English. However, the flexibility and the skills needed to apply communicative approaches, methods, and techniques and the ability to understand the communication needs of learners as future interlocutors are not well established. Currently, teaching and teacher education processes in Vietnam minimally allow for preservice or in-service teachers or trainees to reflect on their own language learning and teaching experiences. A lack of reflection has reinforced a belief that there is one single correct answer or one perfect method for English language teaching. If the teaching skills of English language teachers are to develop, this belief needs to be challenged.

THE VU-HANU PROGRAM

To meet the demands for English language learning in Vietnam, public and private educational institutions have developed many English language education and training programs. In this context, in 1999 VU commenced a partnership with the HANU to deliver postgraduate programs in TESOL. These VU-accredited higher education awards are part of a pathway for participants to achieve a TESOL degree, also taught and awarded by VU in Vietnam. The content of the programs is prescribed by the academic requirements of VU, but it is taught by staff who are mindful of the contexts within which English language teachers work in Vietnam, and the programs are responsive to the social, economic, political, and cultural constraints of such contexts (e.g., Holliday, 1994; Kramsch, 1994; Tollefson, 1995).

Needs analyses and the documented previous experience of the teacher trainers have resulted in an approach in which the prescribed content is delivered flexibly. One example of this flexible delivery is the use of AR projects for assessment purposes. These projects are designed to achieve the program aims and to maintain them on three levels: coordination of the programs, implementation of the programs by the teacher trainers, and implementation of the learning outcomes by the course participants.

The VU-HANU postgraduate TESOL programs attempt to address the issues outlined here, especially the need for Vietnamese teachers of English to become aware of and have opportunities to develop the skills for adopting AR approaches to language teaching. These issues are also related to the need for teachers to develop their individual levels of creativity and the professional confidence and autonomy to address their classroom concerns.

The Participants: Vietnamese Teachers of EFL in Vietnam

There are three groups of participants in the VU-HANU programs: the course participants, the teacher trainers (of which I was one), and the program administrators. The course participants teach different levels of English language learners at a range of public and private educational institutions in rural and urban areas. Although there are many differences among these participants, the precourse needs analyses conducted by the teacher trainers indicate one main similarity. All participants request and require development of language teaching skills relevant to their teaching contexts

The AR tasks described in the Appendix concern two separate groups of 13 course participants who were enrolled in the November 2000 and January 2001 programs. The majority of the participants were from Ho Chi Minh City, although some were from Hanoi and provincial regions. They were working mainly in English language departments of monofaculty universities, state secondary schools, private adult English language centers, or a combination of these workplaces. The participants' teaching experience varied from 1 year to more than 26 years. There were slightly more women (14) than men (12) represented in these two groups.

The institutions from which the participants came also exhibited differences and similarities. All the institutions had extremely limited access to agents of change, language teaching resources, and general teaching resources. They also had large class sizes of 40–50 learners, with mixed-ability groupings. The learners in these classes had different types and levels of motivation. The institutions had preset, examination-driven curricula, and institutional, economic, and social constraints worked against change. The main differences between the institutions related to prestige and the willingness of institutional administrators to support educational change. Although the institutional backgrounds, the individual requirements, and the organizational limitations experienced by the participants were diverse, the teacher trainers managed this diversity, at least in part, by continually adapting the methodologies used in the in-service programs.

The Program: TESOL Postgraduate Teacher Education

Underpinning the VU-HANU programs was a social-constructivist learning theory (Dembo & Eaton, 1997; Jacobsen, Eggen, & Kauchak, 2002). This theory suggests that learners learn best when they are cognitively engaged in constructive learning activities with others. In other words, learners learn best through activities and tasks that are meaningful, situated, developmental, and useful, and that require them to think and be engaged socially. This theory is particularly relevant to language learning, as the use of language is a situated, purposeful, social activity, and much research, at least in Western educational contexts, has demonstrated that second language skills are best developed through useful and meaningful practice (Ellis, 1994). Social-constructivist concepts were taught and practiced during the programs and used in the postcourse AR assessment tasks.

SOLVING TEACHING PUZZLES COLLABORATIVELY

The participants in the VU-HANU programs went beyond simply observing or reading what others had chosen for them. They were required to complete open-ended tasks that were directly related to their specific language teaching needs. Throughout the learning process, the teacher trainers stressed that there was no single, correct answer to the language teaching problems that the participants raised. The trainers encouraged the participants to find their own solutions to their own problems collaboratively within the social settings provided in the programs. The trainers asked the participants to consider using such approaches in their own teaching. For example, one participant wanted to raise issues related to techniques for teaching large, mixed-ability classes. In response, the trainers

- elicited the local concerns related to this matter
- examined the specific factors related to these concerns for the participant

- evaluated techniques other participants had used
- asked the class to suggest possible solutions for the participant to experiment with

The teacher trainers or participants exemplified these solutions in a subsequent lesson, and the success of the solutions was evaluated. The training framework attempted to replicate the course participants' contexts as much as possible, which allowed the participants to implement their own solutions during the programs. This replication was at least realistic, although not real. It involved the use of the same texts and the same classroom resources as were available to the participants in their teaching contexts. The program enabled the participants to reflect on their progress toward possible solutions to their teaching puzzles individually and collaboratively, which is not a common practice in Vietnamese educational contexts. The programs allowed the development of other key aspects of what I would term *successful teacher education.* Among these key aspects were increased levels of creativity in adapting and designing more relevant teaching materials, and the development of the professional confidence to alter a course structure. The chosen assessment mechanism for the programs facilitated another aspect, the application of empirical approaches to language teaching. This was done through AR projects, which formed the basis for continued, independent teacher development after the participants returned to their workplaces. The program encouraged, expected, and planned for the active participation of the course participants in their own development as English language teachers. The teacher trainers chose approaches, methodologies, and techniques based on the information obtained in the precourse needs analyses, the formative needs analyses, the skills and experiences of the teacher trainers and course participants, and the available resources.

VARIED PARTICIPANTS, VARIED TEACHER EDUCATION MODELS

The programs used a variety of teacher education models, chosen because of the diversity of the participants and their institutions. Although many aspects of the methods could be criticized, they were culturally appropriate in the Vietnamese context. Wallace (1991) outlines these methods in detail; in summary, they relate to

- the apprenticeship or craft model, in which the participants observe and follow the examples of master teachers
- the applied science model, in which the participants study theories and research findings related to language teaching and discuss, develop, and implement methodologies related to these theories and findings

- the reflective model, in which the participants teach, observe other teachers, are observed themselves, and recall past teaching and learning experiences

In the reflective model, the trainees reflect on their prior teaching and learning experiences with their colleagues and teacher trainers to work out alternative methods for themselves and their learners. The participants try these revised methods with their colleagues and continue the reflective process.

The programs were also implemented using *modified loop-input* techniques (Woodward, 1991). The techniques in use require the participants to identify specific aspects of their teaching methodology that they want to improve. They then develop strategies for improvement and seek advice from other participants, the teacher trainers, and text-based resources. The participants act on these deliberations during the training, possibly during microteaching situations. The results of these actions are then evaluated and looped back into the programs. This modified loop-input model avoids what could be criticized as prescriptive outcomes that would result if the techniques, as described in Woodward (1991), were strictly applied. The incorporation of an AR cycle into the loop avoided the transmissive approach to teacher education and the prescriptive outcomes implied in the loop-input technique. The content for the looping is determined by the participants themselves and is not predetermined by the teacher trainers. The application of a modified loop-input model requires the participants to carry out what they have planned, not what their trainers have planned for them. This process only occurs after the participants have had opportunities to reflect on and possibly observe the methodologies used by their colleagues and the teacher trainers. In summary, the participants select aspects of their teaching methodology that they would like to change. The trainers ask the participants to reflect on what they want to change and why they want to change it, and to make an action plan for the changes.

The teaching of reflection, observation, and evaluation skills, which are key aspects of empirical and AR approaches, is an additional component of this modified loop-input technique. The programs taught methodological skills and the language related to these skills. These skills were then looped back into the programs. In addition to learning the skills of professional reflection, observation, and evaluation, the participants also discussed and practiced what Richards (1998) terms *pedagogical reasoning skills,* or the ability to make lesson changes on the run. Other reflective approaches, such as using learner journals (e.g., Gray, 1998; Woodfield & Lazarus, 1998) and regular class-based evaluation and feedback sessions (e.g., Wallace, 1991), were also incorporated into the learning activities.

Participants also prepared portfolios containing resources they developed and materials they were given. The participants were expected to use these portfolios when they returned to their institutions. The materials in the portfolios were to be used for independent development of language teaching skills and to be shared with colleagues. The use of the portfolios enabled the participants to sustain their learning after the completion of the programs and to make changes to their teaching methodology to deal with curriculum constraints.

Postcourse Action Research: A Possible Solution

On their return to their teaching institutions, participants were required to complete a major postcourse task involving the use of AR techniques. This formed the main component of the assessment and related to the academic requirements of VU.

There are many definitions of action research, but Nunan's (1992b) definition encapsulates the major elements for teachers. He states that AR is "a form of self-reflective inquiry carried out by practitioners, aimed at solving problems, improving practice, or enhancing understanding. It is often collaborative" (p. 229). The simplest and most flexible AR model offered by Kemmis and McTaggart (1988; see also Burns, 1999; Nunan, 1992a; Richards & Lockhart, 1994; Wallace, 1998) involves four cyclical or spiral stages of planning, acting, observing, and reflecting. The action researcher may also enter a fifth stage of replanning, in which the cycle is repeated. This model of AR underpinned the projects that formed the main assessment mechanism in the VU-HANU programs. In the summary of participants' AR projects found in the Appendix, these stages are labeled as follows:

1. question or problem
2. plan
3. action
4. observation
5. reflection and replanning

Davis (1985) states that

action research enables you to try new ideas with a minimum of risk, it makes the task of bringing about change manageable by forcing you to make improvements step by little step, it allows you to introduce changes gradually so that they are almost imperceptible to others in the environment, who might otherwise be unsympathetic, and it allows you to involve others . . . in the change process. (p. 87)

The need for Vietnamese English language teachers to feel safe and to maintain face while they attempted to make changes was another strategic reason for choosing such an approach in the programs and for the main assessment task.

Those who use AR discover that it is an evolving process and, as one question is answered, other questions arise. At first, this approach to research was problematic for the participants because they expected to find, and be assessed on, the perfect answer. The discovery that there is no one perfect solution, and that any chosen solution creates problems of its own, was part of the participants' growing awareness and contributed to the maintenance, sustainability, and evolution of their professional development. In their AR project reports (see the Appendix), all the participants noted that new problems and directions arose because of their projects. New insights were as simple as "the teacher needs to be more active in each lesson" or "the teacher needs to give clearer instructions," or as complex as "the teacher needs to develop new texts for ESP [English for specific purposes] medical students." Such reflective responses indicated that the completed AR projects were having their desired effect. Postcourse learning was continuing, and the participants were making changes that they previously thought impossible.

Maintaining the Learning

The AR techniques used and taught in the programs required the participants to think about ways to improve their language teaching. In doing AR, the participants planned for the improvements they identified as being needed, implemented these improvements, observed what happened, reflected on their observations, and then replanned. The teacher trainers gave the participants examples of AR procedures in the form of case studies (e.g., Jackson, 1998) that were, as far as possible, specifically related to the participants' EFL teaching contexts. Once participants were familiar with AR procedures, the trainers asked them to identify and clarify their own language teaching needs. The participants were assisted in making plans that developed solutions to meet these needs. The participants then returned to their institutions and implemented their plans. This approach was one way that the participants used and sustained the concepts developed in the programs beyond the programs and after the participants had completed the AR assessment tasks.

After two programs, I completed the summary of the participants' AR tasks as set out in the Appendix. This analysis confirmed that the participants had modified and implemented the AR approaches, the teaching methodologies, and the techniques introduced during the course in ways that were relevant to the participants in their teaching contexts. The submitted tasks demonstrated an encouraging uptake of the main program content. All participants identified relevant methodological issues that had concerned them, such as how to increase learner-to-learner interactions, how to increase talking time, and how to teach grammar communicatively.

Importantly, in terms of sustainability, the submitted AR projects showed a willingness to use AR approaches for future development of language teaching skills. Fifteen of the 26 participants noted the value of the AR approaches in helping them solve their own problems. All noted that they had new problems to solve because they had completed their preliminary AR tasks. This indicated that the participants had developed a disciplined means of taking action and that exploring and reflecting on results are significant skills for language teachers in EFL contexts such as Vietnam. The participants also demonstrated that they were professionally more confident in attempting methodological changes and more creative in their approaches to these changes. A number of the participants asked colleagues to observe their classes, a rarity in Vietnam except when senior teachers observe colleagues for the purposes of inspection and professional assessment. Others developed their own language teaching materials, also a rarity in Vietnam. Still others developed an awareness that learners needed to be active members of the class and that teachers can and should share classroom power for the benefit of the learning process.

The following example from the AR summaries illustrates the social-constructivist concepts of the maintenance of learning used in the programs and demonstrates the value of AR in effecting change. One participant was concerned that his learners were passive in class, and he was "frightened of class silence." He had become aware that his learners needed to be engaged interactively (Brown, 2001) in language learning and that he needed to give them opportunities to practice their second language. In order to address these *puzzles* (Allwright & Bailey, 1991), he planned to try a number of activities and approaches. He decided to use *warmers* (Hadfield, 1998) in his classes in order to

- give all learners an equal chance to talk
- reduce the amount of immediate corrective feedback he gave (Baker & Westrup, 2000)
- organize class presentations and activities more coherently
- encourage and motivate the learners
- allow the learners more thinking time before responding

He initiated actions to fulfill his plan. He surveyed the learners to ascertain their learning styles. He organized more pair and group work, and allowed learners to rearrange the usually fixed seating arrangements. He allowed the learners more thinking time. He asked one of his colleagues to observe his classes to record and compare the amount of student talk and teacher talk. After implementing these actions, he observed that his learners appeared more active, motivated, and engaged in the lessons. The learners reported that they understood more about the language and concepts being taught, and he observed that the number of learner talking events increased fourfold. He noted, however, that the new techniques required him to prepare and plan better, and that this took more time. Because of these observations, in his reflection and replanning he was more able to select suitable exercises, activities (Vale, Scarino, & McKay, 1993), and tasks (Nunan, 1999). He had also learned how to arrange the seating to maximize student talking time.

From my perspective as a teacher trainer, the most encouraging outcome was that his plans for the future included not only using and sustaining the learning outcomes of the program he had attended, but also sharing his new approaches to problem solving. He planned to organize a professional development program during which he would report on his AR project and promote its use among his colleagues. He also planned to apply the methods of AR in attempts to solve new classroom puzzles that had emerged during his reflections, such as gaining access to alternative texts for learner use and developing a bank of classroom activities.

This example, which was fairly typical, shows that the participant could make changes, introduce new techniques, implement new methodologies, develop an institutionally based professional development program for colleagues, and become more creative and confident within his professional context. I am sure that this participant would not have believed that such incremental changes were possible until he had actually completed them. Other methodological puzzles researched for the AR reports included the management of large, mixed-ability classes; the quality and quantity of learner-to-learner interactions in the target language; the introduction of communicative techniques; and the development and maintenance of learner motivation. All these methodological issues are key concerns for Vietnamese EFL teachers and were part of the programs. The summary of the AR tasks also indicates that one of the main concerns for Vietnamese teachers—the development of professional autonomy—could be addressed despite the social, economic, cultural, and institutional constraints that operate in Vietnam.

The summary of the AR projects also indicates that the participants used varieties of new teaching techniques and either observed themselves or were observed by colleagues. In the reflection and replanning aspect of the projects, new methodological concerns emerged from researching the original problem. This implies that the process of learning can extend beyond the prescribed requirements of the VU-HANU academic program and the required Vietnamese institutional curricula. Thus the learning that took place because of this professional development could continue. More than half the respondents stated that they would continue to use AR approaches. This again indicates that teachers can be empowered to enhance their teaching approaches, even within the confines of restrictive EFL curricula, if they are given the tools to do so and if they are given the required practice in using these tools.

Conclusion

Despite the cultural and contextual concerns of the programs, the incorporated AR component developed the participants' English language teaching methodology skills in a manner that encouraged them to continue implementing the knowledge they gained. The AR assessment tasks also encouraged the participants' creativity and professional confidence in developing their skills. Perhaps the most important conclusion to be drawn from the analysis of the AR tasks is that the participants were able to make positive, effective changes in their classes for their learners even though this was not a commonly accepted practice and even though making such changes may have been problematic.

The more general outcomes of the programs in relation to the longer term effects on English language teaching practices in Vietnam would require greater exploration than the brief analysis of the participant AR assessment tasks reported here. Such research would need to include interviews with many stakeholders, workplace visits, intensive and longitudinal classroom observations, and the continuing education of the former participants in the program.

Appendix: Summary of the Postcourse AR Assessment Tasks

These AR summaries are arranged according to their thematic concerns or problems.

THEME 1: MOTIVATING STUDENTS
Question or Problem 1

- The students are very passive.
- The teacher is frightened of class silence.

Plan
- To use warmers
- To give all students a balanced chance to talk
- To lessen correction of students' oral mistakes
- To have better organized activities
- To change order of presentation of materials in the textbooks
- To motivate students
- To develop more confidence in students
- To allow a longer wait time for responses

Action
- Surveying students' learning strategies and learning styles
- Organizing more group and pair activities
- Rearranging seats and students' seating positions
- Providing students with supplementary materials from reference books
- Using warmers at the beginning of each lesson
- Allowing students more thinking time before expecting answers
- Asking colleagues to observe teaching and record student and teacher talking times

Observation
- Students reported that they understood language and concepts better after using supplementary materials.
- Students were more active: Initially, there were 60–80 student talking times; after 3 weeks there were 240–260 student talking times.
- Students were more active, motivated, and interested.
- Teacher required more planning and preparation time.

Reflection and Replanning
- Teacher knows how to select more suitable exercises, activities, and tasks.
- Teacher knows how to best arrange seating and students' seating positions for maximum student talking time.
- Teacher developed a list of 10 most popular and beneficial activities for students' learning.
- Teacher will organize and run a workshop about the AR findings for colleagues.
- Teacher will continue using AR.

Question or Problem 2

- Students find listening classes boring and difficult.

> *Plan*
> - To try new methods of teaching listening skills
> - To make students more active during the listening classes
>
> *Action*
> - Using a questionnaire to find out what students thought of the current listening classes
> - Introducing prelistening, while-listening, and postlistening tasks to assist students' listening skills
> - Asking the students to complete the questionnaire a second time after three lessons using the new teaching techniques to work out students' feelings about the new methods of teaching listening skills
> - Making students do more during the lessons
> - Having the teacher do less during the lesson but more before the lesson
>
> *Observation*
> - Students were more active and interested.
> - Students gradually improved their abilities to improve their listening skills. During Lesson 1, 30% of the students could do the while-listening activities; during Lesson 2, 50% of the students could complete the activities; and during Lesson 3, 60% of the students could complete the while-listening tasks.
> - Students were more relaxed during the classes.
> - Students enjoyed the lessons more.
> - Students did not use the answer keys or tape scripts during the listening.
>
> *Reflection and Replanning*
> - The teacher needs to use listening materials that are more relevant to the students' lives and interests.
> - Prelistening activities may need to take longer than while-listening activities.
> - Students are more interested if they are allowed to have more input into what and how they learn.
> - The teacher's attitude needs to be continually monitored as it influences the activity and performance of the students.

Question or Problem 3

- The development of students' confidence to increase their speaking time in class

Plan
- To reduce students' passivity
- To increase students' confidence
- To increase the number of classroom opportunities students have to speak
- To become a more friendly teacher

Action
- Introducing more group activities for students
- Actively assisting students while they are doing group work by moving among the groups
- Discussing with students the need for changes and involving them in the change procedures
- Using surveys of the students to ascertain their ideas of what needed to be changed
- Changing the way the teacher views mistakes and the manner of correcting mistakes
- Changing the teacher's view about willingness to make changes
- Using self-reflection as a means of identifying, implementing, and evaluating changes to the teacher's methodology
- Replanning of the timing of the components of the syllabus (from easiest to most difficult)
- Using topics that are more relevant and interesting for the students
- Using warmers
- Rearranging the seating in the classes
- Using articles in newspapers and magazines to improve students' general knowledge

Observation
- Many students previously failed the exams; now many students pass the exams.
- Students are more confident speaking in class, especially during group work.
- Students are generally happier in class.
- Students are much happier with the new seating arrangements.
- Students are much happier to regularly change groups for group work.
- Students' expectations and needs are being met more adequately.
- Students find the topics of the lessons more relevant to their lives.
- Students' critical thinking abilities have improved. (They are faster, clearer, and more decisive thinkers.)
- Teacher's method of correcting mistakes does not destroy students' level of confidence.

Reflection and Replanning
- Need to continue to use AR methodologies to improve teacher's teaching and students' learning
- Need for the teacher to continue to be self-reflective and flexible

THEME 2: INTRODUCING NEW METHODS OR CHANGING METHODS

Question or Problem 1

- The introduction of communicative methods

Plan
- To design materials to add to the current college methodology text that describes and uses communicative methodologies
- To have the trainee teachers at the college use these ideas in their practicums

Action
- Using traditional methods of teaching initially, then introducing new communicative methods
- Having students and trainee teachers reflect and comment on the effectiveness of both methods for language learning
- Introducing background reference material about the theory and practice of communicative methodologies to the trainee teachers and discussing this material
- Encouraging teacher trainees to use communicative methodologies during their practicums (The trainees were to trial these methodologies, observe these trials, and reflect and comment on the usefulness of the new methods. The action researcher also observed these trials.)
- Designing and trialing theoretical and practical ideas for a new methodology book

Observation
- The direct comparison of the use of traditional and communicative methodologies received positive comments from all trainee teachers. The students they were teaching during their practicums also gave positive feedback.
- Teachers and trainee teachers were concerned about the amount of time it takes to prepare communicative activities.

Reflection and Replanning
- Need to develop a bank of activities along with the communicative methodology textbook currently under development
- Need to revise the secondary English textbooks to make them more communicatively oriented

Question or Problem 2

- How can I change the methods of teaching English following a teacher education workshop?

Plan
- To make a direct comparison of students' involvement in lessons using old and new methods

Action
- Rearranging the seating in the classes
- Using group work and pair work
- Using role-playing activities
- Using a writing journal

Observation
- Students gradually appreciated the new methods (In Week 1, 35 of 56 students enjoyed the new methods. After 2 weeks, 47 of 56 enjoyed the new methods.)
- Fifty-two of the 56 students passed the oral examination.
- The new methods are worth continuing.

Reflection and Replanning
- Need to continue the AR approach to making changes

Question or Problem 3

- Using new and old methods of teaching English

Plan
- To compare the effectiveness of new methods and old methods
- To train students in the techniques required by the new methods
- To experiment with rearranging the seating in the classroom

Action
- Using new methods at the same time as old methods to allow students to become more comfortable with the new methods
- Trying a variety of seating arrangements and discussing the effectiveness of these seating patterns with the students
- Using more group work
- Preparing lesson plans

Observation
- Students had more chance to participate.
- Students were more motivated.
- Students could share knowledge and skills with each other.
- Students could help each other.

- Students could improve their general knowledge.
- The classroom climate became more effective.

Reflection and Replanning
- There is a need to fight sometimes against traditional Vietnamese learning styles.
- There is a need to spend more time on educating learners about the new methods.
- The strong students became more active, but the weaker students still need a lot of help with the new methods.
- Teachers need to become more involved with their students' learning.

Question or Problem 4

- How can I help students develop their listening skills?

Plan
- To analyze and critically evaluate current methods of teaching listening
- To introduce prelistening, while-listening, and postlistening tasks
- To manage large classes better during listening tasks
- To develop students' confidence
- To conduct a survey of students about preferred methods of teaching

Action
- Spending more time on prelistening tasks
- Teaching the necessary vocabulary before the listening task
- Using a variety of methods to teach the new vocabulary
- Using the three-stage teaching method: prelistening, while-listening, and postlistening
- Rearranging the seating and individual students' positions in the classroom
- Developing a more positive attitude toward the students
- Using a variety of graded tasks and questions for mixed-ability classes
- Selecting listening tasks more carefully
- Preparing lessons more carefully and making lesson plans
- Keeping and using notes of activities and impressions

Observation
- Current methods were not effective.
- New methods were more effective.
- Students became more stimulated when the teacher's attitude was more positive.
- Students are not so afraid of the listening lessons.
- Weak students felt more confident.

Reflection and Replanning
- Continue using AR techniques

Question or Problem 5

- How can I apply new methods of teaching English effectively?
- How can I help students worry less about exams?

Plan
- To rearrange the seating in the classroom
- To use pair work and group work
- To plan activities using pair work and group work
- To create an English environment in the classroom
- To prepare supplementary materials
- To teach grammar communicatively
- To get feedback from the students

Action
- Rearranging the seating in the classroom on many occasions to mix students
- Gradually increasing the amount of time spent speaking English in each lesson
- Preparing materials that are more relevant to the students
- Using grammar games more frequently
- Teaching grammar using the four skills
- Using a variety of activities and asking students what they think of the activities
- Helping students analyze their own learning styles
- Using topics and themes that are interesting for the students

Observation
- Currently, the purpose of teaching English is for the students to pass the exams.
- The exams are too focused on grammar.
- Students lacked opportunities for speaking and listening practice.
- Teachers talk too much in classes, but teacher talking time was reduced from about 90% to about 33% using the new methods.
- Teachers depend on course books too much.
- Rote-learning techniques are used too often.
- Teachers focus too much on correcting students.
- Students cheat too much on the exams.
- Oral tests would be better tests of language.

Reflection and Replanning
- The students were tired but happy.
- The teacher was more tired but happier.
- More time will need to be devoted to preparing lessons.
- The teacher will continue using AR methods in each class.
- Taking note of what students are doing in the classes is useful for future lesson planning.
- Getting evaluative feedback from the students at the end of each lesson is useful for planning.
- Practicing the new methods will help their implementation.

Question or Problem 6

- Teaching reading skills more effectively

Plan
- To identify how reading is taught currently
- To try some of the recommendations for the teaching of reading from the program

Action
- Consciously using a less teacher-centered and more student-centered approach to the teaching of reading
- Using group work for teaching reading skills

Observation
- Only 50% of students used to be engaged in the reading lesson; now more are involved.
- Students are less bored.
- Group work for pre-, while-, and postreading tasks increased students' language practice.

Reflection and Replanning
- Need to continue trying new approaches to and activities for the teaching of reading skills

Question or Problem 7

- How I can teach ESP reading skills to my medical students?

Plan
- To try to improve the students' general reading skills
- To try to improve the students' technical reading skills
- To investigate current teaching practices
- To investigate and trial new methods of teaching reading skills to ESP students

Action
- Trying to define the problem in the classroom
- Developing, administering, and analyzing a student questionnaire on teaching methodology
- Trying new suggestions that come from analysis of questionnaire and observing any changes

Observation
- The use of prereading activities assisted students' comprehension (previous methods, 50% success; new methods, 70%—and increasing—success).
- Preteaching specific vocabulary items assisted comprehension and retention of the new, specialized vocabulary.

Reflection and Replanning
- The time spent on prereading activities is worthwhile.
- The AR process is worthwhile.
- New texts for ESP medical students need to be developed.

THEME 3: INCREASING STUDENT INTERACTIONS AND REDUCING TEACHER TALK

Question or Problem 1

- Increasing students' interactions in a reading lesson

Plan
- To rearrange the students' seating in the class
- To use more group and pair reading activities
- To incorporate a variety of levels of activities for a mixed-ability class
- To mix more-able students with less-able students

Action
- Observing three different classes using three different texts and three different methods, from the traditional method to more communicative methods
- Having a colleague observe these classes and record the interactions
- Having the classes videorecorded for further analysis and reflection
- Carefully planning the reading tasks
- Being more friendly, helpful, and enthusiastic
- Planning a variety of activities for each reading text

Observation
- With the traditional method, only about 50% of the students were involved in the class.
- With the traditional method, the weaker students remained passive, nervous, and silent and relied on the stronger students to answer the questions.
- The traditionally taught lesson was boring for both the teacher and the students.
- The data from observation of the first lesson and the videotape of the second and third lessons, using a more communicative approach, indicated that two thirds of the students were active versus one third in the first lesson.
- Stronger students and weaker students began to enjoy working together.
- The teacher became more of a facilitator rather than a controller.
- Students learned more.
- Students began to feel more relaxed in class than ever before.

> *Reflection and Replanning*
> - Continue using AR techniques
> - Continue to use a more communicative method to teach reading skills
> - Exchange ideas with colleagues about this approach to the teaching of reading

Question or Problem 2

- How can I make students more active in class?
- How can I feel more relaxed when teaching a silent class?

> *Plan*
> - To build the students' confidence
> - To increase the opportunities for students to talk in class
> - To be a friendly teacher
> - To minimize the correcting of students
> - To have well-organized activities
> - To prepare interesting topics
> - To rearrange the class seating to be more suitable
>
> *Action*
> - Using warmers at the beginning of each lesson
> - Using a variety of activities that made sure that all students had some responsibilities during the activities
> - Educating learners about the purposes and processes of pair work and group work
> - Introducing student self-correction techniques
> - Thinking before correcting
> - Preparing interesting topics for the students
> - Allowing students to use their mother tongue when they had tried but were not succeeding in conveying an idea in English
> - Rearranging the seating to suit the activity
> - Educating learners about the seating arrangements and rearrangements
> - Using praise generously
> - Talking less
>
> *Observation*
> - Warmers helped students feel more relaxed.
> - Warmers helped students get the general idea of the lesson.
> - Students had more chances to talk.
> - Students felt more confident when they were not corrected immediately.
> - Students were more interested in the lessons.
> - Passive students became more active.
> - The teacher felt much more tired but happier.
> - Some students spoke in their mother tongue more often than necessary.

> *Reflection and Replanning*
> - Need to continue to develop interesting tasks and activities
> - Note that students are more active when their minds are engaged and at work
> - Try to locate more suitable classrooms with more suitable furniture for group and pair work
> - Attempt to have a proper balance between use of mother tongue and English

Question or Problem 3

- How can I increase student talking time in my classes?

> *Plan*
> - To reflect on and analyze previous methods that were not working
> - To use ideas from different textbooks to develop speaking and listening activities
> - To use previous methods with one class and new methods with another class and then compare the two
>
> *Action*
> - Teaching one class traditionally
> - Teaching the second class using new methods as follows:
>   —Using warmers related to the theme
>   —Spending more time preparing the students for the tasks
>   —Giving clear instructions about the activities
>   —Moving among the students when they are doing pair and group work
>   —Using competitions
>   —Using more elicitation
>
> *Observation*
> - Old methods reflected the way that I had been taught and were now no longer appropriate for nonlanguage students.
> - The new methods worked better than the old methods to solve the problem of class silence.
>
> *Reflection and Replanning*
> - Students are happier and appear to be more confident.
> - Teaching is more enjoyable.
> - There are many more problems to solve about teaching English in Vietnam.

Question or Problem 4

- The students are passive and not doing well in exams.

Plan
- To involve more students in class
- To have students do better in exams

Action
- Having class and individual meetings with students to discuss the plan
- Supplying prelistening activities to set the context
- Initially placing students who are friends in groups and then rearranging these groups
- Breaking down difficult questions into smaller, more understandable components
- Using more warmers and language games
- Using more eye contact
- Giving more positive feedback to students

Observation
- After the changes, all students had at least one chance to use English in class.
- Before the changes, half of the students were involved in classes; after the changes, 90% of students were eager to join activities.
- Students showed more confidence to take chances.
- Classes were more cooperative.
- Students had better listening and speaking skills.

Reflection and Replanning
- Need to continue implementing changes
- Need to think of solution to seating arrangement
- Continue using more games and warmers
- Continue using AR procedures

Question or Problem 5

- How can I engage students more actively in a lesson?

Plan
- To apply group and pair activities

Action
- Changing the seating arrangements and the seating positions of students
- Encouraging competition between groups
- Reminding students of the need to pass the examinations and how using group and pair work is related to this
- Asking students for feedback about each lesson
- Changing lesson plans based on the students' feedback

> *Observation*
> - All students were involved in the lessons.
> - Students reported that they were more interested in the lessons.
> - Students felt more confident speaking.
> - Teacher worked less in the lesson but more before the lesson.
> - Students were evaluated as the best in the college in speaking skills.
>
> *Reflection and Replanning*
> - Need to train students in the new approaches
> - Need to make all instructions clear
> - Need to have stronger students show new approaches to weaker students
> - Continue to use the AR approach

Question or Problem 6

- How can I better use the time spent on communicative activities?

> *Plan*
> - To record different lessons using different ways of using communicative activities
>
> *Action*
> - Only using the stages that were necessary for the communicative activities
> - Organizing roles of the students in the groups (e.g., one student would be a secretary, one a leader)
> - Brainstorming as a whole-class activity and not a part of the group activity
> - Using group work only when relevant to the communicative activity, and using lockstep or pair work if it is more suitable for the communicative activity
> - Recording two lessons to use in analyzing the organization of the communicative activities
> - Using a questionnaire to find out students' feelings about using the new methods of arranging the classes
>
> *Observation*
> - Before the investigation, group work took up too much of the lesson time. After analysis of the recorded lessons and implementation of the strategies, group-work time was more efficiently organized.
> - Group work should not be applied to simple communicative tasks.
>
> *Reflection and Replanning*
> - The teacher must be strict when students are doing group work; that is, the teacher must give clear instructions, and the students must follow these instructions carefully and completely.
> - Some students do not like group work.
> - The teacher needs to continue researching the class.

Question or Problem 7

- Student-to-student interactions are very limited.

Plan
- To rearrange students' seating
- To survey students' needs with regard to activity types
- To survey students' responses to the teacher's teaching style

Action
- Getting students' attention before starting any activity
- Standing in the middle of the room to get students' attention
- After forming pairs or groups, recommending students' attention to listen to instructions about task
- Checking students' understanding of instructions
- Using pair and group work more frequently
- Reducing teacher talking time
- Encouraging, rewarding, and praising student-to-student interactions and all students in general
- Varying interaction types (teacher-student, teacher-students, student-teacher, students-teacher, student-student, students-students)
- Encouraging a more relaxed and friendly learning environment
- Preparing a variety of tasks for the students in mixed-ability classes

Observation
- Positive atmosphere in class was noted.
- Passive students became more active.
- All students participated more.
- Students' self-confidence improved.
- Students' talking time increased.
- Students were more eager to practice.
- Stronger students helped weaker students more enthusiastically.
- All students had at least one chance to speak in each lesson.
- Length of student-to-student interactions increased.

Reflection and Replanning
- Teacher needs to continually plan and prepare materials for mixed-ability classes.
- Teacher needs to plan and prepare materials to be suitable for group and pair work.
- Teacher needs to practice the skills of skimming and scanning.
- Teacher needs to apply AR principles in future.
- Getting evaluative feedback from the students at the end of each lesson is useful for planning.
- Practicing the new methods will help better implementation of these methods.

Question or Problem 8

- The talking time of students is very limited.

Plan
- To use pair work and group work
- To use warmers to increase students' talking time

Action
- Changing textbook exercises into communicative activities
- Using a warmer related to the previous or current lesson at the beginning of each lesson
- Using stronger students to assist weaker students in groups
- Allowing students to use Vietnamese when necessary
- Directing students to change groups regularly

Observation
- Before the changes, 85% of students had low or average marks; after the changes, 85% of students had average to high marks.
- Teacher knows more about students' needs and learning styles.

Reflection and Replanning
- Increase use and scope of future AR plans

Question or Problem 9

- How can I increase students' talking time?

Plan
- To use warmers
- To select suitable materials from the textbook and from reference books
- To use more visual cues
- To allow more time for students to talk
- To not correct students' mistakes immediately
- To organize more motivating activities
- To organize more pair and group work
- To rearrange the seating in the classroom

Action
- Keeping a detailed teacher diary
- Collecting survey data from the students regularly
- Asking colleagues to observe and reflect on teacher's teaching
- Asking students to work in pairs more often than they work individually
- Using warmers at the beginning of each lesson
- Selecting more linguistically suitable and conceptually interesting materials from the textbook and from reference materials

- Rearranging desks to suit the content of lessons
- Rearranging students' seating positions so that less active students are sitting with more active students
- Developing and using information-gap activities
- Reflecting on all the changes made and writing up these reflections in the diary

Observation
- Students were fighting for chances to speak.
- Students were more motivated.
- Students were more active in every lesson.
- Initially, students spoke 70 times in one lesson. After 3 weeks, in one observed lesson students spoke 190 times, with one student speaking 12 times. The lowest number of speaking turns was 3.
- In one lesson, colleagues observed that teacher talking time was 30% and student talking time was 70%.

Reflection and Replanning
- Teacher needs to spend time with each group to help with linguistic and conceptual concerns.
- Teacher needs to actively participate in the students' group work.
- Time for developing materials is sometimes difficult to find.
- Group and pair work are better for students' learning than teacher-centered lessons are.
- For the first time, the teacher felt successful in her profession.

Question or Problem 10

- How can I find out the best grouping arrangements for a listening session?

Plan
- To trial different grouping arrangements to see which is the best
- To increase students' talking time and reduce teacher's talking time
- To increase students' participation and enjoyment

Action
- Surveying a number of students in the class on what they thought of the current methods of teaching listening and how much English they spoke in a listening lesson
- Rearranging the seating of the students into groups and pairs depending on the tasks
- Encouraging students to use each other to answer questions
- Having students help each other assess work
- Using prelistening activities
- Rearranging the seating to allow the teacher to move more freely among all the students

Observation
- Students previously were not using English to learn English; they were only trying to get the correct answers to the textbook questions.
- After rearranging the students into either groups or pairs, students were more interested in using English to answer the questions or complete the tasks.
- The new methods saved a lot of class time.
- Students were more interested, confident, and involved.

Reflection and Replanning
- Gathering information from the students about themselves is useful to continue.
- Teacher needs to change which students sit with which other students in the class so that they are not always with the same partners.
- Creating a variety of activities requires time but is very effective.
- To continue using AR techniques is valuable.

Question or Problem 11

- How can I increase talking time for ESP students?

Plan
- To rearrange the seating in the classroom
- To apply pair work and group work
- To choose more suitable materials to replace the foreign materials in the course book
- To motivate students

Action
- Analyzing why the students were not currently talking in the class
- Rearranging the seating in the classroom so that students could face each other
- Introducing, teaching about, and practicing pair work
- Introducing, teaching about, and practicing group work
- Using reference books to develop new activities and tasks to replace the irrelevant activities and tasks in the current course book
- Using warmers, positive feedback techniques, more appropriate correction methods, better demonstrations, and the teaching of paraphrasing and circumlocution techniques to motivate students

Observation
- Students were more active and more confident.
- Students reported that traditionally taught lessons were boring.
- Teacher talking time decreased from 80% to 40% of the lesson.
- Students' expectations and needs were being met.
- Students still had problems with instructions.

- Some students were still too shy to speak.
- Some students took advantage of the group activities to chat in Vietnamese.
- Colleagues complained of noise.

Reflection and Replanning
- Selecting alternative tasks and activities relevant to the students' backgrounds and needs is a useful but time-consuming practice.
- The teacher needs to be more active in each lesson, moving from group to group or pair to pair.
- Clear instructions are needed.
- There is a need to explain new methods to other teachers.
- The use of AR techniques should be continued to make other positive changes.

THEME 4: DESIGNING THE SYLLABUS
Question or Problem 1

- What type of syllabus can be designed for ESP at the university?

Plan
- To develop a relevant ESP syllabus
- To design, administer, and analyze a student questionnaire to guide the development of a new ESP syllabus

Action
- Developing a questionnaire for undergraduate and postgraduate students
- Administering and analyzing the questionnaire
- Using the questionnaire to inform the development of a more relevant ESP syllabus
- Presenting the questionnaire to colleagues for discussion and appraisal

Observation
- Teachers and students need more relevant methods and materials.
- A new course book needs to be designed for the new syllabus.

Reflection and Replanning
- Sharing opinions with colleagues is useful.

THEME 5: TEACHING LARGE OR MIXED-ABILITY CLASSES
Question or Problem 1

- Managing large, mixed-ability classes
- Incorporating group and pair work into classes

Plan
- To be more learner centered
- To use group and pair work

Action
- Remembering students' names
- Speaking loudly and clearly enough
- Using more eye contact
- Paying attention to weaker students
- Using different exercises for students with different abilities
- Using different students groupings (e.g., weak with strong students)
- Using pair work for drills and group work for freer production
- Giving different roles for students in the groups (e.g., secretary, scribe, monitor)
- Using different seating arrangements (e.g., circle, semicircle, traditional rows)

Observation
- Students performed better in oral examinations. (Before the changes, one third of the students failed, and no student had an excellent grade. After the changes, one ninth of students failed, and two students received an excellent grade.)

Reflection and Replanning
- Students need more education in using the new approaches.
- Teachers need more practice implementing the new approaches.
- New approaches require more careful preparation by teachers.
- New approaches require more effort in planning by teachers.

Question or Problem 2

- Teaching grammar communicatively in large, mixed-ability classes

Plan
- To change the class seating arrangement
- To use more oral practice in classes
- To improve students' confidence
- To change students' attitudes toward making errors and mistakes
- To teach grammar more inductively
- To develop a more cooperative classroom environment

Action
- Using a variety of activities to introduce new grammar points to the students
- Asking students to identify and describe patterns in the new language they are investigating
- Asking students to relate these patterns to grammar they already know
- Giving students explanations of grammar in written form that they read at home
- Using warmer activities related to the new grammar points and for revision of these points
- Using contexts that are directly related to the students' contexts
- Asking and requiring students to write their own grammar rules
- Carefully designing grammar practice activities

Observation
- Students gradually became more active and confident in classes.
- Students gradually became more responsible for their own learning.
- Students gradually became more vocal in classes.
- Classes became more and more smooth in operation.
- Students began to tolerate their own errors and saw them as a natural part of the learning process.
- No method is perfect.

Reflection and Replanning
- Using the new methods takes time for the teacher to prepare.
- Students require education in understanding and using the new methods.
- Teachers need to persist with their efforts to make changes and not give up after a single failure.
- Teachers need to be able to deviate from the planned lessons and feel comfortable about this.
- Colleagues are a vital source of support and new ideas.
- AR is an important process to continue.

Question or Problem 3

- Why are students passive in language classes?
- How can I make students more active in large, mixed-ability classes?

Plan
- To observe what the students currently do during speaking activities
- To self-reflect on current methods of correcting students while they are doing speaking activities
- To analyze the required texts more thoroughly

Action
- Using more pair and group tasks
- Moving among the students while they are doing their pair and group work
- Rearranging the seating in the class to better allow for group work
- Making decisions about whether to correct students' mistakes while they are doing their speaking activities or to wait
- Introducing and using self-correction techniques to the students
- Providing time for end-of-lesson evaluations by students
- Using different types of tasks of differing levels of difficulty in differing student groupings
- Using open-ended questions
- Using warm-up activities
- Varying the methods of reading and the types of reading tasks

Observation
- Formerly passive students are more active in each lesson. (Ninety percent of all students are now active; previously about 50% were.)
- Teacher talks less, and students talk more.
- Students are more confident, even the weak ones.
- Students report that lessons are more practical and interesting.
- The class atmosphere is more positive.
- Students' comprehension has improved.
- The teacher now does not need to be the queen of the class.

Reflection and Replanning
- The students are no longer afraid of each other, the work, or the teacher.
- The teacher is now more able to take risks, be more adventurous with the applied methods, and accept imperfection.
- There is no one best method.

Innovations in Curriculum Development: Crossing Cultures, Crossing Generations

ABIGAIL BROWN AND JENNIFER WHARTON

At the Maui Writers Conference in 2000, Frank McCourt spoke on his years as an English teacher in New York. He mentioned a project in which he had asked high school students to write children's stories, which were then evaluated by elementary school students. The aim of this activity was to establish a meaningful task that would motivate the high school students to develop their writing skills by providing a target audience that would give feedback. As ESL instructors at TransPacific Hawai'i College (TPHC), in the United States, we faced similar problems in motivating students to learn and practice reading and writing skills, and to understand the application of these skills in broader communicative contexts.

We were inspired by McCourt to design a set of instructional materials for a structured, repeatable reading and writing curriculum unit. This project, first piloted in fall 2002, developed a user-friendly unit that was designed to reinforce the established reading and writing competency objectives for two groups of learners by having them cooperate around a specific task. We focused on two student populations, students from a local Hawai'i elementary school and international college students from TPHC. We designed a project that required the groups of students to collaborate in order to produce original children's literature, as illustrated in the excerpt from "Mike and the Star" (page 94), a story created by an elementary school student and a Japanese college student.

In addition to reinforcing specific language skill competencies, we were particularly interested in the effects this social and collaborative activity

Excerpt From "Mike and the Star"

would have on the English language students. We wanted to find ways to make learning these skills enjoyable and to understand how this enjoyment might affect students' motivation to read and write and their attitude toward these activities. The resulting curriculum unit is the product of our curiosity and effort, and our continuing interest in designing memorable and worthwhile learning opportunities for students along a continuum of literacy development.

The literacy unit addressed the following reading and writing learning objectives for both groups of learners:

- to provide meaningful communicative reading activities for a group of college-level language students and a group of elementary school students
- to provide authentic reading materials for and promote reading appreciation among elementary school students
- to develop the reading and writing literacy skills of the college-level language students and the elementary school students
- to provide a meaningful communicative writing task for the ESL students through which they could practice and learn academic language skills, including process writing, product orientation, and basic narrative structure in writing
- to give the elementary students a voice and place in which they could be the expert

- to provide a sense of product and contribution for the ESL students
- to introduce both groups to the concepts of juried products and product marketing
- to foster a sense that reading and writing can be fun
- to facilitate connection and dialogue between international university-level students and primary school students in the Hawai'i community
- to continue TPHC's educational and service-oriented mission in the community

Motivation for the Innovation

Five other factors influenced our interest in designing the curriculum unit and motivated us to proceed with the project. We hoped that the project would reinforce reading and writing competencies for both groups, provide opportunities for the ESL students to use the target language, provide opportunities for both groups to interact outside their own age groups, fulfill TPHC's service-learning mission, and contribute to the development of global citizens.

REINFORCING COMPETENCIES

Our goal was to provide students with a fun and motivating curriculum unit that would reinforce two sets of reading and writing competencies, those set by the college and those set for the children by the Department of Education (DOE; see Hawai'i State Department of Education, 2005). We aimed to achieve this by developing a meaningful task through which the students could apply and practice strategies learned in their regular classrooms.

PROVIDING OPPORTUNITIES FOR TARGET LANGUAGE USE

We were also particularly interested in the effects of a social and collaborative activity on the motivations and attitudes of the foreign English language students toward reading and writing, and in finding ways to make learning these skills fun. Moreover, although the college's intensive academic program is attractive in many ways, it also creates a few challenges. TPHC now has a homogeneous, almost exclusively Japanese student population. Students in the ESL program attend English language classes for 7 hours each day, which limits their opportunities to use English outside the college.

Paradoxically, although the college students sometimes complain of few opportunities for interaction with native speakers, they also express nervousness and a lack of confidence, stemming from their perceived inadequate language proficiency, to create those target language situations on their own. Many teachers have attempted to address this problem by organizing field trips, but opportunities for sustained interaction with native speakers of

English and the rapport necessary for developing more complex communication skills over time are limited because most field trips are a single event. Although teachers can justify taking classes into the community to practice their speaking and listening skills, opportunities for practicing reading and writing are somewhat harder to find or orchestrate. Thus, we also designed the project to give our international ESL students a series of opportunities to interact with English-speaking students during school hours, using a variety of language skills.

DEALING WITH ISOLATION AND MATURATION: DEVELOPMENTAL OBSTACLES

It was clear that both groups of students who were to participate in the project spent a considerable amount of time isolated within their own age groups. Opportunities for communication were generally limited to peers, families or host families, and teacher interactions.

The international students, in particular, were in a somewhat unnatural situation, as they had very little or no contact with children in Hawai'i unless their host families happened to have children. TPHC students are just moving into young adulthood, but they have relatively few opportunities to take on more adult roles and responsibilities because they spend most of their time with people in their own age group, do not work, live with host families, and for the most part are entirely financially supported. In many cases, they do not even see themselves as adults, because the age of adulthood in Japan is 20 and not 18, as it is in the United States. Other than responsibility for schoolwork, students at the college, and new students in particular, do not often encounter situations in which they can learn to handle some of the responsibilities that will come with adult social roles. The project allowed students to begin to take on some of these roles in a supervised context.

FULFILLING THE SERVICE-LEARNING MISSION

A further benefit of the project was that it supported TPHC's service-learning mission. The college has a strong service-learning component in its overall mission and philosophy, and ESL students are provided with service-learning opportunities through an elective volunteering class and a college-wide volunteering program. Approximately 35% of the student population engages in regular volunteering activities.

Participation in service-based programs gives the largely Japanese student population opportunities to become active members of the Hawai'i community, to practice language skills with native speakers of English, and to develop valuable future job skills. We thought that the project would provide incremental social and language practice in a structured environment for the ESL students, who might then sign up for other volunteering activities once they felt more comfortable with and confident about their ability to interact effectively with native speakers.

DEVELOPING A GLOBAL VIEW AND UNDERSTANDING THE CONTINUUM OF LEARNING

TPHC has a clearly stated mission to create global citizens. Murphey and Jacobs (2000) state that "the incremental assuming of control of one's language learning within a community not only accelerates acquisition, but changes group and individual personalities" (p. 228). We hoped that participation in the project would foster an understanding in the students of themselves as members of a global community of learners.

We also hoped that both groups of learners would gain a greater appreciation of the continuum of literacy development, particularly English literacy development, independent of factors such as age, ethnic affiliation, or national group membership. By collaboratively developing texts like the excerpt from "The Naughty Ghost" shown on page 98, both groups of students could begin to see themselves not primarily as second graders, or college students, or U.S. students, or international students, but rather as writers creating a story.

Pedagogical Principles

Our by no means exhaustive review of the literature showed that a number of tested pedagogical practices substantiated the rationale for the unit. The six pedagogical learning principles that guided the development of the curriculum unit are outlined here.

MIXED-AGED READING DYADS

Mixed-aged dyads have a positive effect on the attitudes toward reading of unenthusiastic readers. Research indicates that cross-age reading encourages student motivation and performance on standardized reading and writing measures (Leland & Fitzpatrick, 1994).

Leland and Fitzpatrick (1994) took a class of sixth graders who were "generally unenthusiastic about reading" (p. 292) and paired them with kindergarten students to study the effects of cross-age reading on motivation. The study confirmed that collaboration between mixed-age dyads improved reading and writing motivation as reported by the students, their parents, teachers, and the librarian. The study also indicated that "developing a sense of ownership fosters positive attitudes toward reading and writing" (p. 295) and that putting reading into a social context is beneficial for students. Outside the actual focus of the study, their research also indicated

Excerpt From "The Naughty Ghost"

improvement in some aspects of reading ability and, as reported by the librarian, an increased use of the library. The younger children also reported being positive about reading and writing with the older children (p. 300).

TASK-BASED COMMUNICATIVE ACTIVITIES

First and second language research shows that the classroom use of task-based communicative activities helps second language learners of all ages acquire and practice language skills. When students must negotiate a task, they use and practice language in a meaningful way.

LEARNER-CENTERED CLASSROOMS

There has been a shift in recent years from teacher-fronted classrooms to those that focus on the learner as active participant because of the belief that learner-centered classes are more effective. The role of the teacher has changed, in language classrooms in particular, from that of disseminator of knowledge to that of facilitator of learning through the active construction of opportunities for learning to take place. The teacher does not teach knowledge so much as design classroom situations that will require the students to participate and, in the process of participation, learn the targeted knowledge base or acquire the targeted proficiency (Murphey & Jacobs, 2000).

EXPLICIT DIRECTION IN HELPING BEHAVIORS AND PEER TEACHING STRATEGIES

Klingner and Vaughn (2000), in their study of the effects of helping behaviors in an ESL classroom, indicate that explicit instruction in cooperative learner strategies aids student acquisition of language skills. This is because such strategies give students opportunities for a greater range of language practice. It is also necessary to structure the learning environment so that students know how to help each other learn. After studying the effects of using cooperative strategic reading on reading skill improvement in content classrooms, Klingner and Vaughn concluded that peer interaction and helping behavior facilitate acquisition of reading skills.

COLLABORATIVE LEARNING MODELS

Collaborative learning methods have gained increasing attention in recent years because of a number of studies that have linked these methods to greater student achievement (e.g., Sharon, 1980). Collaboration implies that all learners have something to contribute to the completion of a task. Students must negotiate with each other, decide on roles and tasks, and communicate with each other at different stages as they work toward completion. Murphey's (1998) "near-peer role models" are people who are close to each other in "proximity, time, size, ethnicity, age, sex, interests and learning level" (pp. 201–202). Near-peer role models have a bigger impact on learning than role models who are more distant because they provide input that is more comprehensible to the learner.

Our literacy project required collaboration between participants who could be considered distant in terms of age, nationality, and first language: 7- to 9-year-old U.S. students of diverse ethnicity and 18- to 19-year-old Japanese college students. However, we purposefully chose to combine these particular age groups. We wanted to include learners who were all beginners working on similar skills in reading and writing development and on similar collaborative skills, such as giving feedback politely, thinking critically, asking for further information, and being able to share ideas freely. We also wanted to provide an opportunity for increased interaction that would not be particularly face-threatening or scary for either group of students. We thought each group had distinctive contributions to offer to the task of generating a children's story and would collaborate effectively.

PROCESS WRITING

Process writing, as it currently appears in the literature, presents a series of steps—brainstorming, evaluating, organizing, writing, and editing—that are repeated in a spiral pattern, resulting in a higher quality product. As teachers in a competency-based curriculum, designed to enable second language students to write and read at a college level, we expect students to produce acceptable academic work. It is through the introduction of clear guidelines for each phase that students can complete the process and generate an acceptable product.

The Curriculum Context

THE INSTITUTION

TPHC is a nonprofit, 2-year college in Honolulu accredited by the Western Association of Schools and Colleges. It is dedicated to providing international students from Asia with opportunities to improve their English language skills through its ESL program and to obtain an associate in arts (AA) degree through its college program (see Organization of the ESL and Associate in Arts Programs). The college is quite small, with a maximum enrollment of 280 students and a class size of 16 or fewer students. All incoming students are assigned to a level by an institutional placement test that is later confirmed by performance on the Test of English as a Foreign Language (TOEFL) and by teacher observations.

The ESL program is intensive, with students attending classes 7 hours a day, 4 days a week. The program has two levels: intermediate and advanced. Beginning-level ESL was being piloted at the college at the time of writing but involved a relatively small number of students. The typical student completes the intensive ESL program prior to entering the 18-month AA program. While in ESL, students focus on acquiring and practicing the English language and academic skills they will need to succeed in the AA program. The program adopts a competency-based curriculum and an integrated skills approach in which reading and writing skills and speaking and listening skills are paired. The program uses competency-based assessment along with TOEFL performance as the criteria for advancement through the ESL program and acceptance into the AA program. Students must complete their English proficiency requirements in 9 months, with the average being 6 months, or two terms of 12 weeks.

Students must demonstrate proficiency in clearly articulated competencies at each level in the curriculum. For example, students moving from intermediate-level to advanced-level reading and writing must demonstrate

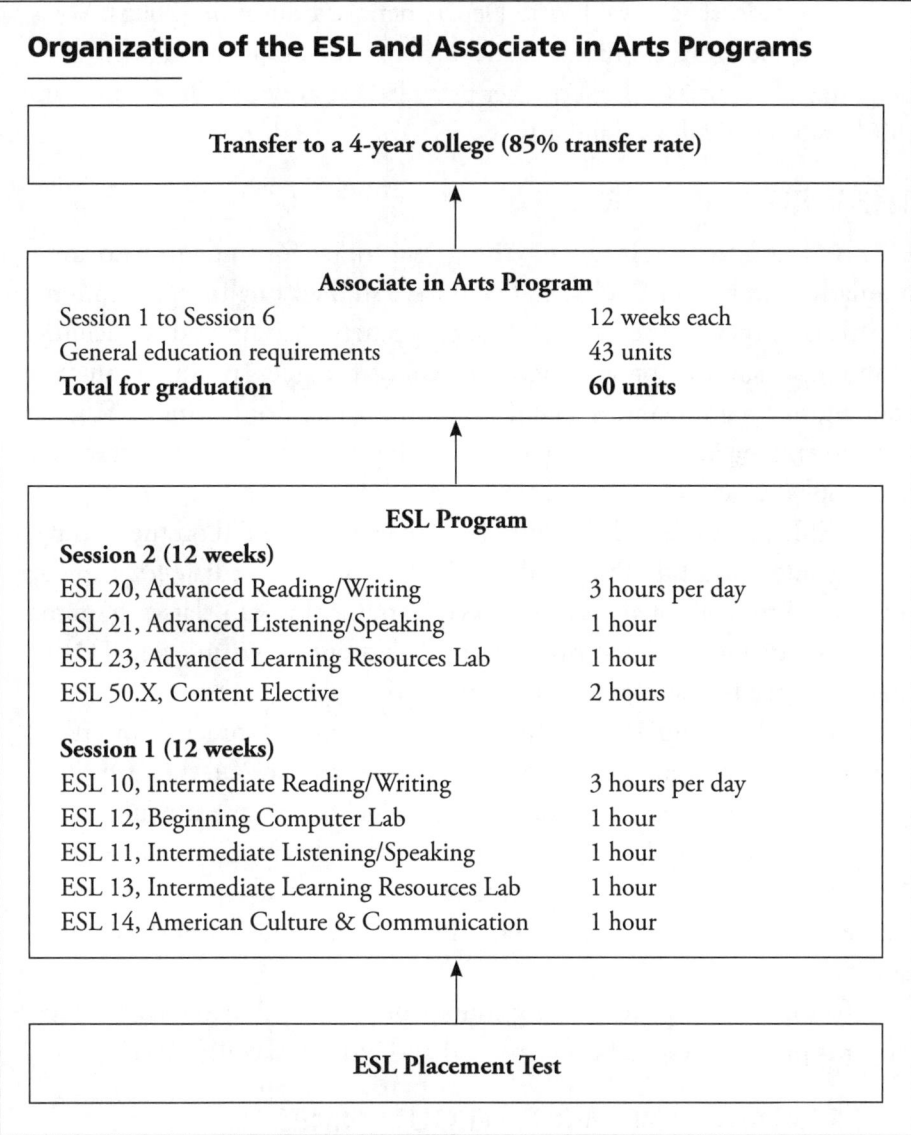

an ability to write an academic paragraph, including a topic sentence, supporting sentences, and a concluding sentence. Similarly, students moving from intermediate-level to advanced-level listening and speaking must demonstrate that they can effectively engage in conversation by making relevant comments, asking questions, signaling comprehension or lack of comprehension, and soliciting and offering opinions. Teaching within this curricular context, we found it natural to design a curriculum unit that encouraged students to practice specific reading, writing, speaking, and listening competencies that were already a required part of the ESL program. The curriculum unit also targeted specific language arts content standards established for second and third grades by the DOE (for a complete list of these standards, see Hawai'i State Department of Education, 2005). We researched the DOE standards at the outset of the project, and one participating elementary school teacher provided expanded DOE second- and third-grade curriculum standards.

THE WRITING COURSE

ESL 10, Intermediate Reading/Writing, is a course for students who are nonnative speakers of English but who have studied English for a minimum of 5 years in their home country. Students practice reading skills, including skimming, scanning, previewing, using context to guess meaning, predicting content, making inferences, and distinguishing fact from opinion. Students learn to employ a process approach to writing and progress from developing paragraphs to developing academic essays.

In ESL 20, Advanced Reading/Writing, students build on the reading, writing, and critical thinking skills learned at the intermediate level and are introduced to additional rhetorical essay patterns. In both classes, grammar structures are reviewed and practiced as they occur in writing, and TOEFL practice in reading and grammar is included.

ESL 20, Reading/Writing Intensive, is a course for students who perform better than average on the ESL placement test and on the TOEFL in their first term. Because the college has adopted a clearly articulated competency-based ESL curriculum and assumes that students will go to AA with this specific knowledge base, these students take one term in ESL before they move to the AA program. In that term, they cover the competencies for both ESL 10 and ESL 20.

The three reading and writing courses in ESL are all designed to prepare students progressively to be able to read and write at a college level.

THE READING AND WRITING OUTCOMES

The following reading and writing competencies from the competency-based curriculum were targeted in the curriculum unit.

1. employ a process approach to writing, including brainstorming, clustering, outlining, revising, rewriting, proofreading, editing, and evaluating
2. develop strategies used in writing coherent and unified academic paragraphs and essays by formulating topic sentences, writing supporting sentences, ordering sentences and paragraphs logically, using transitions, and beginning to master complex grammatical structures
3. write a descriptive or narrative paragraph using spatial or chronological ordering

4. write interesting and effective introductions and conclusions
5. guess vocabulary from context and expand active vocabulary
6. preview and predict the content of a reading selection
7. read a text and answer basic comprehension questions
8. make inferences and be able to answer inference questions
9. increase reading speed
10. engage in extensive reading and demonstrate understanding

The literacy project targeted more than 15 learning objectives from the DOE standards for second and third grades (Hawai'i State Department of Education, 2005), including these:

- read for enjoyment and to gain information
- interact and respond to material presented in a text
- demonstrate fluency in reading
- apply spelling-sound recognition and meaning-based strategies
- relate information and events in a text to the student's own ideas and life experiences
- share reading with others
- share the experiences of others from different cultures through reading and discussion
- write for self and others about familiar topics and topics of interest
- read one's own writing to check for meaning, spelling, and punctuation and to rewrite, add, or delete words to make writing clearer
- share writing at various stages
- illustrate ideas in a text with pictures
- be able to give the rudiments of constructive feedback on written material

The texts that the students produced collaboratively clearly demonstrate these learning objectives. For example, the excerpt from "Scary Story" shown on page 104 displays a developing ability to order sentences logically, use appropriate connectors, and illustrate ideas in a text with pictures.

We had specific areas of concern about TPHC's reading and writing curriculum. We felt that students lacked a real audience for their writing and that they were therefore not producing a finished product that readers would appreciate as a communicative work with a message. Students were not participating fully in the writing process because they did not understand the process approach. Because several rhetorical styles had to be covered at each level in the curriculum, in a 12-week term there was not enough time to undertake a complete process approach with all essay types. We thought that independent practice in writing a children's book would reinforce a process approach to writing as an effective way to generate

Excerpt From "Scary Story"

On the seat next to his seat, a girl is also sleeping. Her name is Jennifer. She does not like studying, but she loves her family very much.

a successful written product. We hoped that by mastering and internalizing process writing techniques, the students would be able to apply these techniques to other rhetorical patterns in the future.

THE STUDENT POPULATIONS

The project involved two student populations, a group of native-Japanese-speaking ESL learners at TPHC and a group of second- and third-grade students at a local public elementary school (see Project Participants). The curriculum unit was piloted for the first time during TPHC's fall session in 2002 and implemented in spring and fall 2003.

For the fall 2002 pilot course, the 12 Japanese-speaking students from TPHC were enrolled in two advanced-level classes: one ESL 20 Intensive class and one ESL 20 class. One of the students in the ESL 20 class was repeating the advanced-level course. The 26 second graders were attending a local public elementary school, and the class included special education students. The students were also taking a once-a-week Japanese language and culture class. Two college-level ESL teachers and one elementary school teacher participated in the project.

In the spring 2003 project implementation, the 56 TPHC students were enrolled in five reading and writing classes: three cohorts of intermediate-

Project Participants		
Fall 2002	**Spring 2003**	**Fall 2003**
12 Japanese college students	56 Japanese college students	12 Japanese college students
26 second graders	51 third graders	25 second graders
2 college teachers	5 college teachers	1 college teacher
1 elementary school teacher	2 elementary school teachers	1 elementary school teacher

level students, one cohort of advanced-level students, and one cohort of intensive-level students. The 51 elementary school students came from two third-grade classes. We were each teaching a reading and writing cohort, one at the intermediate level and another at the intensive level. Three other college-level ESL teachers and two third-grade teachers participated. In the fall 2003 course, one ESL 20 class of 12 TPHC students and one second-grade class with 25 students participated in the project along with one college-level ESL teacher and one elementary school teacher.

Designing and Adapting the Curriculum Unit

THE PILOT

For the pilot, we determined that the two groups of students would need three meetings to complete the project successfully during TPHC's 2002 fall term. The following were the top three items on our first brainstorming list:

1. Match up the project with TPHC's highly structured ESL curriculum.
2. Determine if there are interested teachers at TPHC and at a local elementary school.
3. Decide if we have the time and resources necessary as coordinators to see the project through to the end.

The first item on the list was fairly easy. TPHC's ESL classes are organized around competencies, and many of these agreed very well with the project. We also ran it by the ESL program coordinator, who thought it was a good idea and gave her official approval.

We created a timeline (see Appendix A) to show that the project would take approximately 13 hours for the college instructors and 6 hours for the elementary school teachers. The timeline allowed for completion of the entire unit over 8 weeks. We then wrote letters introducing the project to the teachers and students, and two TPHC teachers immediately replied that they were interested in participating. However, finding an elementary school teacher was not so straightforward. The ESL students are in classes 7 hours each day, and the college does not have a school van, so we wanted to find an elementary school within walking distance. Our preferred local elementary school was one with which TPHC already had an official sister-school relationship; TPHC students had previously volunteered there, and teachers had taken their classes to read to the kindergarten students. We were advised to approach the librarian, who had been a facilitator in the past. Unfortunately, our e-mail and letters went unanswered because, unbeknownst to us, the school was near the end of a grant-writing deadline.

As the weeks passed and the fall semester began, it seemed as if the project would not get off the ground. In a last-ditch effort, we walked across the street to the school at lunchtime and luckily found the librarian available and very willing to meet. She took us directly to the second-grade teacher who she thought would be interested in participating in such a project. The teacher listened to our description of the project and said she would like to participate. Pleased by the growing support, we agreed that we would somehow find the time to complete the project. We crossed off the last item on our list, informed the three interested teachers that the project would proceed, and began to develop the materials that the students and teachers would need to complete the project. We generated a master list of materials and tasks, and then met weekly to work on the project. We also exchanged e-mail, wrote materials, and swapped them for comments and editing. Happily, we discovered that we worked well together, having similar ideas about the project but also complementing each other's strengths and weaknesses. Although we sometimes felt as if we were racing to produce materials for a project that was already in progress, the time constraints kept us on track and focused. In fact, all things considered, the pilot went surprisingly well. Working with experienced and enthusiastic teachers and having an index of basic materials that we planned to develop helped the project move along fairly smoothly.

Although everyone involved agreed that the fall 2002 pilot had been a great success, there were a few problems to sort out. One problem concerned originality. Some of the students were unable to create an original children's story, and their finished product looked suspiciously similar to an already published story. It was clear that subsequent implementations would need to emphasize the importance of originality. This idea aligned with the concepts of plagiarism that were already a part of TPHC's reading and writing curriculum. In addition, we realized that we would need to develop more instructional materials to help the students collaborate. The college students needed more information about how to interact with young children, and the elementary school students needed more preparation activities before each visit. We also realized that three visits did not allow the students enough time to complete the task comfortably, so we decided to add one more visit to the schedule.

THE SPRING 2003 IMPLEMENTATION

After the pilot, we presented the unit at a TPHC ESL meeting in February 2003 (see Appendix B for an overview and Appendix C for the project flowchart). When we said that we would repeat the project during the 2003 spring term, five college teachers volunteered. Their 56 students represented approximately 50% of the ESL population at the college. For the implementation, we could not work with the same second-grade students, so the next big challenge was to find enough elementary school students to participate in the project. Once again, the librarian saved the day by putting us in contact with two third-grade teachers. We ran the unit for the second time with seven teachers and more than 100 students.

We used the feedback we had received from the teachers, students, and personal observation in the pilot project to modify the unit. We added more preunit activities (see Appendix D) and story-development process writing worksheets (see Appendix E). As a result, the unit materials were more complete, and the unit seemed better organized, even though there were a few additional challenges. The sheer number of participants meant more time had to be spent in coordination while we continued to add to the materials base. Balancing the schedules and personalities of so many people, writing new materials, revising existing materials, and teaching a full semester of classes proved quite demanding. However, our belief in the project and the participants' enthusiasm strengthened our resolve to see it through.

During the second implementation, we noticed that although further materials development had improved the curriculum unit, it had also increased the amount of class and homework time needed. Because we did not want the project to become a burden to the reading and writing teachers, we separated some of the more listening-based and speaking-based tasks and asked if the listening/speaking teachers could address these during their classes. Many of the tasks, such as reading aloud, practicing pronunciation, forming questions, and maintaining a conversation, are already competencies in the listening/speaking classes, so justifying the transfer of these tasks was not too difficult.

We thought we had solved the problem very well until we found that our solution had created another minor problem. One very enthusiastic listening and speaking teacher began adapting some of the handouts and making a few additional ones. We grew concerned that veering away from the materials provided could create an imbalance in the curriculum by not allowing students enough time to acquire the other skills in ESL. Luckily, a few conversations corrected the misunderstanding, and we realized that we needed to inform all future teachers that the unit should reinforce but not replace the established curriculum. Because it is now clear that the project naturally targets many of the ESL program speaking/listening competencies, plans to integrate the unit more formally with the listening/speaking ESL curriculum are in development. Another problem that we encountered was that we were not able to obtain consistent feedback from the elementary school teachers. As we were busy coordinating, developing materials, and teaching, we did not always notice that the elementary school data were incomplete. By the time we realized some feedback was missing, one teacher had already moved to a new school. Thus we decided to emphasize at the outset that participating teachers must agree to return feedback and evaluations in a timely manner. A timeline of feedback with dates and check boxes will probably assist in resolving this issue in the future.

Finally, we noticed that some of the TPHC students began to play games with the children and veer off task because some of the children gave very little response to their questions. The students seemed to need more explicit instruction on how to interact with children, how to sustain a conversation, and how to elicit useful feedback. It also became clear to us that the elementary school students needed more information about what they would be doing at each of the meetings so they could be more active participants. As a result, we developed more materials for both groups of students.

In spite of these challenges, the second implementation was a resounding success, and the larger number of participants increased the enthusiasm and excitement. During this implementation, the elementary school students visited TPHC for the final meeting. It was fun to see the students host the children on campus and to observe how well the college students and children had bonded by the end of the project.

THE FALL 2003 IMPLEMENTATION

The curriculum unit ran for a third time during the fall 2003 term with one TPHC class and one second-grade class. By this time, we had assembled all the project materials, checklists, and timelines in a binder for the TPHC teacher, and we were beginning to plan an elementary school resource binder. We met twice with the second-grade teacher to discuss additions to the elementary school materials. Informed by her experience and ideas, we were able to develop more previsit and postvisit materials for the children, and we incorporated some of the children's writing into the feedback process. At this time, we also met with the new elementary school principal, who offered his enthusiastic support for the project, especially because it aligned so well with DOE content standards for the second-grade and third-grade language arts curriculum.

Evaluating the Curriculum Unit

We evaluated the project by using preproject questionnaires, journals, class discussion questions, preproject and postproject student evaluations, postproject teacher evaluations, and anecdotal information gathered from frequent informal discussions with teachers and students. In addition, as project coordinators, one or both of us observed all visits.

Both sets of students reported that learning reading and writing within a cooperative framework was both fun and worthwhile. The project also encouraged some helping behavior, and several college students commented that the children helped them with pronunciation and vocabulary while reading aloud and with creating illustrations for their books. The college students' assessment of the unit's usefulness for language skills improvement was positive, with students reporting that they felt they had improved in all four language skill areas, especially reading and speaking. As expected, a few of the college students had some problems interacting with the children, possibly generated by cross-cultural expectations about child behavior. Some college students were thus motivated to ask their teachers how to communicate better with the children. For example, one student wrote in her journal,

> *I like children [when] the children are good. The children of . . . are fidgety. While a girl read her book, he didn't focus his attention on listening the story. I don't know how to get his attention and what I should do. I wanted to say "bad boy" but I'm not teacher, so I couldn't do anything of him to pay attention. Next time, I wonder about him. I want to know how I can say when I lose their attention.*

Some students found that they liked the interaction more as time went on and that they were able to build a rapport. In their journals as well as on the final project evaluation, we saw comments such as these:

> *First I hate this project but second and third time, I was not.*

> *This times field trip was better than before. I think children were used to speaking with us. Therefore, they was able to be so friendly and relax . . . . I enjoyed the field trip.*

We asked the teachers to evaluate the project in terms of its ease of implementation, usefulness for meeting reading and writing objectives, observations of student motivation, and interest in doing the project in the future. All the teachers said they would like to do the project in the future. They stated that they thought the project was valuable in increasing motivation around reading and writing skill development, providing feedback and evaluation practice, helping vocabulary acquisition, increasing sight-sound association in English due to increased motivation to practice read-aloud skills, and providing additional pronunciation practice. The teachers also pointed to some additional benefits, including integrated language skills development, encouragement of helping behaviors, and increased social opportunities to use English.

The college students demonstrated better facility in writing, such as clearer concepts of developing a story, building a plot, creating suspense, using humor, building cohesion through repetition, and writing for a specific audience. This improvement was greater than what we usually see in strictly academic writing. The students were able to write and illustrate a book in 8 weeks, gained an appreciation for the process of writing for a specific purpose and audience, and generated a final product that was shared with others, as illustrated by the excerpt from "The Beautiful Rainbow." They gained practice in speaking with native speakers and in negotiating a task. They also reported that they enjoyed the project and thought that it improved their language skills. The elementary school students gained experience in hosting a group and in giving feedback. They commented on how hard it is to write a book, but they also expressed interest in wanting to write books for the college students. They commented that they enjoyed helping the college students and especially seemed to like the chance to make college-age friends, with one child asking, "When are they coming back?"

Conclusion

This curriculum unit was integrated with many of the existing course competencies for TPHC's ESL reading and writing classes and the language arts content standards established for second and third grades by the DOE. There has been no institutional assessment of student gains in language skill proficiency resulting from this project. Institutional assessment was not the goal of the project; nor is it possible to assess whether student language skills improved solely as a result of this project or as a result of other classroom instruction received over the course of the 8 weeks. The project was primarily designed to provide a challenging, enjoyable, and motivating task that would require cooperation to complete, necessitate the practice of the targeted competencies, and encourage collaborative learning.

In their study, Leland and Fitzpatrick (1994, p. 300) refer to Mayher's (1990) castor oil syndrome, which holds that learning needs to be unpleas-

Excerpt From "The Beautiful Rainbow"

> "Please stop! I want to cry, too.
> But we should decide to go or not."
>
> But the cat didn't stop crying.
>
> "Come on. I'll leave here.
> I can't stay anymore."
>
> The bird left there.
>
> The cat was left alone, and he was crying, crying, and crying.

ant, painful, or medicinal if it is to be effective. We think that teachers need to move away from this idea and should incorporate learning activities into their classrooms that are effective as well as engaging. We believe this curriculum unit is a concrete step in that direction.

The third cycle of the project went well, and as we begin to prepare for the next implementation, we have much to be proud of. The curriculum unit is popular with teachers and students, we have created more than 60 pages of instructional materials, and we have developed a stronger relationship between the college and the elementary school. We are also currently working with the elementary school principal to standardize the annual meeting times for the project.

We had always hoped that this unit would stand on its own. We know there are many interested and talented teachers who would like to be involved in such a project but who lack the time necessary to develop materials or coordinate plans with teachers at other schools. Our goals for the near future include finalizing project binders so that teachers can preview the unit independently, contact a teacher from a corresponding school, and execute the unit. Meanwhile, the user-friendly curriculum products in the appendixes have been designed as a portable curriculum unit to be used by teachers interested in utilizing task-based collaborative learning principles in their classrooms. We hope our efforts will help facilitate ongoing collaborative learning between diverse groups of students and increase cooperation between teachers at the college and elementary school levels.

Appendix A: Project Timeline

Week	Tasks	Materials	Time
1	1. Introduction to the project for both groups of learners and teachers	Letters	10 min.
	2. Preliminary assessment of reading attitudes for both groups of learners	Prereading questionnaires	15 min.
	3. Introduction to children's literature for college students	Orientation by TPHC librarian and handouts	15 min.
	4. Public library visit by college students to select children's story	Previous handouts	30 min.
	5. Directions for college students on how to read a children's story and how to interact with young learners	Handout on how to read a story; handout on how to interact with young learners	25 min.
2	6. Instruction in cross-cultural communication for elementary school students	Handout on cross-cultural communication	20 min.
	7. Practice by college students in reading their stories with partners in class over two 30-minute sessions	Children's books; peer feedback checklist; guided journal questions	1 hour plus 15 min. of journal writing
	8. First meeting of college students and elementary students; reading of stories to each other and discussion of what kinds of books they like best	Books; handout on interview questions	60 min. to meet; 15 min. to travel
	9. Follow-up activity about school visit for college students	Guided journal questions; small-group discussion questions	20 min.

Week	Tasks	Materials	Time
	10. Follow-up activity for elementary school children	Discussion questions	10–15 min.
3, 4	11. Brainstorming by college students on story ideas; outlining of one or two stories	Brainstorming handouts; outlining handouts	60 min.
	12. Second meeting of college students and elementary school students; discussion of possible story ideas; beginning of collaboration on story development and illustration ideas	Previous handouts; story-development handout	60 min. to meet; 15 min. to travel
5, 6	13. Follow-up activity for college students	Guided journal questions	15 min.
	14. Writing of an original children's story using a process approach to writing (college students). Suggested breakdown of the four days: • Day 1: Refine outline (30 min.) • Day 2: Write the text of the first draft, no illustrations (60 min.) • Day 3: Give peer feedback (30 min.) • Day 4: Revise (30 min.)	Handout on introduction to text; graphics handout; peer feedback evaluation form; revising checklist	4 days
	15. Third meeting of college students and elementary school students; reading of stories to children and elicitation of feedback from them	Original stories; evaluation handouts	60 min. to meet; 15 min. to travel
	16. Follow-up activity for college students 7	Guided journal questions	15 min.
7	17. Revision, editing, and illustration of college students' original stories based on the elementary school students' feedback and peer revision; final decisions for integration of text and graphics	Draft of earlier work; peer feedback information	60 min.; can be spread across week
8	18. Completion of final versions of their stories; binding of the book; fourth and final meeting of college students and elementary school students to share finished products, reflect on the project, and celebrate	Binding materials; binding machine; completed stories	90 min.
	19. Final evaluation of project by both groups	Evaluation questionnaires	30 min.

Appendix B: Overview of the Unit

The curriculum unit involves four meetings between the college students and the elementary school students. The exact days and times can be arranged at the teachers' convenience. In brief, the project includes the following phases extending across the four meetings:

1. At the start of the project, both groups of learners complete a survey about their reading interests. The college students are introduced to the basic concepts required to understand children's literature. They select appropriate children's books for use with elementary school students and practice reading their selected books aloud, paying attention to intonation, pace, and storytelling techniques for use with children. The elementary school students also choose a story they would like to read to the college students. Before the first meeting between the two groups, the elementary school students and their teacher discuss cross-cultural communication.

FIRST MEETING

2. The students meet for the first time, and both groups of learners read their selected stories aloud in English. The college students lead a follow-up discussion to elicit feedback from the elementary school students about what books they like to read and why.

SECOND MEETING

3. Before the meeting, the college students brainstorm possible story ideas and draft outlines using the learning materials provided. They share their story ideas with the elementary school children at the second meeting and receive feedback. The two groups of learners collaboratively discuss story development and illustration ideas.

THIRD MEETING

4. Before the meeting, the college students each write a draft of and begin to illustrate an original children's story, using an academic process approach to writing. They read these drafts to the elementary students at the third meeting, and the children then give formal feedback, through provided assessment tools, about what was most effective in the literature. The college students also gather more information to make decisions about final illustrations and text layout for their books.

5. The college students revise, edit, and bind their original work based on feedback and revision by the elementary school students.

FOURTH MEETING

6. At the last meeting, the college students read the final versions of their stories and invite the elementary school students to evaluate the final products as well as share their opinions about the entire project.

Appendix C: Project Flowchart

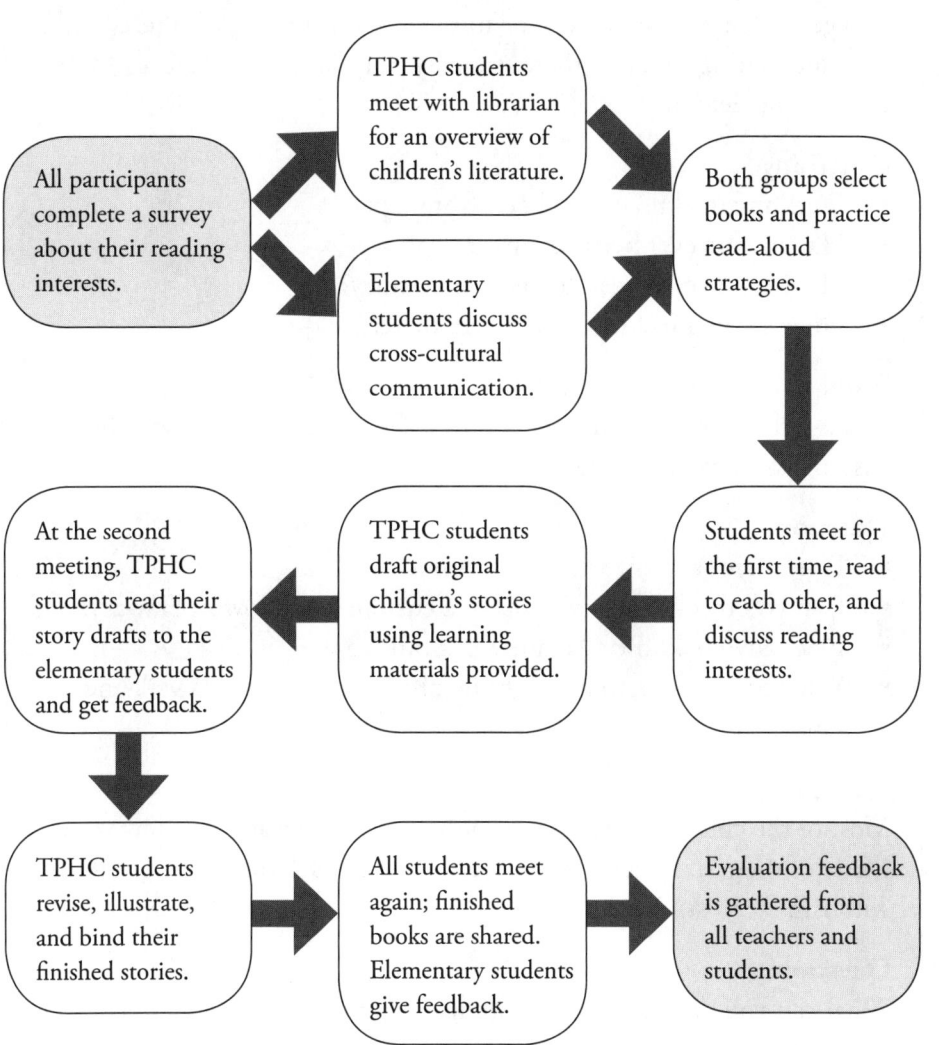

Appendix D: Sample Activity: Guided Discussion

Purpose: To help prepare the elementary school children for their first visit with the international college students

Method: Use for whole-class activity.

**CROSS-CULTURAL COMMUNICATION
GUIDED DISCUSSION QUESTIONS**

Prompt
You are going to do a reading and writing project with international college students from Japan. The most important thing is to relax and have fun getting to know these students from Japan; they are also very excited to meet you!

Questions
- Does anyone know somebody from Japan?
- Has anyone ever been to Japan?
- Has anyone ever been to another country?
- How did you feel when you were there?

Prompt
Because they are from another country, the students may have different customs than we do in Hawaiʻi.

Questions
- Does anyone know what a custom is?
- Can you think of an example of a custom we follow in Hawaiʻi?
- Does anyone know a Japanese custom?
- What kinds of customs might be different between Hawaiʻi and Japan?

Prompt
Most of the college students have only been in Hawaiʻi for a few weeks. Many of them have never been in an American school before or talked with American students.

Question
What can you do to help the students feel more comfortable in your classroom?

Prompt
It might be nice to introduce yourself to the college students the first time you meet them.

> **Question**
> What could you say to introduce yourself?
>
> **Prompt**
> Sometimes, asking someone a question makes them feel better.
>
> **Question**
> What is a question you could ask the students?
>
> **Prompt**
> Because English is not their native language, the students may feel a little nervous speaking English. Their pronunciation may sound different, and they may not know some vocabulary words in the stories.
>
> **Questions**
> - Has anyone ever studied another language before?
> - If yes, did you like it? What part was fun? What part was hard?
> - Were you sometimes shy to speak in the second language?
> - What are some things you can do to help the college students as they read to you?
> - What are some things you can do to help them understand you as you read to them?

Appendix E: Sample Activity: Storyboarding

Purpose: To help college students develop original story ideas

Method: Students draft two detailed story outlines using the handouts below. They present their two potential story ideas and get feedback from the children.

> **Storyboard Ideas: The Beginning**
>
> 1. I am thinking of writing a _____ story about _____.
>
> 2. What is the setting (time and place) of the story? For example, does it take place near the ocean, mountains, city, or outer space? Think of when the story occurs, such as now, in the future, or 100 years ago.
>
> 3. Who are the characters? How many main characters are there (minimum two)? Are they people, animals, magical creatures,

or objects? Describe each character's personality and appearance. Be specific.
- Describe Character 1 . . .
- Describe Character 2 . . .
- Describe Character 3 . . .
- Describe Character 4 . . .

Storyboard Ideas: The Middle

The middle of the story is where the plot develops. A narrative story develops chronologically through a series of events, scenes, or dialogue. The characters are usually trying to achieve a goal. There is often a problem or several problems that make reaching this goal difficult. How the characters try to solve the problem is part of what makes the story interesting. One scene will be the climax, the most exciting scene. The climax is where the problem or difficulty gets resolved.

How does your story develop?
- First . . .
- Then . . .
- Next . . .
- After that . . .
- Suddenly . . .
- In the end . . .

Storyboard Ideas: The End

Stories can end in many different ways. Some stories have happy, sad, or surprising endings. Some stories end thoughtfully, with a lesson or strong message to the reader. Sometimes the ending tells you exactly what happens to each character. On the other hand, sometimes readers must use their imaginations to decide what really happened.

How does your story end?
- Idea 1 . . .
- Idea 2 . . .
- Idea 3 . . .

Foreign Eyes on Thailand: An ESP Project for EFL Learners

JOHN KNOX

This chapter documents a language learning project developed and implemented for an English for specific purposes (ESP) course, English for Tourism III (EFT III), at a private university in Thailand. This project required learners, in groups of three or four, to interview departing foreign tourists at Bangkok International Airport and report on their findings. The class was a final-year course for learners majoring in tourism in a 4-year bachelor's program in the Faculty of Liberal Arts. It was the third of three required English for Tourism courses for these learners, and was taught for 3 hours per week across a semester of approximately 15 weeks.

The specific content and materials of the course were not prescribed, but EFT III was the culmination of English language studies for the tourism students in our faculty, and hence a range of requirements and expectations had to be met. All learners were fee paying, and maintaining a curriculum recognized as relevant and effective by prospective students and by industry was the basis for the viability of the Faculty of Liberal Arts. Generally, the course content focused on tourism-related language, and, more specifically, there was a requirement to focus on language and situations related to travel within Thailand, or *inbound* tourism. This requirement was to balance the focus on *outbound* tourism, travel outside Thailand, of the first two EFT courses (see English for Tourism Classes on page 120 for an overview of the three courses).

After 3 years of studying grammar-based and skills-based English courses, the learners, quite reasonably, had strong expectations that the EFT

English for Tourism Classes			
Course	**Hours**	**Focus**	**Materials**
English for Tourism I (Semester 1)	45	Outbound tourism	Stott & Holt (1991)
English for Tourism II (Semester 1)	45	Outbound tourism	Stott & Holt (1991)
English for Tourism III (Semester 2)	45	Inbound tourism, including Temple Tour Project	Teacher developed

courses would enable them to apply their language knowledge and skills in situations relevant to their chosen major. The head of the English Department, colleagues in the Tourism Department, and colleagues in the English Department shared this expectation and also expected that the courses would be rigorous, consistent with the other courses in the curriculum and with the learners' needs.

There were three ESP strands in the faculty—English for Tourism, English for Hotel Management, and English for Secretarial Science—and a number of informal and formal mechanisms were in place to ensure that the EFT courses met stakeholders' requirements. These courses had strong project-based components, and in some cases colleagues not teaching on a particular ESP course were involved in assessment in that course, most typically in spoken presentations. This was part of the strong collegiality in the department and led to a healthy environment of sharing ideas and an enthusiasm among teachers to maintain high standards.

As a formal part of a degree program, final examinations were compulsory and were vetted by the departmental exam committee. Grades were assigned according to university rules, and they counted toward the learners' grade point averages and completion of the bachelor's degree. Additional assessment procedures, such as oral proficiency interviews and projects, were common in a number of courses, but the nature of the department meant that assessment procedures in any given course were widely known among the teachers and were required to be rigorous, transparent, and clearly related to the course objectives.

The Motivation for the Innovation

In such a curriculum environment, introducing a student-centered, student-generated (Hall, 2001) project proved a significant challenge. The primary goal of the EFT courses was to prepare learners for employment in the tourism industry by teaching them the English language knowledge and skills they needed in such work. Often, however, as in any ESP course, it was difficult to clearly differentiate where language teaching stopped and real-world teaching began, and the courses tended to integrate the teaching of both language and real-world knowledge and skills.

In EFT I and II, learners used a set text and practiced English in simulated situations that were meant to resemble conditions in authentic outbound tourism contexts. The second half of EFT III was devoted to the Temple Tour Project, which had been introduced and developed by a colleague. The project, in which learners gave guided tours of various temples in Bangkok, had generally gained wide acceptance and popularity among staff and learners, as learners saw the project as immediately relevant and useful. However, the first half of EFT III was based on a range of eclectic units that were constantly revised and changed, including Festivals, Handicrafts and Shopping, Transport, Food, Customs and Traditions, Ecotourism, and Airports and Airlines. The available textbook written for the inbound Thai tourism context had been tried and deemed unsuitable for EFT III. Learner interest varied from topic to topic, and the time-consuming job of materials development added to my responsibilities. As EFT course manager, I was hindered by the lack of available materials and by the problems inherent in developing materials from scratch with limited resources, including the most crucial resource of time.

MOTIVATING AUTHENTIC COMMUNICATION IN ENGLISH

While working as EFT course manager, I was undertaking studies for my master's degree at Macquarie University, in Australia, and I was motivated to explore alternative approaches to curriculum development. Project-based learning, in particular, appeared to be a challenging and thought-provoking model, and one that was likely to be feasible as projects of different kinds were already commonly used throughout the department. Project learning is defined by Legutke and Thomas (1991) as

> *a theme and task centered mode of teaching and learning which results from a joint process of negotiation between all participants. It allows for a wide scope of self-determined action for both the individual and the small group of learners within a general framework of a plan which defines goals and procedures. Project learning realizes a dynamic balance between a process and a product orientation. (p. 160)*

Colleagues and I had formed the strong impression that learners benefited significantly from the Temple Tour Project, and I believed that this was due to its authentic nature. After approximately 15 years of predominantly traditional classroom learning, learners had to communicate in English for this project. I made the decision to introduce an additional project in which learners would go to Bangkok International Airport to interview departing foreign tourists about their experiences in Thailand, an idea triggered by Legutke and Thomas's (1991) brief description of similar airport projects (pp. 161–162). The requirement to interview foreign tourists provided a clear and imminent need for learners to use English for a genuine purpose, in an authentic context, beyond the security of the classroom. The Airport Project in EFT III represented "a further movement away from the conventional practice of learning for some undefined future purpose toward learning for a more specific purpose which can be realized immediately" (p. 215). I believed that the experience of interviewing foreign tourists and of designing, implementing, and reporting on a research project in English would provide another authentic context for using English.

> *If a teacher is to provide students with tools to learn language outside the classroom, the main aim has to be to give students confidence in their ability to communicate despite difficulties, to the point where they can: (a) initiate communicative events, and (b) persist with the attempted communication even when it becomes difficult. (Hall, 2001, p. 231)*

In addition to improving their English language skills, I believed the interviews and the following classwork, based on the data collected by the learners, would expand their real-world knowledge about their chosen field of study.

The interviews themselves were an authentic communicative activity in which learners were required to use English in order to collect information for a research project. Lessons in the classroom, which prepared the learners for the interviews, did not focus on practicing language as a collection of items such as vocabulary, grammar rules, and functions (McCarthy & Carter, 2001). Instead, the focus was on how to use language to achieve a *target task* or *real-world task* (Coleman, 1987; Legutke & Thomas, 1991, pp. 166–169; Nunan, 1988, pp. 85–86). Learners were required to use language heuristically to develop their questionnaires, collect the data, and finally report in English, creating a tangible English language product. The project therefore required a discourse-based approach in which language is viewed "not just as isolated, decontextualized bits of language" (McCarthy & Carter, 1994, p. 38). Such an approach "involves examining how bits of language contribute to the making of complete texts. It involves exploring the relationship between the linguistic patterns of complete texts and the social contexts in which they function" (p. 38). This applied not only to the discourse of the interviews but also to the reporting of the data.

GIVING LEARNERS A STAKE IN THE CURRICULUM

The Airport Project also acknowledged the learners' status as young adults in their final year of undergraduate study who were about to enter the workforce or, in many cases, to live abroad and further their studies. Consequently, the learners were required to

- form their own groups
- decide on their topics of interest within the broad constraints of the topic—the experience of a tourist in Thailand
- develop their own interview questions
- approach the tourists independently
- decide on the form of their report
- be involved in their own assessment and the assessment of their peers

These requirements provided the learners with a real stake in the curriculum and gave them the power and responsibility that comes with determining the direction of one's own learning. The project positioned them, in Kenny's (1993) terms, as *producers* rather than *consumers:* "This is the other dimension to autonomy, in which learners do not just choose, select, and re-arrange, but produce, create, clarify issues, propose solutions and make a difference to the world through their learning processes" (p. 434).

As the project designer, I was convinced that the philosophies underlying the project were worthwhile and appropriate, and I had the support of my teaching colleague. Our challenge was to design and implement a curriculum that could realize the educational philosophies we held and at the same time meet the requirements imposed on us by the curriculum context, including the expectations of the other stakeholders in the EFT courses.

The Curriculum Context

THE COURSE AND THE ENGLISH LANGUAGE CURRICULUM

EFT III was compulsory study for students in the bachelor of arts degree, majoring in tourism, and was the third of the three EFT courses. Over the 7 years I taught the courses, learners consistently indicated that approximately two thirds of each class intended to go immediately into employment in the tourism industry, with approximately one third planning to become tour guides and one third planning to work in airline-related jobs. The remaining third planned to undertake postgraduate study. The large proportion of learners expecting to go on to English-medium postgraduate study meant that in some units of the EFT courses, tourism content, such as ecotourism, was approached from an academic rather than a vocational perspective. The rationale was that these learners might gain greater familiarity with the language and academic skills required of them in postgraduate study. This was also part of the rationale for the research-based approach to learner reports in the Airport Project.

In any given year, there were typically two or three EFT classes, with 20–30 learners in each. In the year the Airport Project was introduced, there were two classes. My class had 21 female and 4 male learners, and the other class had 25 learners with a similar female-to-male ratio. This ratio was typical across the 7 years I taught the EFT courses. The learners ranged in age from approximately 21 to 23 years, and most came from middle-class or wealthy families.

Students majoring in tourism studied 21 English language courses across their 4-year program, as detailed in Overview of the English Language Curriculum.

The other EFT III teacher and I were both native-English-speaking males in our late 20s. We shared common philosophies of education and teaching approaches, both favoring approaches that could be described broadly as communicative. My colleague was enthusiastic and supportive of the Airport Project, and although I was responsible for its conceptualiza-

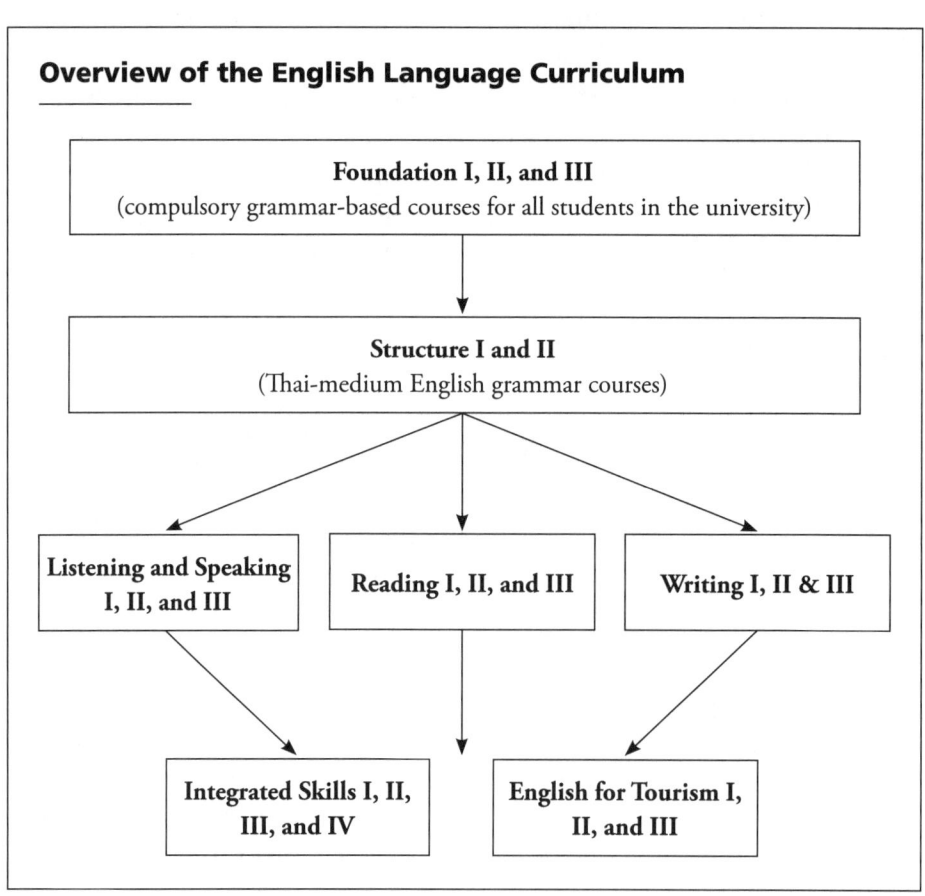

tion and initial development, its implementation and ongoing adjustment were collaborative. As course manager, I was officially responsible for the administration of the EFT courses. It had become the practice in the skills-based and ESP courses in the department for course managers to provide all teachers on a given course with teaching outlines. These outlines would detail the content to be covered in each lesson, and teachers would generally cover the same material at the same time across all classes. For the two EFT classes, this meant that my colleague and I would commonly visit each other's classrooms during lessons. The fact that we were familiar with each other's teaching styles and comfortable with collaboration and consultation, even during class time, became particularly useful during the implementation of the Airport Project, as unexpected problems arose and we needed to react quickly and with consistency between the two classes.

THE PLACE OF THE PROJECT IN THE CURRICULUM

The official course description for EFT III (translated from the Thai version in the University Handbook) read as follows: "Practice using English in authentic tour-guide situations and other situations; learn how to perform the job of tour guide with greater efficiency." The Temple Tour Project already provided practice in one authentic tour guide situation, yet in the actual temple tours, the learners' language was, unsurprisingly, predominately monologic and often memorized, and many learners showed little ability to deal with questions or enter into any dialogic exchange in English. Consequently, there was a sound pedagogic reason to introduce the Airport Project, and the following practical issues made the project suitable for these learners and palatable for the various stakeholders:

- The airport was situated near the university, a particularly relevant issue in Bangkok.
- The airport was a convenient and rich source of English speakers from a variety of language backgrounds, providing a representative sample of the English speakers the learners would encounter in the tourism industry.
- The departing tourists, who were the interviewees, had recent, relevant experience of the Thai tourism industry and were thus a valuable source of information.
- A trip to the airport to interview tourists had face validity in an ESP course on tourism and was therefore acceptable to the university administration.
- Former and current learners often expressed a desire to go to the airport as part of one of the EFT courses, so learner motivation was generally high.

In terms of the existing EFT curriculum, the project drew on the EFT I and II courses by enabling the learners to apply their language knowledge and skills in an authentic context. The learners had the scope to determine the content or subject area themselves, and the information gathered by the class in this project was surprising to many of the learners. It helped them develop a greater sensitivity to the needs and wants of foreign tourists and facilitated their preparation for and method of conducting the temple tours. Also, the contact with English speakers from all over the world increased their confidence and experience in dealing with, and speaking to, foreign tourists. In this way, it helped bridge the gap between the EFT courses, on one hand, and the Temple Tour Project, on the other.

The Process of Designing the Project

A learner-centered or learner-generated curriculum does not require an extensive, predetermined, teacher-generated syllabus (Nunan, 1988, pp. 5, 45). In fact, such a syllabus can be seen as antithetical to a learner-centered curriculum (Candlin, 1984; Hall & Kenny, 1988). However, it was suitable to produce one for the Airport Project for a number of reasons. The first, which I have discussed at length, was institutional accountability. Secondly, though my colleague was enthusiastic, a let-the-learners-work-it-out course plan would have been highly unlikely to win favor with him. With an outline, the "what-am-I-going-to-do" question (Macdonald, 1965, cited in Brindley, 1989, p. 6) faced by all teachers was answered.

Thirdly, from a cultural viewpoint, the learners had very little, if any, experience in generating content or taking responsibility for the direction of a curriculum. My suspicion was that their idea of teacher and learner roles was unlikely to fit comfortably, at least initially, with that implied by a learner-centered, learner-generated curriculum (Nunan, 1988, pp. 95–96; Wright, 1991, pp. 15–16). An activity the learners were very familiar with, however, was bargaining, so we presented a course outline to them as the teacher's first offer in a bargained curriculum (Benson, 2001, pp. 55–58). Finally, as learner-teacher negotiation was an essential component of the outline, the syllabus outline was always a point of departure rather than a fait accompli.

DEVELOPING THE SYLLABUS

Needs analysis for the EFT courses was conducted both formally and informally on an ongoing basis, in conjunction with the evaluation of previous courses. Learners were routinely consulted about their impressions and their expectations of each course. This meant that the EFT courses were continually developed in response to learner feedback, and the conceptualization of the Airport Project was itself a part of this process. In the year that the Airport Project was introduced, all learners had completed the Needs Analysis Form at the completion of EFT II.

With the information from this initial formal needs analysis, I adapted the prospective outline of the project that I had completed as part of my master's degree studies into a more specific syllabus plan, including the dates of the visit to the airport and assessment procedures. In developing the syllabus plan, I devoted considerable energy to detailing the objectives of the project. It was vital to convince the stakeholders that the project would be much more than simply "a gambit by means of which a fun element can be introduced into an otherwise lifeless and dreary classroom" (Legutke & Thomas, 1991, p. 158). This was particularly important because the entire EFT III curriculum would now consist of two projects without any set textbook, unlike any other course in the department. By developing detailed objectives and assessment activities, I documented the intention to provide learners with experience in, and knowledge about, the linguistic and practical requirements of dealing with foreign tourists in face-to-face English

---

Needs Analysis Form

NAME: _____

This form has two aims:

1. to start you thinking about EFT III
2. to get some ideas about what you want in EFT III

Please answer every question and give as much information as you can.

- What kind of language learning activities do you enjoy the most?
- What activities DON'T you enjoy?

In EFT III, we will have two projects. In the first one, you will go to the airport and interview foreign tourists.

- What would you like to interview the tourists about?
- What language skills do you want to practice before we go to the airport?

After the interviews, you will organize your information and report it to your class and the teacher, and to people outside the class.

- How would you like to report your information? (In writing? By speaking? Both? Another way?)
- Do you have any suggestions or questions about the project?
- Is there anything else you would like to include?
- Is there anything you DON'T want to do?

language encounters as well as guide them through the process of developing research skills and knowledge about foreigners' perspectives of tourism in Thailand.

SETTING THE OBJECTIVES

The overall objectives for the project were expressed as behavioral objectives, or objectives that focus on the outcomes of the teaching/learning encounter. For each timetabled lesson, objectives specified the activities learners would undertake but not the outcomes of those activities (Brindley, 1989, p. 9). These objectives assisted in the development of lesson plans and helped keep learners and teachers focused on the task at hand throughout the implementation of the curriculum. Institutionally, detailed objectives gave us the language we needed to address criticisms of the project and to justify the project to the English Department, the Tourism Department, the university, the Airports Authority of Thailand (AAT), and the learners. The objectives were also, obviously, central to assessment and were in fact used in the Self-Assessment Instrument.

With the objectives and syllabus outline in hand, I discussed the proposed project with the head of English, who was enthusiastic. We cosigned a letter to the dean of the Faculty, who granted approval, and, with these administrative steps in place, a formal request for permission to go behind the immigration and customs barriers at Bangkok International Airport and interview departing tourists was drafted, translated, and hand-delivered to the AAT by two learners who had worked there in a previous semester. Permission was granted.

The Project

The project design was adapted from Legutke and Thomas's (1991) six stages of a project. Project Stages (page 130) compares Legutke and Thomas's stages of development with those of the Airport Project.

The project represented a negotiated, learner-generated curriculum, and much of the real curriculum development took place during its implementation. Curriculum Overview (page 130) indicates the timeframe for the project.

LESSONS 1 AND 2: OPENING AND ORIENTATION

Legutke and Thomas's (1991) first stage, called *opening*, was not completely relevant to this project as the tourism students were already a community by the time they were in the fourth-year EFT courses. Therefore, the first two lessons integrated some aspects of opening, or introducing the target community as a resource base for language learning, introducing textual data for research activities with topic orientation, sensitizing learners toward the

Self-Assessment Instrument

Project 1

1. Look at the list of course objectives below. Write *YES* next to the ones you think you have achieved, *NO* next to the ones you think you have not achieved, and *MAYBE* next to the ones you are not sure about.

Objectives

By the end of the project, you should be able to:

___ consider issues about tourism in Thailand from your point of view and from a foreigner's point of view and discuss and/or write about them in English

___ plan an interview and interview a foreigner in English

___ use English to give and ask for feelings, opinions, observations, judgments, and conclusions

___ use English to explain, justify, and give reasons

___ keep a learning diary in English

___ use language to learn, solve problems, and develop ideas

___ develop and recognize different ways to learn

___ define a task or a goal, decide what to do to achieve it, and finally achieve it

___ work with other people as a group to achieve a task

___ collect information from interviews, readings, and other English language sources

___ evaluate and organize information

___ present information clearly in English

___ evaluate your own learning and achievement

___ evaluate other people's achievement

2. Now think about the value of the objectives. Discuss them with a partner.
   a. Would you take any off the list? If yes, cross them off.
   b. Are there any you think should be changed? If yes, rewrite them here.
   c. Would you add any objectives? If yes, write them here.

---

theme, mobilizing existing knowledge, arousing curiosity, and allowing for exchange of personal experiences (Legutke & Thomas, 1991, pp. 171–173). During these lessons, learners discussed in pairs and groups which aspects of tourism in Thailand interested them. Other activities were designed to help the learners begin to consider Thailand from a foreigner's perspective. The stimulus material included a series of authentic, short quotes from foreigners

Project Stages

Legutke and Thomas's (1991) Typical Project Stages	Airport Project Stages	
1. Opening	1. Opening and orientation	
2. Topic orientation		
3. Research and data collection	2. Research and data collection	
4. Preparing data presentation	3. Reorientation	Evaluation
	4. Preparing data presentation	
5. Presentation	5. Presentation	
6. Evaluation		

recounting their initial experiences of Thailand. Activities included groups of learners choosing a tourist destination in Thailand and considering what and whom foreigners would encounter there, and how they might react.

The first misstep came in the very first lesson, in which we handed

Curriculum Overview

Lesson	Project Stage	Sample Activities
1, 2	Opening and orientation	• Whole-class discussion of project • Brainstorming and group discussion of foreign tourists' experiences in Thailand
3, 4, 5, 6	Research and data collection	• Group work on developing questionnaires • Teacher-centered language instruction • Listening and note-taking • Role-playing interviews
7	At the airport	• N/A
8	Reorientation	• Group discussion of airport experience • Evaluation of interviews • Peer assessment
9, 10	Preparing data presentation	• Individual preparation of reports • Learner-teacher conferencing • Evaluation of project
11	Data presentation	• Presentation of spoken reports and video documentaries

out and discussed the overview of the course, the first offer in a bargained curriculum. The learners' initial reaction was far less enthusiastic than I had anticipated, particularly given the positive reactions to the concept of the project that we had received from these same learners in the previous semester. It was my colleague who pointed out that too much information was not always a good thing, and though my motivations had been honorable, I had included too much information on the educational philosophy and theory of the project in the outline. He suggested that we write and distribute a more learner-friendly, step-by-step overview in the following lesson, and learners responded far more positively to this (see Appendix A for both outlines).

LESSONS 3–6: RESEARCH AND DATA COLLECTION

This part of the curriculum involved the learners in backward planning, beginning with a consideration of the target task and deciding what needed to be done in order to achieve it. Learners formed their groups for the interviews and considered what language knowledge and abilities would be needed and what else they would need to prepare. Materials included a listening activity in which a foreign tourist (played by me) was interviewed (by my teaching colleague), and language dealt with in the lessons included the grammar and intonation of questions, backchannel signals, nonverbal communication, listening and note-taking, approaching strangers, asking for permission to record, closing an interview, and dealing with impolite or rude tourists. The learners suggested approximately half of the language content of this part of the curriculum.

The last lesson before the interviews involved both classes working together outside the classroom to role-play and record actual interviews with one another and any native-speaking teachers who happened to pass by. This lesson was crucial as the learners had an opportunity to run through the logistics of approaching people in groups in a nonthreatening manner and of establishing a division of labor for interviews involving recording, questioning, supporting the questioner (clarifying questions and answers where miscommunication occurred), taking notes, and so on. Isolated cases of recording problems during this dress rehearsal also made learners aware of the limitations of and proper ways to use their recording equipment and of the need for contingency plans.

One of the problems we faced during this stage of the curriculum was that once learners formed groups, they worked together outside class to produce their questionnaires immediately. This was a very positive sign in terms of motivation but left something of a gap in the class time that we had set aside to do this. Furthermore, learners were somewhat reluctant to review and refine their questionnaires beyond making changes explicitly suggested by their teacher. Similarly, after one class activity in which they role-played interviewing classmates in pairs, using the questionnaires, they were reluctant to do other, similar activities. However, we negotiated this period by insisting that learners consider the overall organization of their questionnaires, eliminate repetition, and refine their questions so that they would elicit the kind of data the learners wanted. We also ensured that the questions were grammatically accurate and that each learner's pronunciation of each question was clear and intelligible.

Although it became apparent that I had allowed too much time to prepare for the interviews, we were unable to move the interviews forward due to the bureaucratic approval for the interviews from the Faculty of Liberal Arts and the AAT. In later years, we reduced the number of preparation lessons for the interviews, collected questionnaires in the third lesson, returned them with extensive feedback (written and spoken) in the fourth lesson, and assigned them a score out of 5% for the course.

LESSON 7: AT THE AIRPORT

The seventh lesson was waived in lieu of the actual interviews. The trip to the airport was a very positive experience, and the learners were understandably excited. After meeting in the public area of the departure terminal, we were given passes and escorted behind the barriers. My colleague and I sat in an open area while the learners interviewed tourists and returned occasionally to where we were sitting to ask questions, recount their successes and mishaps, play us funny incidents from their recordings, and generally share the experience. All groups interviewed a number of tourists, and the success of the day could be judged by the fact that a number of the groups returned independently to the airport on the following weekend to interview more tourists at the check-in area of the departure terminal.

LESSON 8: REORIENTATION

The fourth of Legutke and Thomas's (1991) six stages, preparation of data presentation, was separated into two parts: reorientation and preparation of data presentation. The first part was a lesson devoted to reviewing, evaluating, and sharing experiences of the interviews. This lesson also served to remotivate the learners and focus them on completing the product of the project (Legutke & Thomas, 1991, p. 178).

Learners worked in their interview groups to list good and bad experiences, funny events, surprises, and what they had learned. These groups were then split up, and the learners formed new groups to share their experiences again. The new groups also considered what they would change if they did the project again, and shared suggestions with the entire class. These suggestions included being able to conduct the interviews at a time of their own choosing and being able to go to places other than the airport. Both these suggestions were incorporated into the project in following years. Learners completed the Interview Evaluation shown here. Each learner also completed one copy of the Group Evaluation Form for each of their group members anonymously and in private, and returned them to the teacher.

The teacher compiled marks for each learner and assigned each learner an average of the peer scores. Comments were compiled, typed, and distributed to each learner. The following comments received by two learners are indicative of those received across the cohort.

Interview Evaluation

A. The Interviews
  1. Did you enjoy the interviews? Why or why not?
  2. What lessons and class activities do you think helped you in the interviews?
  3. Which lessons and activities do you think were not helpful?
  4. Did anything happen in the interviews that we did not learn about first? What?
  5. What extra activities would you suggest before the interviews?

B. Your Performance
  1. What grade would you give your performance in the interviews? (A? C+?) _____ (THIS GRADE WILL NOT COUNT TOWARD YOUR MARK.)
  2. How could you improve your performance?
  3. Any other comments?

Group Evaluation Form

Name of student being evaluated (NOT your name!!): _____

Please rate the student using the following scale:
  1 = excellent   2 = very good   3 = good   4 = not so good   5 = poor

- Works as part of the team   _____
- Contributes to group work in class   _____
- Contributes out of class   _____
- Responsibility—performs agreed duties   _____

Please write a short comment for each of the following:
- Strengths in English   _____
- Other strengths   _____
- Weaknesses in English   _____
- Other weaknesses   _____
- Other comments   _____

Student A

STRENGTHS IN ENGLISH: conversation and reading; speaks loud; quite good at listening

OTHER STRENGTHS: smiles all day and a joker; pays attention to learning

WEAKNESSES IN ENGLISH: vocab and grammar; doesn't speak well; not so good at speaking and writing

OTHER WEAKNESSES: smoking—in my opinion if she feels crazy she should go to play sport; speaks slow; has few ideas for group

OTHER COMMENTS: I'm proud of her because she works and studies at the same time; She has responsibility for her duties

Student B

STRENGTHS IN ENGLISH: listening and speaking and writing; very good because she's good at grammar and speaking; good pronunciation and action

OTHER STRENGTHS: very good personality and very confident to talk with farang [Western foreigners]; self-confident, responsible for duties, good personality

WEAKNESSES IN ENGLISH: confused when speaking, structure of sentence; listening to foreigners with strange accents (e.g., French); thinking is too fast and speech cannot follow, not smooth

OTHER WEAKNESSES: hard to understand when she speaks fast; quite quick-tempered; sometimes overconfident

OTHER COMMENTS: She's very good and has responsibility to work in a group; Makes many mistakes when she loves to speak quickly; OK

LESSONS 9 AND 10: PREPARING DATA PRESENTATION

About half of the total cohort submitted written reports. Learners from two groups, one from each class, submitted video documentaries, and the remainder gave spoken presentations. I expected that the lessons at this stage of the project would be characterized by focused, self-determined work in the classroom, in conjunction with teacher and perhaps peer consultation, and this turned out to be the case for a number of the weaker writers in the class. These learners benefited from this class time, and I spent time developing a template with them, which they found useful and which was adapted and incorporated into the assessment task in later years. A number of the weaker writers in the class turned in written assignments far better than any work I had ever received from them, which was gratifying for all of us. A number of the learners with stronger communicative abilities in English also presented some of the best work I had seen from them.

As with the preparation of the questionnaires, we were surprised at the amount of work all the learners did on the project in their own time. The learners who produced video documentaries spent a considerable amount of time, and their own money, producing their videos in a professional editing studio, as the technology for digital recording and editing was not widely available at that time. The last class activity was completing a self-assessment and final evaluation form, which learners worked through individually and then in pairs. They then brought the completed form to a final interview with the teacher for discussion after the presentations.

LESSON 11: DATA PRESENTATION

For this lesson, the two classes came together to watch the video documentaries and listen to the spoken presentations. Both teachers rated each presentation. A number of other teachers in the English Department, including the head of department, were invited and came, and a number of the written reports were edited and collated with the two video documentaries into a report, which was submitted to the AAT and to the head of the English Department.

Assessment and Evaluation

ASSESSMENT PROCEDURES

The assessment of the project counted for 50% of the grade for EFT III. The other 50% came from the Temple Tour Project. An examination was a university requirement and included a listening task in which a foreign tourist was interviewed about his or her experience in Thailand. Assessment Procedures (page 136) outlines the assessment processes and the weighting given to each assessment task in the Airport Project.

At a number of stages in the curriculum, the learners completed structured activities involving learner diaries, which were collected in the final lesson. In the reorientation stage, when nearly all the learners had experiences they wanted to record and share, the diary was most effective as an extension of class activities and as a means of beginning the process of writing the first stage of the report. My colleague and I assigned marks according to the amount of work each learner had put into the diary, judged in terms of quality and quantity. Assigning grades was a subjective and difficult process. Unlike the experiences reported by Legutke and Thomas

Assessment Procedures

Procedure	Lesson	Weighting	Description
Learner diary	2–9	10%	Personal reflection on a range of set tasks
Peer assessment	8	5%	Evaluation of peer contribution to group
Report	11	20%	Data-based research report on foreign tourists' impressions of Thailand
Self-assessment	Exam period	5%	Completion of form and interview with teacher discussing achievement of project objectives
Exam	Exam period	10%	Formal examination including sections on vocabulary, listening, reading, and writing

(1991), the learners rarely responded enthusiastically to the diary activities, and in subsequent years the learner diary was dropped.

The peer assessment made members of each group accountable to one another and ensured that some recognition of commitment and work was rewarded in the project marks. It also gave learners an increased level of responsibility in the curriculum, and widened the number of judges who determined the grades and the range of activities used as a basis for assessment. Learners responded very positively to the opportunity to rate their group contributions and appreciated the feedback they received.

The process of self-assessment required learners to complete the Self-Assessment Instrument (page 129) and then to individually discuss their achievement of the course objectives with the teacher. At the conclusion of this discussion, they assigned themselves a mark out of 5. The process was very interesting. In all but a few cases, learners had difficulty relating their activities to the project objectives, and it was a productive experience for them and for me to sit together and discuss the various processes and products of the interviews in terms of the objectives. The common tendency was for the learners to assign themselves poor marks initially. At the end of the process, only one learner had assigned herself a full mark of 5, and she did so only after I assured her it was all right to do so. One learner who had arrived at the airport late and did not do his share of the work in his group assigned himself a mark of 2. All other learners fell into the range of 3–4½.

The written and spoken reports were divided into two sections. The first was a report on the experience of the project, which included a discussion of the rationale for the questionnaire and a report of what happened at the airport. The second section required learners to present their data and to present conclusions and recommendations based on those data. The learners who produced video documentaries preferred to work without explicit structure and were allowed to do so. We found it very difficult to judge video documentaries against written reports against spoken presentations and to do justice to all learners, and in later years all learners were required to submit a written report in order to ensure equity and reliability in this assessment procedure. Additionally, we later dropped the section requiring a report on the experience of the project and introduced the Language Analysis Assignment, which required transcription of a portion of an interview together with language analysis and commentary. This assignment became one of the most successful elements of the project in later years and provided a contextualized and motivating basis for investigating language content,

---

Language Analysis Assignment

Language Analysis (10 marks)
300–500 words (NOT including transcript)   Due: _____

- Find a part of one of the interviews where there was some kind of misunderstanding, confusion, or problem in communication.
- Transcribe that part of the interview. Your transcript should be between 45 seconds and 90 seconds long. It should be double-spaced, and each line should be numbered.
- Answer these questions. You are expected to *consider* the questions and write thoughtful, organized, analytical answers. Try to give details in your answers, and refer directly to the transcript. Remember the word limits.

1. **What caused the misunderstanding or confusion?** Try to explain how the problem occurred. Was it a problem with pronunciation, or vocabulary, or cultural differences, or a combination of causes, or something else?
2. **How did you all deal with the problem?** For example, did you ask them [or they ask you] to say it again, or did they ask you [you ask them] to explain, or did you all ignore the problem, or did you [they] explain in another way, or something else?
3. **Can you suggest other ways to solve communication problems like this?** Try to make realistic, practical suggestions. These are called communication strategies, and include using language [asking questions, speaking more slowly, etc.] and other ideas too [using gestures and facial expressions, etc.]

such as the differences between spoken and written language, intercultural communication and miscommunication, and linguistic and nonlinguistic strategies for effective communication.

EVALUATION

At different times in the various stages of the project, learners were asked to reflect on the requirements of the project, their own performance, the performance of their peers and their teachers, and the objectives of the project. Evaluation was a part of what Davies (1989, cited in Legutke & Thomas, 1991, p. 218) calls the *experiential cycle*. Although informal methods, such as casual conversation between learners and teachers in and out of class, and formal evaluation instruments were used throughout the project, the formal evaluation took place exclusively in the review section of the Davies cycle, shown here.

Formal evaluation instruments included an evaluation form completed in class after the interviews, a peer assessment form, and a final self-assessment form (see page 129). Both formal and informal evaluations from learners were overwhelmingly positive, and the generally high quality of the final reports produced by the learners confirmed the project's success. In a very real sense, the implementation of the project was the experience element for my colleague and myself, and after review we made changes in

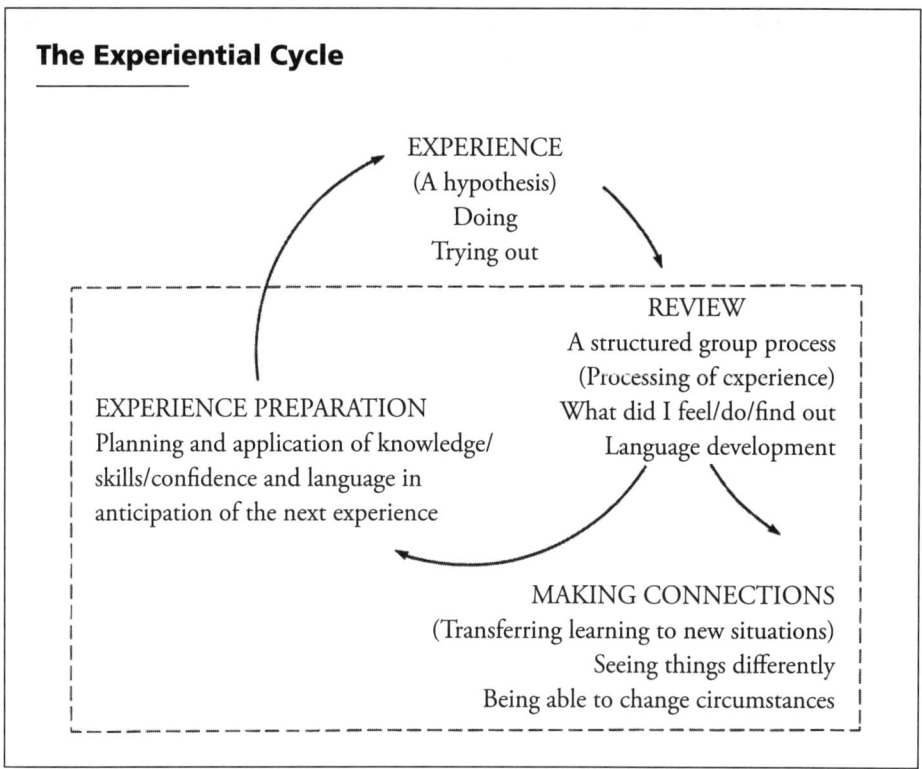

preparation for the next experience of this type. I kept notes of our discussions regarding what did and did not work, and based on these and on the learner feedback discussed above, we made a number of changes in subsequent years. Changes already discussed included a reduction in the number of lessons devoted to preparing for the interviews and changes to the assessment procedures, that is, dropping the learner diaries, requiring all learners to submit a written report, and introducing a language analysis task.

Two other fundamental changes introduced in subsequent years came primarily as a result of feedback from learners. One was that we dropped the requirement to interview tourists at the airport and that part of the preparation for the interviews became a consideration of what kind of tourists the learners wanted to interview, and where and when learners might be able to find these tourists. This led to interviews being conducted at the airport and in Chinatown, outside (and in one case in the lobby of) five-star hotels, in backpacker districts, and in night markets. In addition, learners were not as comfortable with an entirely project-based course as I was. Due in part to the success of the Airport Project, I was able to argue successfully that the separation of inbound and outbound content into different courses was not necessary. As a result, the courses were restructured, and the Airport Project became the first project in EFT I, framing the content of the three courses and introducing learners at the outset to the demands of English language communication with the people who would ultimately become their clientele.

Conclusion

Reconciling my own pedagogical beliefs and intentions with the constraints imposed by the requirements of the curriculum was both challenging and time-consuming. Like Hall and Kenny (1988), I found that "the setting-up of this course required an energy-sapping amount of [administrative] work, informal contacts and semialliances, letter writing, opportunism, and struggles against hostility in some quarters" (p. 30). Ultimately, though, the investment of time and energy was more than worthwhile, and the process was an overwhelmingly positive educational and social experience for teachers and learners alike.

Acknowledgments

I thank David Hall from the Linguistics Department at Macquarie University for helpful comments on an earlier paper from which this chapter was developed, and Simon Offley for his input and participation in the project.

Appendix A: Initial and Revised Course Outlines Distributed to Learners

INITIAL COURSE OUTLINE
English for Tourism III—Course Outline

- Practice using English in authentic tour-guide situations and other situations.
- Learn how to perform the job of tour guide with greater efficiency. (translation of course description from the university calendar)

English for Tourism III is a project-based course. There will be two projects. You will work in groups for both projects, but you will be marked individually. The first project aims to help you understand foreign tourists more, and to feel confident when you communicate. The second project aims to give you practice at being a tour guide in a real situation and use the skills you have learned.

For the first project, you will go to the airport in groups and interview departing tourists about their experience in Thailand. Then you will make a report or a presentation using the information you get from your interviews.

For the second project, you will give a tour of a temple in groups. You will get more information about the second project after midterm.

It is important for this course that you come to class and work with your group. If one person in the group does not help, everyone in the group will share the problem. You must be responsible for yourself and to your friends.

Project 1
OBJECTIVES
By the end of the first project (midterm), you should be able to:

- consider issues about tourism in Thailand from your point of view and from a foreigner's point of view, and discuss and/or write about them and other tourism-related topics clearly in English
- plan an interview and interview a foreigner in English
- use English to give and ask for feelings, opinions, observations, judgments, and conclusions
- use English to explain, justify, and give reasons
- keep a learning diary in English
- use language to learn, solve problems, and develop ideas
- develop and recognize different ways to learn
- define a task or a goal, decide what to do to achieve it, and finally achieve it
- work with other people as a group to achieve a task

- collect information from interviews, readings, and other English language sources
- evaluate and organize information
- present information clearly in English
- evaluate your own learning and achievement
- evaluate other people's achievement

ASSESSMENT

Project 1 is worth 50% of your grade for this course. Project 2 is also worth 50%.

- Self-assessment: At the end of the project, you will assess your achievement of the course objectives, and after talking about it with your teacher, will give yourself a mark. (5 marks)
- Group assessment: After the interviews, you will give the people in your group a mark for the amount of work they did for your group. Your friends will also give you a mark. (5 marks)
- Diary: Your teacher will check your diary, and you will receive a mark for the quality and quantity of your writing, and for how much you can explain what you have learned. (10 marks)
- Report/presentation: You will decide what form your report or presentation will be in. It might be a written report, or a video documentary, or a play, or a speech, or something else. Your teacher will help you decide. (20 marks)
- Exam: The midterm exam will test the language skills you develop during the project. (10 marks)

The idea of this project is to give you responsibility for your own learning. This gives you freedom but also requires responsibility. The teacher's job is to help you, to give advice, and to teach the language skills and knowledge that you need to complete the project successfully.

You will decide what to interview the tourists about. You will decide what your report or presentation will be like. You will help decide your own marks and your friends' marks.

If you plan to work in the tourism industry after you graduate, this course will give you knowledge about your future customers and experience in dealing with them. If you plan to continue studying after you graduate, this course will give you experience in conducting research, organizing information, and making conclusions.

Whatever you do after you graduate, this course aims to develop your English skills by getting you to use English to communicate in real situations, and to help you understand the ways that YOU learn English, so you can practice those skills long after you finish this course.

REVISED OVERVIEW DISTRIBUTED TO LEARNERS
Airport Project 1996

Section	Dates	Details
Introduction	Oct. 31, Nov. 5	
Preparing for interviews	Nov. 7 Nov. 12 Nov. 14 Nov. 19 Nov. 21	Forming groups Working out questions Interview techniques Planning Practicing
Interviews	Nov. 21	At the airport
Preparing for presentation/report	Nov. 26 Nov. 28 Dec. 3	Sharing interviewing experiences Evaluation of group Interviews Lessons Sharing information Planning and preparing report/presentation
Presentation/report	Dec. 12	

No Textbook? No Problem! Reading and Writing With a Nonfiction Bestseller

SARAH DODSON-KNIGHT

This chapter describes the processes and results of modifying an existing curriculum for an advanced reading and composition class of adults in an intensive English program (IEP). Instead of a traditional composition textbook, I used the nonfiction bestseller *Longitude: The True Story of a Lone Genius Who Solved the Greatest Scientific Problem of His Time* (Sobel, 1995). The book is a compelling example of effective academic writing conventions, and I used it as a springboard to improve student writing. Through the book, I was able to integrate reading and writing instruction and practice in a way that engaged the students and made more efficient use of class time.

This approach had many positive results. The students were proud that they had read, discussed, and written about a book designed for adult native speakers, and they were better prepared for working within academic discourse when they advanced to classes at the university. I succeeded in making the class more student centered, and, of equal importance, the students and I enjoyed this departure from the traditional ESL composition class.

The Motivation for the Innovation

I sat down over the semester break to prepare for a new class that I had been assigned to teach, an advanced reading and composition class for an IEP in the United States. While preparing, I realized that I wanted to try something different. My supervisor had given me a syllabus (Intensive English Program, 2001) with a list of what to teach and a textbook, *Foundations of*

Writing: Developing Research and Academic Writing Skills (Spencer & Arbon, 1997). However, the syllabus did not match the textbook. For example, many of the concepts in the textbook were not listed to be taught at this level, and the order of presentation in the syllabus differed significantly from that in the textbook.

In the reading component of the program, the students were expected to read many chapters from a college textbook from their specific fields of study, and I did not know how to address these textbooks in class. I was also unsure how I would evaluate the students' understanding of these textbooks and how I would connect them to any of the writing assignments. Overall, I felt disorganized before I had even started. I therefore decided to modify the course by finding a way to integrate the reading and writing components of the syllabus.

In the syllabus, AD302: Advanced Reading and Composition was described in this way:

> *In this course, students learn to summarize as well as paraphrase. Work with the structure of essays continues. Providing adequate support from outside sources is emphasized and practiced in three major writing assignments: summary report, expository essay [specified elsewhere in the course materials as a "cause/effect" essay] and persuasive essay. Students continue working on sentence variety with both compound and complex sentences as well as spelling, punctuation and verb tenses. Reading skills to be reinforced include: general comprehension, scanning, skimming, inferences, vocabulary from context, affixes and dictionary practice. (Intensive English Program, 2001)*

The syllabus also devoted a week to preparing students to write exam essays by covering the necessary vocabulary for understanding questions and practicing timed, written responses.

Although the textbook included readings, they were short texts and sample essays written for nonnative speakers. They were not representative of what students would encounter at university. In fact, I felt the readings disadvantaged my students in the context of university study, where the textbooks and articles would be written for native speakers of English. Leki (1993) explains the disadvantages of these brief, unrelated readings: "Short texts are, in fact, likely to be more difficult to read since students never read enough about the subject to build the knowledge about it" (p. 14).

I wanted to prepare my students to read nonfiction, but I realized that the required reading in the syllabus would have to change. I would not have time to read all their different textbooks, and it would be impossible to use these textbooks in class or adequately check the students' comprehension.

I suspected that the students would be wasting their time and would be frustrated if I did not integrate their outside-of-class reading into the course. Having a common text that everyone could read together meant that we could analyze it in class, practice vocabulary strategies with it, and use it as a springboard to writing. Integration of reading and composition is seen as desirable by writers such as Johns (1993), who states that "it is now agreed that at least two of the academic skills, reading and writing, cannot be separated either in terms of research or practice" (p. 274).

Books and articles about extensive reading instruction in the ESL classroom tend to center on the strategies and benefits of using literature rather than nonfiction works. However, I believe that many of these strategies and benefits apply to nonfiction books. In planning AD302, I kept in mind Aebersold and Field's (1997) justification for and cautions about working with longer texts: "The task is not to have students study literature; it is to plan lessons around works of literature, beginning with the shaping of goals and objectives that will focus their language learning" (p. 163). Aebersold and Field conclude their chapter on using literature by reminding teachers that "the main reason for using any text is to improve the students' language skills. Thus, the teacher needs to set appropriate objectives . . . that focus on language development rather than the study of literary forms" (p. 166). This reassured me that I could indeed use a nonfiction book, in lieu of the standard textbook, as a tool for writing instruction.

I believed I could make the course less disjointed by integrating the reading and writing assignments, using a common reading text as a springboard to writing, and teaching reading and writing skills within a familiar context. My instincts were based on my having taught composition to native speakers at a U.S. university, where the essays the students read and the essays they wrote were always connected, and these instincts were supported by research in second language (L2) reading and writing pedagogy. Carson (1993) endorses this reading-to-write approach, explaining that "it underscores the fact that most writing, particularly in academic contexts, depends to a large extent on reading input—either directly from source texts, or indirectly from background knowledge, which itself results from experience with texts" (p. 99). However, Leki (1993), in an article summarizing then-recent research on reading and writing instruction, found that, for several reasons, "adult ESL classrooms are only beginning to consider how to effectively integrate both reading and writing" (p. 10). This is despite the fact that "teaching reading and writing in separate courses has had dramatic consequences on reading instruction, robbing reading of its natural purpose and ignoring its social dimensions" (p. 12). I was determined to make my classroom one where students were truly reading to write.

The Curriculum Context

AD302 was the third in a series of four 7-week undergraduate reading and writing courses offered through an IEP at a large state university in the United States. Approximately 125 students were enrolled in the IEP at the time, with the majority of students from the Middle East, Japan, and Korea. As well as the reading and composition course, students were generally taking an oral communication class, a grammar class, and an elective such as Business English, Pronunciation, or Film.

My class met every day for 80 minutes over the 7-week term. There were 12 students in my class. Most of them were under 25 years of age, with an equal number of men and women. The students' first languages were Arabic, Chinese, Japanese, Korean, and Spanish. Many of the students were planning to pursue undergraduate or graduate degrees at the university, and others intended to return to their home countries after the IEP.

This course was their first writing course in which the focus was not on reading short fiction and writing personal essays. The students would need to be able to write expository research papers, using academic writing conventions, in classes with native speakers. I wanted to highlight writing skills such as summarizing, paraphrasing, and citing sources, and to reinforce concepts that had been introduced in earlier classes and that were important in expository writing, such as thesis statements, topic sentences, text organization, and the use of cohesive devices.

The student population was known for wanting a great deal of grammar instruction, and I feared that my students might be suspicious about studying a nonacademic book, which they might see as not directly relevant to their fields of study. I feared that my idea about a common reading text would only complicate the teaching situation. The challenge of finding a nonfiction book seemed impossible at times, given the following criteria I had established for the ideal book:

- The theme of the book must be related to science or engineering.
- The topic of the book should engage the students and the teacher for 7 weeks.
- The target audience of the book must be adults or young adults, not children or adolescents.
- The book must not be set in the contemporary United States to avoid the need to spend class time explaining references, U.S. history and traditions, or other background knowledge.
- The book must present many examples of writing that the students need.

- The book must be structured with a plot rather than be a purely theoretical or informational book.
- The book must present concepts that could lead to writing assignments and further research.
- The book must be short enough to read in 7 weeks.
- The book must be available in an inexpensive paperback edition.
- The book must have an obvious recycling of vocabulary that will mirror what occurs in textbooks and allow for instruction in word-attack strategies.

I felt comfortable teaching the conventions of academic writing, and I hoped that once I found a book that fulfilled my criteria, the rest of the course would fall into place. The only problem I anticipated was possible student reluctance to adapt to a course format centered around a book that was not a textbook.

Modifying the Syllabus

Although I did not want to, or need to, change the goals of the course, I thought that I could modify the way we accomplished them by not separating the reading tasks from the writing tasks. Therefore, with approval from my supervisor, I combed the bookstores, determined to find a nonfiction book with an engaging and accessible plot to use as the primary textbook for my class. I chose the bestseller *Longitude* (Sobel, 1995) as an excellent example of good academic writing. Although the book is a historical account of the 17th-century quest to develop a method for determining longitude at sea, it is also a plot-driven story with vividly drawn characters. In the book, Sobel uses the skills my students needed to acquire, such as summarizing, paraphrasing, using quotations, synthesizing information, citing sources, and providing an extensive bibliography. It appealed to my students because they did not have to be familiar with U.S. culture to understand it, and because Sobel touches on the disciplines of physics, astronomy, politics, psychology, geography, and economics, which some of my students were planning to study at the university.

The next step was to redesign the class and rewrite the syllabus to incorporate *Longitude* and use it as a springboard to writing. I started by setting these course objectives:

Students will practice reading and writing in English by

- using authentic English texts, including newspaper and magazine articles, encyclopedias, and Web sites

- summarizing, paraphrasing, and quoting
- writing multiple drafts of essays
- writing three out-of-class essays (summary, cause and effect, and persuasive)
- developing essay-exam strategies
- learning and practicing academic conventions
- reading a nonfiction book (*Longitude*)
- communicating with the instructor and other students in the class though a Web forum discussion
- reacting to material covered in class by posting to the Web forum, doing other in-class writing, or participating in class or reading-circle discussions
- improving editing and proofreading skills

I also developed the Course Timetable shown here, which I presented as a 7-week course calendar.

On the first day of class, I wanted to excite the students about the book, so I explained and justified the format of the class by using the following strategies:

Course Timetable	
Week 1	Introduction Summarizing Web forum posting
Week 2	Chapters 1–3 of *Longitude* Draft summary essay
Week 3	Chapters 4–6 of *Longitude* Final draft of summary due Start cause-effect writing
Week 4	Chapters 7–9 of *Longitude* Draft cause-effect essay Practice taking essay exams with midterm
Week 5	Chapters 10–12 of *Longitude* Final draft of cause-effect essay due Start persuasive writing
Week 6	Chapters 13–15 of *Longitude* Follow-up to *Longitude* Draft persuasive essay
Week 7	Final draft of persuasive essay due Practice essay for final exam

- I told the students that they would not need to spend $30 or more on several textbooks.
- I showed them clips from a PBS Nova video (Angier, 1998) that was based on the book.
- I prepared printouts of Web pages with pictures and diagrams on the topic of the book, and we completed an exercise in which the students each read different pages, devised titles for each section, and put the pages in a logical order.
- We previewed the book, and students examined the front and back covers, table of contents, pictures and graphs, and bibliography and then predicted what the first few chapters would be about.
- I explained what the reading, writing, and research tasks would be in the IEP composition class and at the college level, and how reading this book and writing about it would prepare students for those tasks. I also explained that in order to move up to the next course, AD402, the students would need to show that they could read and understand texts written for general native-speaker audiences and write well-organized essays, incorporating information from sources appropriately and with enough detail.
- I shared with the students my feelings of pride and confidence when I first read an entire book in my L2.

Over the 7-week course, we read three chapters of the book per week and spent one day each week discussing it in a *reading circle* (Daniels, 2002; Neamon & Strong, 1992). Reading circles grew out of native-speaker reading classes in elementary schools and are also known as *literature circles* or *literacy circles*. With this methodology, students are divided into groups of three to five, and all members of the group read the same material. However, each member is assigned a different role (see Appendix A) and prepares a different written assignment, thus becoming an expert on a different aspect of the reading. For each new reading assignment, members change roles. The roles I assigned to the students were

- summarizer: This student writes a paragraph explaining the assigned reading.
- teacher: This student writes discussion questions.
- dictionary: This student prepares a list of vocabulary from the reading. Each prepared entry must include related information, such as other forms of the word, synonyms, antonyms, idioms, and expressions using the key term.
- psychologist: This student writes two paragraphs analyzing one of the main characters and his actions.

- artist: This student creates a visual representation of an important scene from the reading and explains its importance to the overall work. The visual representation can take the form of a drawing, a collage, a comic strip, clip art, and so on.

The students in my class were expected to bring copies of their prepared work for each member of the group. This meant that the students would not have to reread the book at the end of the term before taking the exam, as they could use the summaries and questions for review purposes. Student who were going to be absent on a reading-circle day had to e-mail their written assignments to the teacher and the group members. The students worked in their groups for part or all of the class period to share what they had prepared and to discuss the assigned chapters. I found that they read more carefully and wrote better texts because their target audience was wider than just the teacher and because the other group members were depending on them to convey information thoroughly and accurately. Aebersold and Field (1997) highlight the importance of cooperative learning in L2 classes, which I wanted my students to experience through studying *Longitude*:

> *It is through reading, talking, sharing, arguing, and trying to put into writing their ideas that students truly learn. L2/FL [foreign language] classes function best this way. Students who have tasks to complete— using the second language to complete them—are safer, better supported, and more likely to learn in a group. Students who have tasks to complete in small groups in the L2 risk less, have access to expanded resources, and experience increased motivation to learn. (p. 190)*

In the remaining four sessions each week, we studied how Sobel used academic writing techniques such as paraphrasing, summarizing, and introducing quotations. I also developed a range of in-class activities focusing on reading and writing skills and various types of academic writing. Some of these activities and their intended focus are described below:

- prediction: Students were asked to read chapter titles and imagine what would happen next. The reading-circle group that best predicted the subsequent chapter received a prize.
- skimming and scanning: Students searched the text for specific pieces of information or for the name of a person who spoke a given line of dialogue. This activity was structured like a game, with different reading-circle groups competing against each other for points.
- vocabulary through context: Students highlighted new words and found phrases in the surrounding sentences that gave clues to their meaning.
- cohesive devices: Students highlighted words and phrases that indicated

chronological order, cause and effect, contrast, and other rhetorical patterns. Students also identified the function of the word or phrase.
- summarizing: I provided examples of strong and weak summaries, and the students critiqued them before writing their own summaries of sections in the book. They practiced writing summaries of individual pages, then one chapter at a time, then several chapters, and finally of the entire book. Students practiced writing summaries of progressively shorter lengths, first 200 words, then 100, then 50, and finally 25.
- paraphrasing: Students reread a paragraph in class, and then I showed examples of strong and weak paraphrases, which students critiqued. The students then created and compared their own paraphrases. (See Appendix B for a sample paraphrasing activity.)
- quotations: Students searched for direct quotations in the text and identified different ways in which the quotations had been introduced and integrated into the paragraph. They were asked to notice which ideas were quoted, which were summarized or paraphrased, and what the resulting effect of the direct quote was. Students then worked on smoothly incorporating quotations from the text into their summaries.
- book reviews: Students wrote customer reviews of the book for the online merchant Amazon.com (http://www.amazon.com/).
- chat rooms: Students engaged in wide-ranging discussions, for example, on questions that I prepared, the themes of the book, and the writing process.
- forums: The students and I held discussions through online asynchronous forum postings. For example, I wrote questions or made suggestions on a computer forum such as a bulletin board, and the students responded in writing. The students then responded to each other's ideas.
- music: Students were asked to find a song that had something in common with the reading, to listen to it, and to discuss it. For example, I shared "Galileo" (Saliers, 1992) by the Indigo Girls.
- role play: Some students took on the roles of the characters from the book, while others acted as journalists or television talk show hosts who interviewed the characters. They then wrote newspaper articles about what they had learned.

During the second week of class, when many of the students confessed that they did not always understand parts of the assigned reading, I decided to begin posting a reading guide on our class forum, listing names and concepts important to the current chapters. I told my students that if they remembered the people and ideas, then they had understood all the main ideas, which they could discuss in detail in class. My students rose to the challenge and ultimately praised the book and the experience, as seen in these edited customer reviews they posted on the commercial Web site Amazon.com:

I found the book really interesting, because she has turned an historical fact into an interesting and fascinating story. Through her book I could realize not only the importance of the Harrison's invention, but also how a man can do anything if he puts passion and energy into what he wants. (Aristizabal, 2000)

I would like to teach this book to my students. If you have never read this book, first pick it up and read. Then from that time, you will travel in a world of time. (Kim, 2000)

Actually I couldn't understand the meanings of many word, but I am very glad I read it. I now know about longitude history which I have never thought about . . . . Even though it's about science history, it was not difficult to understand the story. (Choi, 2000)

As the course continued, the students moved from recognition to production and practiced academic writing techniques. They completed in-class writing tasks and online research, learned essay exam strategies, and undertook a midterm assessment with essay questions based on *Longitude*.

I engaged students in two types of informal writing tasks: in-class writing and online writing. In class, students handwrote answers to questions on the board at the beginning of class. This helped focus their attention on the writing class and the current material. Two days per week, when we met in the IEP computer laboratory, the students asked and answered questions that I posted to an asynchronous discussion forum and in chat rooms. This online writing was read by their groups, by me, and sometimes by the whole class, thus forcing the students to consider their audience even when writing a simple paragraph. The following sample writing prompts show how informal writing tasks targeted different learning objectives.

Some prompts addressed the process of reading and writing in English:

- What are your goals for this class? Be specific: How do you want to improve your reading and writing?
- Last night, you wrote a couple of paragraphs trying to convince future IEP teachers to teach, or not to teach, *Longitude*. This is called *persuasive* writing. What does *persuade* mean to you? What do you think you should include in persuasive writing?
- What is the most challenging part of the essay you are working on now? Do you have any questions for me?
- What are the strengths of your essay? What parts need more attention? What would you like me to focus on when I read it?

- Look at the list of goals that you wrote on the first day of the course. Have you started to accomplish any of them? Do you want to add anything new to your list? Do you have any questions for me?

Other prompts addressed understanding of content:

- What are your impressions of the first chapter of *Longitude*? What are the most important facts you learned from this chapter?
- What did you find most surprising about these chapters? What was most difficult to understand?
- What else do you want to know about Galileo? If you were writing an article in English about Galileo for international students, what information would you include? What would you leave out?
- What information do these two articles about Galileo have in common? Make a list of the main ideas. In your opinion, what else is important?

The music and role-play activities worked well on reading-circle days when group discussions petered out but I wanted the students to keep focusing on the ideas in the book.

My students were supposed to practice essay exams and to write three source-based essays: summary essays, cause-effect essays, and persuasive essays. As anticipated, I was able to plan the big writing assignments around topics presented in the book. Using the themes in *Longitude*, I wrote essay questions for the midterm assessment, for example, *Discuss the problems that sailors experienced in the years before a method for determining longitude was introduced* and *Compare and contrast the Lunar Distance Method with the Clock Method.* I also assigned the following longer papers:

1. a report about Galileo, drawing from outside sources that the students synthesized
2. an essay about new developments or events from the book and their effects
3. an essay through which the students had to persuade the Longitude Committee to award the substantial monetary prize to John Harrison, the protagonist, who ultimately did not receive all he deserved for a lifetime of hard work that changed navigational history

According to the IEP assessment guidelines, students were to produce three drafts of each paper. The first two were graded on content and organization on a 10-point scale. The third was also graded on grammar and mechanics, and the scores for the final draft were recorded. Other grades came from reading-circle assignments, prewriting exercises in class, posts to the class forum, and so forth. According to IEP policy, students had to receive a score of 80 or higher to advance to the next level, with 45% of the overall mark for in-class assignments, 45% for outside-class assignments, and 10% for homework and class participation.

Unfortunately, I had not predicted that, by the middle of the term, when we began working on the second essay, the students would be tired of dealing with *Longitude* every day. They asked if all their papers had to be about the book. At this point, I wondered if the book was too advanced for them and whether they did not feel confident writing about the material.

I had no intention of discontinuing the outside reading and the in-class reading circles, but I did not want the students to find the in-class writing exercises and out-of-class assignments tedious because they were all on similar topics. I still felt strongly that writing should not exist in a vacuum, and I therefore decided to empower the students by giving them a choice of topics for the second and third essays. However, I wanted to ensure that any alternative options would enable students to draw from the same readings and that they would not have to reset their schema and start from scratch with the research. The alternate topic became *studying abroad,* and students had the option of writing the cause-effect essay about one specific cause or effect of studying abroad. For the persuasive essay, they had to convince a specific group of people to study abroad, in a specific place. The students were pleased with these choices, and the majority of them wrote the last two papers on the alternative topic.

Evaluating the Course

At the end of the 7 weeks, each student had written three research-based papers and completed two exams: the midterm assessment and the IEP common final assessment, which was graded anonymously by two other writing teachers. They had also read and thoroughly discussed a full-length nonfiction book. They had shared their writing with me and with their peers through reading-circle assignments, during peer-editing sessions, and in online writing. They had also shared their views with the outside world via reader reviews on Amazon.com. Leki (1993) champions peer review when she states that "by reading each others' texts in a reading/writing class, students directly confront the elusive, slippery nature of reading" (p. 22).

Overall, the students in my AD302 class achieved the course goals with varied success. Although I feel that all the students improved their reading skills and reading speed, they nevertheless had trouble comprehending *Longitude,* and many were still struggling with some of the writing skills, particularly paraphrasing and citation. My supervisor assured me, and I have since seen with other classes, that these are particularly difficult skills that L2 students cannot be expected to master in 7 weeks.

At the end of each term, IEP students complete evaluation forms about the course and the teacher, but the administrators and supervisors at the institution do not provide written feedback to the teacher. In the student evaluations, the students rate 16 statements and questions from 1 to 5, with a score of 5 being the highest. The following average ratings focus on the statements related to my modifications of the course:

- The teacher was well prepared and well organized. (4.9)
- The teacher used examples and illustrations effectively. (4.7)
- In this class I made progress in my study of English. (4.2)
- In this class the textbook and other class materials were helpful. (4.1)
- Overall, how would you rate this teacher? (4.7)
- Overall, how would you rate this course? (4.2)

Student comments in the evaluation are optional and anonymous. Evaluative comments from my students about my teaching included the following edited assessments:

She used the network computer more effectively and it was very interesting class.

I think I could improved in this class. However I have one complaint about the book. In fact, that book we read was interesting, but it was a kind of treatise on some specific major. I couldn't have much interested in that book. In just my interest, I prefer historical book not about scientific event.

The final should be in the lab to correct the mistakes.

There should be more time to do the essay and I think that in the Term we should write two essays not 3 because we don't have time.

This class was very helpful for me. But I wanted free topic in my essay. (Of course, you did ask us about last draft. I thanked you for that). Especially I liked chatroom. I wanted more time about chatroom. It was really funny.

From these comments, I can see that, for the most part, my students were not fazed by the changes I incorporated. Some particularly enjoyed the computer-assisted language learning components, and they felt as if they had accomplished a great deal in the class.

I am also certain that, despite their difficulties with *Longitude,* the students understood it better than they would have understood a textbook that they had read outside class and had never discussed. Participating in reading circles each week helped keep the class student centered and allowed for more practice of oral language skills, thus preparing the students for future class discussions at the university level. Overall, I feel that my changes to the course prepared the students well to cope with future academic reading and writing tasks.

Conclusion

As a result of teaching this class, I have become an even stronger proponent of the reading-to-write approach. In other courses, I have used complete texts rather than excerpts, and I have used these texts, or the concepts they present, as a springboard for informal in-class writing, at-home journal writing, and formal compositions. I have even endeavored to introduce more nonfiction into beginning-level and intermediate-level courses, and I am now reading more nonfiction in my own free time.

I believe that working with a common, extended text makes it easier for the teacher to illustrate writing conventions and for the students to understand and practice them. I am convinced that in the course described in this chapter, it was easier for students to come to terms with difficult academic writing concepts and skills because they were working with the same topic throughout the term. They did not have to jump from one unrelated reading or set of examples to another and continually reset their schema. They did not have to spend precious class time trying to understand the meaning of new texts before attempting to write a summary or paraphrase. Concentrating on one text made cohesive devices and citation much less abstract.

I believe that the concepts described in this chapter could be applied to other courses. Teachers could certainly employ these ideas at other levels by using fiction, children's books, or magazines to illustrate skills, organization, and grammatical structures. In oral communication classes, teachers could develop a wide range of listening and speaking activities to improve spoken language skills by integrating reading circles into traditionally teacher-centered classes and by using a common book as a springboard to discussion.

Appendix A: Reading Circle Handout

This handout was distributed at the beginning of the term.

Name _____

Group _____

AD302 Reading Circles

For the next 6 weeks, we'll be reading *Longitude* by Dava Sobel (1995), a bestselling nonfiction book. You will be responsible for reading three chapters per week and preparing materials to share with your Reading Circle group. Your group will meet for 20–30 minutes during class to discuss the book. I won't explain or lecture about the book to the whole class, so you must work together to understand it.

To prepare for your Reading Circle, you will do a different writing assignment, which you will bring to your group on Mondays. Change roles each week, so that you can gain experience with each role. The different roles are:

- **Role 1: Summarizer:** Write a two-paragraph summary of the three chapters that includes information about the most important people and events.
- **Role 2: Teacher:** Make a list of 8–10 discussion questions. Note: avoid yes/no questions and ones with very short answers. You'll be leading the discussion, so you want to ask questions that will make everyone else do the talking. Try to go beyond the simple facts, for example, not just *What did Harrison decide?* but rather *Why did Harrison react that way?* You can also ask for opinions, such as *What would you do in this situation?* or *Do you approve or disapprove of this judgment? Why?*
- **Role 3: Dictionary:** Choose 8–10 important words or phrases from these chapters and give a definition (in English). Indicate the page number for each word. Also provide the part(s) of speech and some other pieces of information, for example, synonyms, antonyms, other forms of the word, idiomatic expressions using this word, and so on.
- **Role 4: Psychologist:** Write two paragraphs analyzing one of the main characters and his actions. What did he do? Why? How did he feel about it? What were the effects? And so on.
- **Role 5: Artist:** Choose a scene from the chapters that you think is particularly interesting, surprising or important and make a picture of it. The picture can be a drawing, computer clip art, a comic strip or a collage. Then write one paragraph explaining why you chose this scene and explain what is happening in the picture.

IMPORTANT

Bring four copies of your material to class: one for me to grade and one for each member of your group. If you keep all the information together, you will have a handy glossary and enough information to study for the exams without needing to reread the entire book.

Your classmates are counting on you to keep up with the reading and bring in this information, so if you know that you will be absent on a Monday, please e-mail the homework to me and to your group. Also, I'd prefer for you to type your homework, but I will accept handwritten work. You'll have to pay to photocopy it, though.

Appendix B: Paraphrasing Exercise for *Longitude* (Sobel, 1995)

1. **Original (p. 22)**

   Solar and lunar eclipses, however, occurred far too rarely to provide any meaningful aid to navigation. With luck, one could hope to get a longitude fix once a year by this technique. Sailors needed an everyday heavenly occurrence.

   Paraphrase

   Eclipses of the sun and the moon, however, happened far too rarely to provide any meaningful navigation help. One could hope to find longitude once a year by this technique, with luck. What was needed by sailors was a heavenly occurrence every day.

2. **Original (p. 35)**

   Some clock enthusiasts suspected that good timekeepers might suffice to solve the longitude problem, by enabling mariners to carry the home-port time aboard ship with them, like a barrel of water or a side of beef. Starting in 1530, Flemish astronomer Gemma Frisius hailed the mechanical clock as a contender in the effort to find longitude at sea.

   Paraphrase

   Frisius thought that sailors could carry clocks.

3. **Original (p. 12)**

   Launched on a mix of bravery and greed, the sea captains of the fifteenth, sixteenth, and seventeenth centuries relied on "dead reckoning" to gauge their distance east or west of home port. The captain would throw a log overboard and observe how quickly the ship receded from this temporary guidepost. He noted the crude speedometer reading in his ship's logbook, along with the direction of travel, which he took from the stars or a compass, and the length of time on a particular course, counted with a sandglass or a pocket watch. Factoring in the effects of ocean currents, fickle winds and errors in judgment, he then determined his longitude.

   Paraphrase

   In order to find longitude at sea, 400 years ago captains of ships used a technique called "dead reckoning." This involved throwing a log off the boat and noting how fast the log moved away. Then the captain checked the approximate speed of the boat, what direction they were heading, and the time they'd been on that course. Then he also considered possible mistakes, inconsistent winds and ocean currents. These factors gave him the ship's longitude.

4. **Original (p. 21)**

   As Admiral Shovell and Commodore Anson showed, even the best sailors lost their bearings once they lost sight of land, for the sea offered no useful clue about longitude. The sky, however, held out hope. Perhaps there was a way to read longitude in the relative positions of the celestial bodies.

   Paraphrase

   No ship captains, not even Shovell and Anson, were good enough to determine longitude accurately at sea, unless they could already see land in the distance. However, people hoped that they could use information from the sun, the moon and the stars.

NOTE: In the first example, the paraphrase too closely resembles the original, and the second is much too short and is a summary rather than a paraphrase. The last two meet the requirements for a good paraphrase.

When Writing Is *Murder*: Transforming a Composition Course With a Mystery Novel

8

TODD HEYDEN

Writing is murder when a class doesn't care and the students don't write regularly or with commitment. This is a story in which the mystery of motivating such a class to write was solved. It describes an ESL freshman composition course in which students read a murder mystery, *The Alienist* (Carr, 1994), and then researched and wrote about its historical setting and immigrant life on the Lower East Side of New York, in the United States.

The Motivation for the Innovation

ESL students must write regularly in order to develop fluent and clear written language. Previously, my students had not been doing enough writing to achieve either of these aims, but, in a course designed around a mystery novel, they were able to write extensively. Addressing the second challenge of commitment to writing is crucial. Otherwise, students remain disengaged and cannot use writing to discover and refine an idea. Inspiring my own students to commit to writing was a tough challenge until I committed myself to transforming my English department's ESL freshman composition course curriculum.

On the surface, this transformation required two clear changes. The first was to assign a single novel rather than the standard anthology of essays, and the second was to modify the prescribed writing handbook by adding writing activities designed to promote fluency. At a deeper level, transforming the curriculum required two pedagogic shifts:

1. In assigning a single novel instead of an essay anthology, the course would be based on a "sustained, content-based" approach (Pally, 2000, p. 14), instead of the longstanding departmental approach, based on the study of an anthology of rhetorical essay forms, such as persuasion and description.
2. Using writing activities along with the departmental writing handbook implied that fluency came first and correctness was to be postponed (MacGowan-Gilhooly, 1996).

Once these shifts had been made, the students' success was nothing short of inspiring. However, obtaining permission to make the changes took some time and a great deal of persuasion. The course guidelines established by the university English department had been in place for over a decade, and attempts to alter them had to be made with finesse. The departmental commitment to traditional ideas about teaching writing was a major obstacle to overcome. The curriculum required students to write short essays in rhetorical forms and a longer research paper. There were two required texts: an essay anthology and a writing handbook. Students were to use the writings in the anthology as models for composing their own essays, and they were to refer to the handbook when writing the research paper. However, I felt that this curriculum was not effectively serving the ESL students, who were largely alienated readers and unproductive writers. As one colleague pointed out, "These kids can't do English, and we have to do something about it." The faculty was concerned about the poor quality of what had come to be known as "the dreaded research paper," and this concern provided a climate conducive to my proposed changes. I felt certain that the students could write a successful research paper if the class provided a better context in which to write.

THE CASE FOR ASSIGNING ONE NOVEL

Any changes to the curriculum could be implemented only if the departmental curriculum committee could see credible reasons for change. When I proposed using a single novel instead of the usual anthology of essays, one curriculum committee member found this proposal "altogether too touchy-feely for our department."

However, explaining the research in favor of such a shift helped pave the way, and most committee members welcomed an alternative as long as it was undertaken as an experiment involving only my students. I argued that the use of "sustained content" (Pally, 2000, p. 14) to support the development of writing skills among ESL students in college had been shown to be highly effective. In a course based on sustained content, learners could focus on a single discipline and context for all in-class writing. Familiarity with content would enable them to develop expertise and to write with more confidence, especially when it came to the research paper. By using this rationale, I was able to persuade the department to allow me to replace the usual text with the novel *The Alienist* (Carr, 1994).

THE CASE FOR FLUENCY-ORIENTED WRITING ASSIGNMENTS

Obtaining permission to supplement the writing handbook with writing activities designed to promote fluency was the next hurdle. Here I argued that ESL freshmen need to develop fluency before they can develop accuracy. However, the departmental curriculum was based on the belief that writers must learn to write accurately before they can write fluently. As one colleague said, "The more they write, the more errors they make." The concern was that errors would be reinforced if students were allowed to write without first mastering grammar.

When I asked committee members if they were aware of any research that might support this belief, the frequent reply was that it was common sense. In response to this, I suggested that learning to write can also be characterized as a developmental process in which the initial emphasis is on fluency. Writers first build fluency before they gradually shift toward clarity and correctness (MacGowan-Gilhooly, 1996; Mayher, Lester, & Pradl, 1983). We reached a compromise: The students would still be required to use the writing handbook in order to learn correct citation; the handbook grammar chapters could be supplemented with writing activities based on the course content.

I had won support for revising the curriculum, changing both the textbook and the approach to writing, with the understanding that it would be an experiment involving only my students. However, a further challenge awaited: How would the ESL freshmen students take to reading and writing in this modified curriculum?

The Curriculum Context

THE STUDENTS

Within the university context, most of the responsibility for teaching writing falls to the English department, which, understandably, is primarily interested in teaching literature. As such, instructing second language writers is not a priority. However, the university attracts a large number of immigrant students, the majority of whom go on to careers in business and computer science. These students are admitted to the university on the strength of their standardized test scores in math and English, and my school uses the SAT Reasoning Test, which is the test most frequently employed by colleges and universities in the United States. However, most of the students still need more time and, especially, more practice to develop the writing skills that will make them bona fide graduates. Neither the university nor the students fully recognize how essential writing is, especially as a tool for learning. In such a setting, it is no wonder that students had been resistant to learning to write.

The class consisted of 30 immigrants, 21 women and 9 men. All the students had been in the United States for less than a year. Nineteen were Chinese, and 11 were Russian. The Russian students were in their mid-30s and had held professional positions in either medicine or engineering before coming to the United States. In contrast, the Chinese students were in their teens and early 20s, and had had no substantial work experience.

THE COURSE

In the past, my students had approached writing as an irrelevant task, which they were obliged to undertake only in a composition course. They would not engage with what they were writing, and responded to assignments with "anti-writing" (Neel, 1989, p. 171), the kind of prose that seems to indicate that no one wrote it and that it is just a string of words to satisfy the teacher and complete an assignment. The writing process remained an empty exercise of composing and revising, without the students feeling committed to developing an idea. It is not unusual for students to hold this limited view that writing is merely a game one plays at school (Brooke, 1991). However, I wanted my students to become engaged to such a degree that they would come to write, to their surprise and pleasure, "a text they genuinely inhabited" (Summerfield & Summerfield, 1989, p. 21), and this required a major shift in the design of the departmental freshman writing course.

For the most part, the specified curriculum had been divided into units, each focusing on the mastery of rhetorical forms such as argumentation or comparison and contrast, or into even smaller units on paragraphing or sentence patterns. However, this division of writing into discrete units had proved ineffective, and the challenge was to create a more cohesive curriculum in which students would have the necessary writing practice and be able to commit to developing an idea they genuinely cared about. The solution lay in providing students with a single frame of reference, a novel, that they could engage with as readers and as writers over a whole semester. One student characterized the semester this way: "I felt like I was inside a world I liked learning about." Ultimately, the students were able to experience success, and this was largely because using a single text maintained a clear context for writing.

For first-year ESL students, a course in composition can feel like a semester of freshman *dis*orientation. Not only is academic writing unfamiliar to them (Green, 1989), but the course content can seem confusingly disjointed. An anthology of essays, written on a variety of subjects by different authors, keeps shifting the context for writing, which is analogous to the old joke about the man who tours all of Europe in 7 days: *If it's Thursday, it must be Belgium.* As the frame of reference keeps changing with each new essay, a student can become similarly disoriented: *If it's Tuesday, it must be Amy Tan.* A single text is easier to read than a series of disconnected ones because it recycles key concepts and vocabulary, allowing students to develop familiarity with the subject about which they write. The departmental anthology of essays on rhetorical devices generated little interest or motivation among the students, and they produced only small amounts of writing. This was a cause for concern because developing writing skills in ESL students requires "an abundance of reading and writing" (MacGowan-Gilhooly, 1996, p. 42).

The Process of Adapting the Course

SELECTING A NOVEL

The essay anthology was replaced with a novel, *The Alienist* (Carr, 1994), and the writing assignments were focused on its historical setting and immigrant life on Manhattan's Lower East Side. My decision to use a novel was based on case studies in which academic writing skills improved when students studied a single content area over time (Pally, 2000). This choice was also supported by findings that suggest that focusing on one content area can increase students' interest in learning (Brinton, Snow, & Wesche, 1989). McCourt (1999), author of *Angela's Ashes* (1996), recalls finding a cache of essays written by earlier generations of students in the high school where he was teaching. His previously listless students became energized by reading these essays, which had been written by their own relatives at fascinating times in history, such as the Great Depression and World War II. Once McCourt based the course content solely on these essays, students began to read and write with an enthusiasm that had seemed improbable.

I selected *The Alienist* for its setting and because it is an engrossing murder mystery. In the novel, an alienist (or psychiatrist) tracks a serial killer who preys on immigrants on Manhattan's Lower East Side. The book is engrossing, both as a mystery and as an evocative recreation of 19th-century life in New York City. The setting was likely to interest the students, who were immigrants living and studying near the Lower East Side, and the plot twists would serve to motivate them to read. The intention was for students to learn the content gradually and incrementally over a 14-week semester so that they would come to feel a sense of expertise and be more able to write about what they learned. In fact, by the end of the semester, they were able to do more than this, discovering in themselves an energy for writing that they had not known before. Students read more than had previous learners in the course, and, to their surprise and obvious pleasure, they actually read the entire book. The reading was spread over the semester, with the students reading approximately 50 pages per week. As they read further each week, they knew where they were and where they were going, and there was the feeling that they were building on what they learned, as one student explained: "I know the characters like classmates. Every week I want to see what happens to them."

Many ESL teachers do not always have the luxury of assigning a whole novel because they teach in shorter programs or they cannot find a novel set in the locale of their writing class. However, these teachers should feel encouraged to use shorter texts that they believe will be of value and interest to their students. For example, entries from Anne Frank's diary (1947/1993) have been used to create a highly successful course in writing and research (Rosser, 1995).

DISCUSSING THE NOVEL ON AN ONLINE DISCUSSION BOARD

To start the students reading the novel, I set up short tasks on a discussion board, using the course management software Blackboard (2006). Students went online and carried out assignments in which they wrote chapter summaries, composed letters in the voice of a character, discussed plot twists, and so on (see Discussion Board Assignments).

By means of Blackboard, the students corresponded with each other about *The Alienist*. In contrast to their lack of productivity in the past, every student wrote, and even the ones who were silent in class joined the discussions online. The discussion board allowed every student, even the quietest ones, opportunities to contribute comments. The conversation was not monopolized by a small number of more outgoing students, as was often the case during in-class discussions. I used the discussion board for two main purposes: to provide a relaxed forum for discussing the novel and to create a context in which students would have to use writing and, in the process, increase their written fluency. A further benefit was the development of a sense of community among the learners. Students were grouped in class and then asked to respond to their group members on the discussion board. I had often been amazed at how the animated ESL students I observed around campus, gossiping on cell phones in the hallways, chatting online in the library, or making witty comments in the elevator, became mute once they entered my freshman composition class. Not only were many silent

Discussion Board Assignments		
Week	Book Section	Assignments
1	*The Alienist*, 1–50	Post double-entry journal Respond to team members
2	*The Alienist*, 51–100	Write character letter Respond to team members
3	*The Alienist*, 101–150	Write summary
4	*The Alienist*, 151–200	Post double-entry journal Respond to team members
5	*The Alienist*, 201–250	Write letter to Dr. Lazlo Respond to team members
6	*The Alienist*, 251–300	Write summary
7	*The Alienist*, 301–350	Write letter to the murderer Respond to team members
8	*The Alienist*, 351–400	Write Summary
9	*The Alienist*, 401–450	Post double-entry journal Respond to team members
10	*The Alienist*, 451–500	Write letter to the author Respond to team members
11	*The Alienist*, 501–550	Write summary
12	*The Alienist*, 551–end	Post double-entry journal Respond to team members

and withdrawn during discussions, but they were also reluctant to engage in informal in-class writing activities.

Having ESL writers work together online has much to offer, as it becomes a context for learning together beyond the classroom. For example, the students wrote letters to characters in the novel and posted these on the discussion board. Then they sent replies to the letters and received answers. Pedagogically, the letters were highly effective informal writing tasks that increased written fluency. The learning that takes place in cafeterias and dormitories supports classroom learning, and building a sense of community among writing students is invaluable in developing language skills. However, in freshman writing courses, students are often isolated outside the classroom and have limited opportunities for interactive learning. The regular writing on the discussion board enabled the students to participate in productive and collaborative written interactions. Writing about what they were reading became a social act (LeFevre, 1989) in which the students responded to ideas and interpretations about the characters and events in the novel. As one student stated, "I feel comfortable 'talking' about the book chapters from home, on my laptop." The playfulness in the letters, which can be seen in Sample Letters to Characters in the Novel, is indicative of the rapport that developed as students regularly wrote to group members.

As a follow-up activity, I distributed copies of one student letter that had already been responded to and had the students discuss it in class. This second reading produced more complex discussions about the book than would have developed had I merely raised a point in class and asked the students to talk about it. As an interactive medium, the discussion board promoted a sense of community among the students, and as the semester progressed, the students came to see their peers, and not just the teacher, as a resource.

Student comments written while discussing the novel on the discussion board suggested that, as newcomers to New York City, the students quickly felt at home in the world of *The Alienist*. This familiarity grew directly out of two circumstances. First, students read only in the context of the novel and thus became more comfortable with this single frame of reference as readers. In other words, they did not have to keep reorienting themselves as they would if they had been reading an anthology of essays on disparate topics. Second, the novel is set in an area of New York that is near the school, and students passed locales from the book each day. Living and studying near the locales described in the novel made the course content come alive, as one student explained: "When I read about streets I know and places near our school, I feel I am living in the book." Many of the characters in the

Sample Letters to Characters in the Novel	
Dear Doctor Lazlo,	My Dearest Dmitriy
Your story is boring right now. In the homework chapter it goes on and on (and on and on …) about finding the killer by investigating his childhood. I think you shouldn't waste time this way. Let the regular police do the job their way. You are too slow. And why care that the killer maybe had abuse in his past? Focus on now. I am totally bored with this chapter of the book and it is your fault. Too much describing about you and no action.	Maybe you don't understand me? The chapter tells that just like the killer I was abused by a violent relative when I was young. If you know this, you understand why I chase the killer using my psychology style. Also, remember that 'alienist' is name for 'psychologist.' Maybe you should see one if you keep having trouble reading the book (ha!)
Sincerely, Dmitriy	Yours truly, Dr. Lazlo

Note: Doctor Lazlo is the main character in *The Alienist* (Carr, 1994).

novel were, like the students, immigrants living in New York City: "I am also immigrant like ones in the novel who come to Lower East Side in 1890s." Getting to know the characters over time also allowed the students to develop personal connections to the course content, as one student described: "I was a pediatrician in my country. To read about condition of immigrant children's lives was amazing thing." Learning about the historic figures in the book was also a motivating factor: "I like learning about Roosevelt and J. P. Morgan at same time I am reading about how to catch the murderer. I want to know how the story comes out."

WRITING DOUBLE-ENTRY JOURNALS

Double-entry journals are used to encourage students to engage in a dialogue with a text they are reading. Calkins (1986) and others have suggested that readers benefit from using a double-entry ledger as a means of reacting to a book. For my students, the most exciting outcome of reading *The Alienist* was the amount of writing it generated, and double-entry journals were one of the factors that led to this increase in writing. In addition to the letters written on the discussion board, students completed 40 pages of informal writing and a 12-page research project, an unprecedented achievement for them. All the reading and writing activities paved the way for the research project. Students knew about the project from the very start of the course, which gave a focus to their reading and writing. Informal writing was particularly important in this regard as it prepared students to select and synthesize significant information, which they would need to do in the research project. In this way, all the writing they did about the novel served as preliminary research in which they became experts on the book's plot, characters, and historical setting as well as its vocabulary and key concepts. The more practice they had with writing about the novel, the more competent and confident they became in using the specific language and historical information they would use when they wrote their research papers.

For each reading assignment, students wrote double-entry journals in which they responded to quotes from *The Alienist*. This work was meant not only to prepare them to write their research projects, but also to provide much-needed writing practice. The students were required to hand in hard copies of two additional types of informal assignments, listed below. They had to photocopy and share these in small groups each week so that they would benefit from reading insights and observations about the book from their peers (Vygotsky, 1972).

1. The students selected quotes from the novel that interested them and wrote personal reactions to them (see Reacting to Quotations From the Novel, page 170).

Reacting to Quotations From the Novel	
"Not the devil, sir," said a small frightened voice from somewhere back by the door to the stairs. "A saint." (*The Alienist*, p. 216)	This quote made me so curious and impatient to find out who is *the voice*. This made think that someone who is telling this could know who the killer is, so that's why I read the next chapter fast.
"Some people in my job like it when we suffer," the young man said. (*The Alienist*, p. 220)	I know it's selfish, but I was so happy to don't have this poor immigrant kid's terrible job. I am waitress right now and it is not so bad. When I read this I was thinking, what if I was a young immigrant 100 years ago? What would be the things I had to go through? Would I live in tiny Lower East Side tenement with my big family? What would my job be? Would I be the one in charge of my destiny?

2. The students rewrote passages from the novel in the voice of another character, as in the example on page 171, in which a student cites a scene from the novel described by the narrator, John, and then imagines how another character, Sara, might describe it. John is a newspaper reporter assigned to the case, and Sara is a detective. Students were amused by the shift in typical gender roles: John often appears tentative and passive, whereas Sara is bolder and more decisive. The objective in the writing task was to move students from passively observing the story to actively engaging with it. This kind of writing tapped into students' intrinsic motivation to play and invent. It also introduced them to the concept of *voice* in writing. Although I did not provide a model for the assignment, we brainstormed in class how different characters in *The Alienist* might recount a scene from their own perspective.

In previous terms, reading a variety of disparate essays had made it difficult for students to maintain interest in journal writing. However, reading the novel and writing the journals consistently unified pedagogic purposes, and the journals proved crucial to the students' keeping up with the weekly reading schedule. They were writing to learn (Mayher et al., 1983) and were using the journals to help them make sense of what they were reading. Significantly, as familiarity with the novel increased, so did confidence in writing, as one student explained: "I am feeling in the middle of the book much more confidence about writing." The students were able to write extensively, using the journals to explore their own observations and initial thoughts (Rosenblatt, 1938/1977): "This kind of assignment is very effective

Rewriting a Passage in a Different Voice	
John's Voice	**Sara's Voice**
Sara only clutched her bag tightly without a word; and when the two thugs appeared at the rear end of the hall, apparently sealing our fates, she reached into it. "Don't worry, John," she said confidently. "I won't let anything happen to you." And with that she withdrew a .45 caliber Army Model Colt revolver, with a four-and-a-half-inch barrel . . . . (*The Alienist*, p. 85)	John is pathetic. He is nice, but he is weak. The two bad guys were after us. Somebody had to do something. In a minute they could capture us. Maybe kill. John was looking so scared. I told him don't worry, I can protect you. I reached into my purse and pulled out big gun. Those bad guys disappeared. John always says the woman should not carry gun. Maybe now he will stop telling me be "a lady."

to me. I do not during these journals focus on the grammar, instead I try to express my reflections about the reading." The students needed to write in order to read more deeply: "I like writing about the chapters. It helps me think about what is happening in the book. When I only read I cannot go so far."

WRITING THE DREADED RESEARCH PAPER

What students had come to think of as "the dreaded research paper" was transformed into something altogether more enjoyable. This was because they had the support of a semester-long relationship with what they were investigating and writing about. These projects had often gone awry in the past, with students losing their way in the lengthy process of finding a topic, conducting research, and writing it up. Many handed in reams of unreadable information. My usual warning at the start of each term had been "Look, you can't just hand in a lump of stuff. It has to be synthesized and readable," but this had not helped matters.

However, this time, because the students had concentrated their research on the novel's historical setting and immigrant life on New York's Lower East Side, things were different. The students were more involved and wrote engaging research projects. The Research Paper Schedule (page 172) was designed to help the students organize their research and writing. They completed the tasks one at a time over the course of the semester.

Before writing the research paper proposal, the students generated topics during brainstorming sessions in class and from areas of interest that emerged in weekly journals. All the topics had to be derived from *The Alienist*, so that students could write about social issues that figured strongly in the lives of the characters. Topics might be the living conditions of

Research Paper Schedule	
I. Proposal (2 pages)	State your reasons for investigating your topic.
II. Site visit (2 pages)	Describe your visit to a locale from *The Alienist* directly related to your project.
III. Research report (3 pages)	Summarize data from three sources: a book chapter, an article, and a Web site.
IV. Synthesis (2 pages)	Present a portion of your research in the voice of a character from *The Alienist*.
V. Reflection (2 pages)	Tell a story about your experience of doing the research project. What stands out? What do you feel you learned?
VI. Bibliography (1 page)	Cite all sources using Modern Language Association style.

immigrant children in Manhattan in the 1890s; tenements in Manhattan's Lower East Side, where significant dramatic action takes place; or a historical figure important to the plot, such as Theodore Roosevelt or J. P. Morgan. For example, one student, a pediatrician in her home country, formulated her research topic in this way: "As a pediatrician I want to know more about lives of immigrant children. When I read about Jacob Riis in our novel, I want to know more about children's life conditions." Once topics were established, the students had to narrow these to a manageable size. Writing the proposal enabled the students to articulate and justify their areas of research interest and to come to terms with the feasibility of their projects. Once their proposals were completed, the students were ready to begin research.

The site visit was a crucial step in the research process, and the students found it appealing because the novel takes place near their school. They were curious about the places described in the story and were eager to go beyond the book and research the locale in which it is set, as one student described:

> After I finished reading today's chapter, my mind wouldn't stop thinking. I wanted to see how those people lived, so I visited the Lower East Side Tenement Museum. As I entered this old building on Orchard Street, I felt like I was in the Santorelli home. I felt a lack of air, and it was so dark I couldn't see down the hall.

The physical fact of standing on a spot where a scene in *The Alienist* takes place was not only exciting but also grounding. The notes taken on this experience had to contain specific details and concrete examples that made subsequent writing about the locales in the research paper more effective.

The research report required students to go beyond merely locating and citing sources. They had to summarize what they felt was most pertinent and give a short quote from each source. In this way, students had to think about their findings and be highly selective about what they chose to present to the reader, as this excerpt from one student's writing shows:

> *When Jacob Riis says "how the other half lives" he means the terrible conditions that immigrants had to live in, which is what Carr is talking about in his descriptions of immigrant children in "The Alienist." Riis was living in the 19th Century, so what he did had a real purpose. To make the uptown people of power realize they had responsibility to take action and help these people.*

The objective of the research report was to compel the students to go beyond a mere listing of quotes or citing of sources. They had to articulate the value of a particular source, especially in terms of its relevance to the social context of the novel, as can be seen in the sample of student writing above. Here the student links the poverty and social injustice documented in *How the Other Half Lives* (Riis & Sante, 1890/1997) with the social context of the novel.

I also required students to include a synthesis in which they presented a portion of their research in the voice of a character from the novel. To prepare them to do this, I first assigned the double-entry journals described in the previous section, in which they rewrote scenes from the book in the voice of another character. In the past, students had had no trouble finding data on their topics, but presenting these data had proved far more challenging. I was particularly concerned that they could present their research as more than a listing of facts and that they could demonstrate genuine engagement with their research material. One student presented his research as a diary kept by the murderer when he was living in a tenement on the Lower East Side. His research focused on the living conditions of immigrants in tenement housing:

> *The dim light admitted by the airshaft shines on my diary, which I can barely see what I am writing. I am living in this wretched tenement, a brick building six stories high with a storefront on the first floor. There are four noisy families on my floor and we all share the bathroom. The staircase is dark. I live like everyone else in the city, except the rich people living uptown.*

Another student imagined herself as a detective taking part in the murder investigation in *The Alienist*. Her research concerned Theodore Roosevelt's term as New York City police commissioner.

The year was 1898, and I, Karin M. was working on a case what was very different from others in my career in The New York City Police Department. A seven year old Italian immigrant named Georgio Santorelli had just been murdered on the Lower East Side. I was asked by Commissioner Theodore Roosevelt to aid in catching the killer and I joined at once.

A further purpose of the synthesis was for students to learn about making their research accessible and interesting to a reader. The two examples of student writing above show that the students were able to present their research in ways that were not only informative but also engaging and compelling. Earlier assignments, particularly those in which students composed letters to characters or described a scene in the voice of a character, prepared them to complete this task successfully.

In the reflection phase of the Research Paper Schedule, the students narrated their individual experiences of working on the project. Interestingly, some wrote in terms of what they had learned about themselves as writers and readers. For example, one student wrote,

My favorite writing was from my notes about the site which I visited (Ellis Island). It is easy writing when I take notes first . . . . My classmates checked my writing. Some said, "Too much information." One said organize Ellis Island notes like a story. Organization is always my problem. Someone else told "Be more careful with tenses!" I mix them a lot. I need to get better at checking tenses.

Writing a reflection compelled the students to become more conscious of their writing processes. I hoped that this awareness would transfer to other writing tasks the students would have to undertake in the future because they would know how to anticipate and avoid particular pitfalls as well as what strategies to rely on.

Conclusion and Critical Insights

As the students developed a genuine connection to *The Alienist*, they became more engaged with writing about it. They knew where they were as readers and researchers and where they were going as writers; as one student explains: "I know this topic already, so my mind is free to think more on how I am writing." Significantly, they were supported by their semester-long relationship with the course content, which helped them to write with newfound confidence. As writers, they moved from tentatively stitching together phrases to fuller written expression, going beyond the plain listing of facts to a more richly synthesized presentation of research. This was evident in the research papers, which displayed confidence in their knowledge of the subject matter. The students were able to take risks that resulted in a more creative and effective presentation of research (Romano, 1995). The consistent focus provided by a single narrative throughout the semester was significant. As students did informal writing and read further each week, they felt that they were building on what they had learned. Focusing the course on a single, comprehensible theme held the students' interest and motivated them to read and write extensively. In the end, their writing improved as they used language for purposes that interested and made sense to them.

The course managed to meet institutional requirements and engage student interest at the same time. In terms of institutional requirements, students satisfied the English department course objectives. They were able to read a complex text and identify its controlling ideas as well as generate ideas and develop them throughout a well-developed research essay. As far as engaging student interest was concerned, 100% of the class gave the course the highest rating on the departmental course opinion survey. The survey asked students to evaluate the class in terms of the clarity of course objectives, the effectiveness of the course materials, and the instructor's ability to stimulate interest in the subject.

A critical insight emerging from this experience is that educators need to do more to facilitate writing among college ESL students. Curricula should encourage students to engage fully in learning to write. Curricula that, albeit unintentionally, impede the development of writing skills need to be overhauled. Educators need to recognize that writing instruction is often presented in ways that make it manageable for teachers but inhibiting for learners. In particular, developers of college ESL curricula need to reevaluate the use of essay anthologies, the teaching of rhetorical essay forms, and the insistence on grammatical correctness before the development of fluency. It is also imperative that curricula begin to integrate technology, such as discussion boards, into the teaching of writing.

Effecting change within my English department remains a long-term goal. I presented the student research papers that resulted from the writing course at a faculty development seminar. Some colleagues expressed surprise that they were "such a pleasure to read," whereas others voiced concern over unedited errors. These different reactions indicate both the value and the limitations of the approaches used in the course. However, the key point is that students wrote with unprecedented enthusiasm. Considering how little writing previous students had produced, the course can be counted as a qualified success. Ultimately, the value of the revised curriculum is that it put students on the road to learning to write. The hope is that extensive writing practice leads to clearer and more correct writing in the long term (MacGowan-Gilhooly, 1996). These student writers clearly developed their writing skills, and this outcome suggests that this adaptation of a standard curriculum has something to offer others working with college ESL writers. I encourage teachers interested in experimenting with the approach described here to use a popular novel that sustains student interest and has a readily comprehensible frame of reference. The course did not just run as a one-off experiment, and I am pleased to say that it continues to be offered each semester in my teaching institution.

9

The Motive, Means, Method, and Magic of Using the Arts in a Grammar-Based Adult ESL Program

KRISTIN LEMS

"Kristin!" My former student rushed across the wide sidewalk, eagerly embracing me. With shopping bags in tow, she looked more confident and seasoned than years before, when she had been a new arrival in the United States studying in my weekend ESL class. She spoke warmly: "I still remember our class. I still remember our singing. And do you know, I heard 'Que Sera, Sera' on the television a couple of weeks ago and I said to my husband, 'I learned that in Kristin's class!'"

Such enthusiastic reunions with my former students have recurred over the years, and they always fill me with happiness. The students, even those who failed the program, invariably recall shared singing or poetry projects and smile. Innovation through the arts can enrich and enhance a curriculum and draw on the wealth of knowledge (Moll & Gonzalez, 1994) that adult students bring to the classroom. It can be said that the melody never fades, because the arts are a gift that never grows old and rewards both giver and receiver. In this chapter, I describe the motive, means, and methods by which I bring music and poetry into my adult ESL classroom. However, there is a little magic in it, too, because what arises from the arts is so much greater than the sum of the parts.

The Curriculum Context

The setting in which I taught for more than a dozen years was a rigorous English for academic purposes program at a private university located in a large midwestern city in the United States. The five-level, semi-intensive program was designed to move postsecondary immigrant students from zero-level English into the academic mainstream in just five 10-week terms, with each course running for 14 hours per week.

A TIGHTLY CONTROLLED CURRICULUM

A number of features of the curriculum made it fixed and inflexible. First, the upper three levels of the program awarded undergraduate academic credit and letter grades. The academic, credit-bearing nature of the program meant that interdepartmental faculty curriculum committees scrutinized the course outlines. This academic profile of the program made it popular with immigrants in the area and differentiated it from freestanding programs at other local colleges, which did not award undergraduate credit.

Sometimes, as many as six teachers taught different sections of a course at the same level because of the large enrollment of up to 600 students per term. Many of these teachers were new to a particular level or new to the school, with some being assigned to a course the weekend before the first day of class or assigned to a different level at the last minute. The working adults enrolled in the program often needed to switch their schedules among morning, evening, and weekend classes as job schedules and carpooling needs changed. The tightly controlled curriculum minimized the possible negative consequences of having so many new teachers, last-minute teacher assignments, and students changing classes.

The curriculum was highly elaborated. A set of carefully sequenced grammar points formed the core of each level, with a precise set of pages and exercises prescribed from grammar books. If a teacher drifted away from the assigned pages or covered an extra exercise on the same page, it could deprive a teacher at the next level of a planned item. The curriculum specified the order in which the items were to be presented, and deviations were rare, although an occasional rebel teacher might teach a grammar point across the entire 10 weeks instead of during the assigned week.

The program moved forward at a rapid pace and included nightly homework in addition to regular quizzes, compositions, and readings. Each teacher had to cover every component listed in the curriculum, right down to the list of vocabulary words and idioms assigned for each level. Teachers who strayed from the syllabus or dallied in the presentation of the material would disadvantage their students in their preparations for the final examination.

A HIGH-STAKES EXAMINATION

Each course culminated in a very long final examination, administered in the 10th week. The exam, which ran to at least 15 pages, focused on grammar and vocabulary points. It had become famous, or perhaps infamous, among students, with the more pious bringing religious medals and icons to the exam room. Several students became ill from stress, and even the most outstanding students arrived shaking with dread. Students who did not score a minimum of 70% were required to retake the whole course, even if their score was 68%, and very few exceptions were made. The answer key was meticulous, specifying each point, and, to ensure uniformity, the graded exams were submitted to a coordinator and spot-checked again.

The importance of student achievement on the final examination was clearly acknowledged by the program director, who kept track of the mean scores on the final examination for each class. If a class scored consistently below the mean scores of other classes at the same level, either a faculty coordinator or the program director raised this issue with the teacher. Part-time teachers, of course, felt the most vulnerable, worrying that their employment might terminate if their students scored significantly below other students. The number of students who failed the course or received incompletes was also tallied for each instructor, and the figures were distributed at departmental meetings. Although results were never used as the basis for not rehiring a teacher, notice was taken if a large number of students failed or received incompletes, and teachers were expected to have an explanation.

Teachers cared about student progress, mainly because they were caring professionals but also because their own success relied to some extent on shepherding their students successfully through to the next equally challenging level. The teachers who were rumored to have successfully moved a large number of students to the next level were in demand at registration. Due to all these factors, teaching in the program was intellectually challenging, stressful, but sometimes stultifying—because the program's structure and content worked against innovation and creativity.

The program was perfect for academically well-prepared and highly motivated immigrants from Eastern Europe who were under the age of 30. These students had clear goals and the discipline to reach them, and they accepted the rigidly structured program format. However, other students, many of them Hispanic or older learners who had had less academic preparation or had studied their native language in a more holistic way than the Eastern Europeans, were less likely to succeed. About 25% of students in the program had failed, and 5% had failed twice.

The Process of Adapting the Course

At first, I began to insert short musical and artistic activities, such as songs and poems, into the curriculum (Guglielmino, 1986) to serve the needs of the less successful students, or perhaps just to comfort them. I hoped to provide an alternative English language experience for those that were not thriving in the grammar-centered program. Even when students failed the course, these alternate experiences seemed to provide some affirmation for them and to build a sense of community. I also added creative arts activities because the communicative and cultural aspects of language learning were mostly absent from the curriculum or embedded in reading or idiom activities. This meant that students might not receive some of the important background information that would make living in their adopted country easier. The arts were a way to push comprehensible output (Swain, 1985) while conveying culturally relevant concepts.

I also introduced creative arts into the curriculum in order to entertain myself. I had learned over the years that a bored teacher is a boring teacher. As a part-time teacher, I had been assigned to the same course for 8 years, and this repetition became tedious and demotivating. Listening to music, reading poems, and singing with the students refreshed my teaching. The activities also appealed to the students, and in their evaluations of the class, they always agreed most strongly with the statement *The teacher liked to teach us*. Arts activities kept me, and still keep me, everlastingly involved, engaged, and cheerful, and I believe this has had a positive influence on student morale.

At first, the curriculum changes I introduced were tentative, but as I gained confidence that arts-based activities enhanced and did not undermine the curriculum, I extended them until the curriculum innovations occupied a larger part of the lessons. The activities I describe in this chapter evolved over a period of several years, often through trial and error.

An American Poetry Performance Project

A line from a poem by cummings (1998)—"who pays any attention to the syntax of things" (p. 74)—nicely summarizes what poetry can accomplish that prose cannot. In poetry, the affect of language counts more than its grammatical correctness. For this reason, an ESL curriculum that includes poetry can provide a meaningful reading experience (Rosenblatt, 1964) for students at many levels of English language proficiency.

I believe that it is never too early to introduce poetry. It is merely a matter of finding the right set of poems to match the proficiency level of students. Many great poems in English are linguistically manageable, and teachers should never assume poetry is too hard to introduce to beginning-level or intermediate-level students. On the contrary, students can find it very satisfying to read poetry at a sophisticated semantic level without necessarily straining their reading limits in terms of syntactic complexity. Students often understand the meaning of a poem before they can read prose at a similar level because poems are shorter and have a different textual format. In addition, the broken, shortened lines of poetry often provide syntactic clues, as they tend to break at the end of clauses or phrases. With poetry, speed does not matter, as a student can read slowly, carefully, and repeatedly, and get more from a poem with every reading. In other kinds of reading, faster readers are likely to be at an advantage.

PREPARING TO TEACH THE UNIT

As Level 3 coordinator, I was responsible for training and assisting a new teacher as he learned to cover the grammar and vocabulary components of the curriculum. The poetry performance project arose as I was mentoring this teacher, who was a creative soul by nature and temperament. He was depressed by the lockstep nature of the curriculum, yearning to add his own touch. The previous term, we had discussed our concern about the lack of literature in the program and the consequent lack of opportunities for students to explore the beauty of English.

Poetry was one way of introducing students to a little American literature and potentially enabling them to explore it later in more depth. So, during the course break, I began developing a poetry unit for my class. I invited the other teacher to teach it in his class at the same time, and he readily agreed. The unit consisted of reading short poems in class, writing about them in dialogue journals and in compositions, and choosing one to perform from memory for the rest of the class. The in-class poetry reading was to be used for pronunciation and fluency practice and for vocabulary development. Even though it had to be added to an already full curriculum, the poetry project did not take up too much class time.

After perusing many anthologies, I found 20 short American poems with a manageable vocabulary load that I thought would be of high interest. I made the decision to use only American poetry because all students were immigrants planning to the stay in the United States. However, an equally exciting project could use poetry written in English from around the world or even poetry from other languages translated into English. Poems Recommended for English Language Classes (page 182) lists poems that I have successfully used.

> **Poems Recommended for American English Language Classes**
>
> - "Richard Cory" (Robinson, 1922)
> - "Annabel Lee" (Poe, 1850)
> - "Recuerdo" (Millay, 1962b)
> - "The Arrow and the Song" (Longfellow, 1962)
> - "Hope Is the Thing With Feathers" (Dickinson, 1962)
> - "Dream Deferred" (Hughes, 1998)
> - "The Road Not Taken" (Frost, 1962a)
> - "Stopping by Woods on a Snowy Evening" (Frost, 1962b)
> - "Solitude" (Wilcox, 1998)
> - "since feeling is first" (cummings, 1998)
> - "Life Doesn't Frighten Me" (Angelou, 1981)
> - "Love Is Not All" (Millay, 1962a)
> - "The Wind" (Stevenson, 1989)
> - "Sea Fever" (Masefield, 1967)
> - "Mother to Son" (Hughes, 1949)
> - "Trees" (Kilmer, 1919)

TEACHING THE UNIT

The other Level 3 teacher and I gave the poems to our students on the first day of class. As we taught the activities, we found that a good way to ensure the success of the poetry project was to integrate it into several aspects of the curriculum rather than treating it as a stand-alone unit (Lems, 2001). If arts activities are woven into the curriculum, students are more likely to take them seriously. I also discovered that having a peer with whom to discuss the curriculum innovation lent the project a special value.

Throughout the term, the classes studied each poem, with as much focus on the sound and pronunciation as on literary analysis. Because I had chosen poems that did not have a heavy vocabulary load, we had to preteach a few key vocabulary words, but grammar was not explicitly addressed. After teaching these words, we introduced each new poem by reading it aloud, and the class briefly discussed what the poem was about. The classes then read the poem together, and, in pairs, the students practiced rereading the poem to each other. Students kept dialogue journals and wrote a response to each of the poems as part of their homework. We also used the poems as composition topics, including an assignment asking the students to compare two of the poems and to explain why they preferred one to the other.

Meanwhile, my colleague and I kept a dialogue journal of our own. We tried to introduce the poems in the same order so that the first teacher to try the poem could offer teaching tips to the second. Each Sunday, at the close of my weekend classes, I deposited the dialogue journal in the other teacher's mailbox, and each Thursday, when he left for the week, he replaced it in mine. We found each other's comments very helpful and sometimes startling. For example, an unexpectedly intense class discussion occurred after sharing the poem "Richard Cory" (Robinson, 1922) and playing the musical version (Simon, 1966). The poem recounts how a man who seems to have everything goes home quietly one night and kills himself. Students in the other class were very agitated about the suicide. It was deeply upsetting to some students that a wealthy man living the American dream could possibly commit suicide.

The project also included a performance piece, and each student was asked to choose one poem to memorize. The students performed the poems near the end of the term, after weekly practice sessions in small groups. By the performance date, students were fully prepared, with the poems completely memorized, and, to my delight, the students dressed up for the big event, to which we had invited family members as well as the college dean. I served refreshments and videotaped the whole event, later making copies for the students. Another wonderful by-product of the project was the dean's enthusiasm. Her videotaped praise was later shown to the class, to their immense satisfaction and mine.

Some of my U.S. colleagues expressed concern that students would be squeamish about performing a piece of literature in front of others, but I did not find this to be the case. In fact, I found that students from many different cultures and contexts had had experience performing poetry and enjoyed it. Even now, years later, when I meet the students who performed poems during this time, they grin and immediately launch into a recitation of their poems, perfectly intact, as if they had been performed only the previous day.

USING HAIKUS

Another kind of poetry that works well in a strictly structured curriculum is the haiku. Short and to the point, the haiku bypasses the exigencies of the declarative sentence. Its sparse form, taken from Japanese Zen Buddhism, lends itself well to ESL writing. Because the haiku format is achieved through syllable counting in a structure of five, seven, then five syllables per line, it also serves the didactic purpose of reinforcing the concept of the syllable and encouraging phonological awareness. Once the form is introduced, haiku activities of reading, writing, or illustrating take just a few minutes, with little sacrifice of class time.

Teachers can present samples of classical haikus to a class and encourage students to write and illustrate their own haikus and share them with classmates. The haikus produced by the class can be collected into an anthology.

Although I have included haikus in several courses, my most memorable haiku unit was in a summer exchange program with Korean undergraduate students. I introduced the haiku form just before a field trip to the Botanic Gardens. With the poem's syllable structure and a sense of the haiku's impressionistic nature clearly in mind, the students took their journals on the long bus ride, and came back with a glorious variety of haikus about nature, space, and time. I asked them to handwrite and illustrate their work, and they willingly did so, providing wonderful and skillful illustrations. From these illustrated works, I created books, which were presented to the students as souvenirs on the last day of class. Haikus Written After Field Trips shows some of the poems written and published in the book. The first two followed the visit to the Botanic Gardens, and second two were written in response to field trips around Chicago. The third one refers to the complex system of train lines in downtown Chicago called The Loop. The poem was illustrated with a cutout from a downtown train map. The final poem helped explain the student's late arrival and sluggishness in my morning class.

These haikus illustrate what intermediate-level English language learners can achieve. The great attraction of using haikus is that students can experience them on several levels. If students are resistant to poetry writing, they can have fun with syllable counting. If they lack confidence about extensive writing because of insecurities over English grammar, they can successfully write a finished poem using just a few phrases. Most important, poems

---

Haikus Written After Field Trips

Here are rose gardens
Many colorful roses
I want to snap them!   (Sunnyeo Joo)

Look at the flowers
They are tossing their faces
To show their beauty.   (Yun Hwa Jeong)

Life differs from Loop
Can see the right track or not
It is not easy   (Young Ji Hong)

City of Jazz
Drinking Beefeater
My heart becomes drenched with that
Just jazz music.   (Jung Jun Lim)

are not "wrong," as they can break rules creatively to express emotions or imagery, "since feeling is first" (cummings, 1998). Writing haikus in English is also an acknowledgement of respect and appreciation for a non-Western form of poetry.

INCORPORATING MUSIC INTO THE CURRICULUM

Like poetry, music can invigorate a highly structured curriculum and refresh the students while not taking up a great deal of class time. A well-developed musical activity can be a short segment if the lesson is carefully planned. Music can be used for listening, for singing, and as a topic for student presentations. By listening to songs, students can build phonological awareness, vocabulary, and idioms. In instrumental form, music can stimulate visualization and relaxation. Singing can build camaraderie and painlessly provide pronunciation and fluency practice. It also provides a rich reservoir of topics for both oral and written reports.

Listening to Music

The cloze activity (Wajnryb, 1990) involves students completing a text by filling in missing words. Although originally intended for reading, a cloze works well with song lyrics. To make a musical cloze, the teacher picks a popular song and blanks out words in the lyrics at regular intervals or to focus on a grammar point. As the song plays, students fill in the blanks. Before trying this activity with a new song, I check that there is enough time between blanks for students to write the missing words while listening. After students have listened to the song once or twice, I provide a complete lyric sheet and let them check their answers.

In order to adhere to the curriculum requirements, I select specific grammar items as the focus of the cloze, for example, conditionals or articles. I do this to increase student interest in the grammar exercises and to show the meanings in a musical context. I have also focused some clozes on prosodic features, such as the sounds created when two words are placed beside each other, such as the hidden *j* sound between the two words *did you*.

A possible variation on song clozes is to have students fill in the blanks before listening and then see if they have successfully predicted the missing words correctly, either semantically or syntactically. This activity helps students learn to predict meaning, a valuable reading skill. Another variation is to do a jigsaw song transcription. Using a song with slow, clear lyrics divided into verses with a repeating chorus, I put the students in small groups and give each group responsibility for writing down the words of one verse. At the same time, all students are responsible for the chorus. I play the song several times, stopping after each performance of the song, to give each group time to complete their verse and then to write it on the board. The students then listen to the whole song while reading the words they have written on the board. Often members of one group can hear words that another group has missed. Finally, I pass out a copy of the lyrics, and students compare their own versions with the lyrics. If appropriate, the whole class then sings the song, using the lyric sheet. This activity is usually very effective in building class spirit and developing a sense of enjoyment.

Lyrics are not necessary to have a rich musical listening experience. Classes can listen to instrumental music, such as classical or folk music, either for relaxation or as an end in itself. Instrumental music can spark compositions, poetry writing, or conversations about what different people see in the music (Cranmer & Laroy, 1992). My favorite nonverbal music is that of Cirque du Soleil, the renowned international circus troupe.

Singing
Teachers do not have to be singers to encourage students to sing, but the teacher must be willing to sing with the same brio and at the same volume as everyone else. Teachers might also use karaoke CDs with thousands of songs on them. Like reciting poetry, singing in a group or alone is a pastime enjoyed worldwide, and the vast majority of students are delighted to have a chance to do it.

For singing activities in my adult ESL class, I compile my favorite songs, provide students with lyrics, and introduce one song a week, at a regular time, for about 10 minutes. It has hardly any measurable impact on class time but has a positive impact on student morale and energy. I find that songs from contemporary folk and easy-pop repertoires are very popular. I look for songs that are not very wordy, are catchy and easy to sing, and express universal human emotions (Murphey, 1990). Songs that students have enjoyed singing in my classes are listed in Songs Recommended for English Classes.

Over the course of a term, I often find that when I introduce a new song, the students first want to sing all the songs they have learned previously. By the end of the term, students have memorized the songs introduced in the first few weeks and can sing them effortlessly. Even students who begin rather cynically or doubtfully join in over time. Consequently, I need to factor in a few additional minutes each week, as students sing a longer list of songs. During examination week, nobody wants to sing, but at the end-of-term party, students sing all of the songs with great gusto.

Using Music as a Topic for Presentations or Compositions
Another way to use music successfully in a grammar-based class is to have students present a talk on their favorite musician, style of music, or individual piece of music. I ask them to bring a CD of their chosen music or

Songs Recommended for English Classes

- "Que Sera, Sera" (Livingston & Evans, 1955)
- "500 Miles" (1962)
- "The Rose" (McBroom, 1977)
- "Mbube (Wimoweh)" (Linda, 1939)
- "This Land Is Your Land" (Guthrie, 1947)
- "Will You Still Love Me Tomorrow?" (Goffin & King, 1960)
- "All I Have to Do is Dream" (Bryant & Bryant, 1958)
- "Sixteen Tons" (Travis, 1955)
- "My Heart Will Go On" (Jennings & Horner, 1997)
- "Michael Row the Boat Ashore" (1994)
- "Bridge Over Troubled Water" (Simon, 1970)
- "Where Have All the Flowers Gone" (Seeger, 1961)
- "Blowin' in the Wind" (Dylan, 1962)
- "Kumbaya" (Frey, 1939)
- "Take Me Home, Country Roads" (Danoff & Nivert, 1971)

song to class. In some cases, the students in my courses have been semiprofessional musicians in their homeland and have given live performances for the class, a wonderful and unexpected bonus.

When students bring recorded music, the whole class listens to the musical works and enjoys them aesthetically before the students explain why the music is special to them. Sometimes the music is instrumental, ranging from classical to techno and everything in between. At other times, the student supplies lyrics to the class, and sometimes other members of the class already know and love the selections. For example, when the movie *Titanic* was first released, the song "My Heart Will Go On" (Jennings & Horner, 1997) seemed to be a very popular choice and became more or less the theme song for the whole course.

Music topics are also fertile ground for student compositions (Lo & Fai Li, 1998). Adult students enjoy writing about styles of music, particular songs, and favorite performers that are part of their lives. It is rewarding to read such compositions because the resulting writing is invariably motivating and heartfelt. Using music as a writing prompt is consistent with all of the goals of an academic curriculum.

It seems that, no matter what culture students come from, they bring enthusiasm and passion for the topic of music. In my courses, music often serves as the glue that holds the whole class together on an affective level. For many students, who are tired after a working day, being able to relax and enjoy music together is a very affirming experience. Although I rarely see student feedback extolling the benefits of learning the present perfect tense or knowing all definitions of a new word, student comments such as the following are frequently included in my class evaluations: "I liked the music"; "I enjoyed the singing!"; "The songs relaxed me." What is more, the melodies seem to linger in their minds after the course, as the encounter described at the beginning of this chapter attests.

Reflections

I believe that the creative arts and musical activities I strove to include in my grammar-based courses enhanced student participation and motivation. Although I cannot claim that these activities resulted in higher test scores for my students, I can report that they did not result in any decreases in their scores, which were always comfortably within the bell curve. I do know that the music and poetry topics produced superb compositions and oral presentations, and I can show videos capturing the poetry performances that attest to the high level at which my intermediate-level students were able to expressively recite American poetry.

A considerable obstacle to introducing arts activities into a grammar-based program is that administrators, faculty, and even students may dismiss the value of such activities. Some see these kinds of activities as a poor use of class time or, worse, a dumbing-down of the curriculum. ESL educators and curriculum developers, who were themselves educated in a transmission model of language learning, may believe that organizing instruction around grammar is an effective approach. Ironically, however, some also admit that pattern practice and grammar study were not effective in their own study of foreign languages. Many adult immigrant students have experienced top-down educational cultures that stress rote memorization, so they expect to find the same approach in classrooms in their adopted country. The vast majority, however, relish the idea of learning language with an arts component, and I believe that a classroom in which the arts are considered part of the content area of English language study, and in which students have opportunities for aesthetic experiences, will result in high learner achievement.

The arts add wonder and delight to daily life and create a classroom environment that is both comforting and deeply exciting. Based on my own experiences, I would encourage teachers in classrooms around the world to harness the power of student motivation that comes from enjoying music and poetry. If you embark on an artistic path with your adult students, you will all enjoy not just the motive, means, and method of doing so, but all of the magic along the way.

Responding to Learners' Language Needs in an Oral EFL Class

10

JOHN McANDREW

This chapter describes a curriculum development that arose as a response to the English language needs of a group of university freshman learners in Japan. The chapter discusses the contextual factors that motivated and facilitated the response, the curriculum development as a whole, and details of materials and activities that realized the pedagogy of the response.

Essentially, this response consisted of taking a learner-to-learner-generated conversation, assessing it for areas to be improved, and building a course that scaffolded the learners toward socially appropriate use of language. Underlying this approach was an understanding of language as discourse, that is, as socially situated language in use (Candlin, 1997). It is also important to recognize that the choices made in constructing this course occurred in a particular sociocultural and institutional context, the affordances and constraints of which helped shape the course.

The Motivation for the Adaptation

The impetus for the course came largely from my dissatisfaction with the original syllabus that was in place. I had used a fairly popular communicative language teaching (CLT) textbook as the basis for instruction with a freshman class the previous year. The textbook was useful for encouraging learners to talk, but it seemed not to address the learners' specific language needs in a strategic way, nor did it raise awareness of how social relationships affect the language chosen by speakers. Gradually, I had come to feel that the learners were missing opportunities to learn, that they were not using language meaningfully, and that they were not aware of what constituted appropriate language use in social contexts. This lack of recognition of the social nature of texts seemed to encourage the learners to communicate in a decontextualized way, that is, in a way inappropriate to social contexts of language use.

In order to address this problem, I decided to discontinue the use of the textbook with the goal of becoming more responsive to the learners' language needs. I attempted this shift by looking at the discourse the learners were producing in learner-to-learner conversations and using this as a starting point from which to build a course.

Theoretical Foundations of the Course

CONTEXT OF SITUATION

Language use always occurs in a particular social context. Halliday and Hasan (1985) describe the context of situation as consisting of three major variables: field, tenor, and mode. *Field* refers to what is happening in the situation, that is, the social activity that is occurring at the time, such as playing a rugby game, cooking, boarding an airplane, or engaging in casual chat. *Tenor* refers to the relationship between the speakers in the situation, such as friendly or unfriendly, and to the relative status of the speakers. *Mode* refers to how distant the language is in time and space from what it is describing. Language choices will be different if the speakers are face-to-face or a long distance apart, if the speakers are talking in real time, or if there is a delay between the event and communication about that event.

The configuration of field, tenor, and mode form the language register of a particular context of situation and dictate the meanings that are appropriate to that context. For example, one would seldom speak of apples and oranges when buying a television set. It is important to understand that there is a two-way relationship between the context of situation and the language being used in that context. The context influences the language choices, and the language choices function, in part, to construct the context. For example, if one uses friendly language, then one can create a friendly relationship. This concept of context of situation gave me a framework within which to explore whether the language choices made by the learners in a particular situation were appropriate.

TEXT-BASED APPROACH

A text-based approach sees language "as whole texts which are embedded in the social contexts in which they are used" (Feez, 1998, p. 3). It is concerned with focusing students' attention on the words and wordings used to arrive at the particular meanings in a whole text and on the surrounding sociological factors that affect the choice of language. The characteristics of a text-based syllabus are discussed by Feez, who states that "the text-based syllabus is a response to changing views of language and language learning. It incorporates an increasing understanding of how language is used in social contexts" (p. 3; see Characteristics of the Text-Based Syllabus).

The primary method of teaching in a text-based approach is through the analysis and deconstruction of whole texts and then through a collaborative reconstruction of similar texts, until learners are themselves able to produce socially appropriate language. Thus the processes I used drew on the teaching-learning cycle described in the following section.

SCAFFOLDING AND THE TEACHING-LEARNING CYCLE

Scaffolding offers a focused and systematic approach to supporting learning. It allows the learner to push out from an existing point of knowledge toward a target point of knowledge. As Wilhelm, Baker, and Dube (2001) state,

Characteristics of the Text-Based Syllabus (Feez, 1998, pp. 3–4)	
Syllabus type	A text-based syllabus can be thought of as a type of mixed syllabus. This is because all the elements of various other syllabus types can constitute a repertoire from which a text-based syllabus can be designed.
View of language	Language occurs as whole texts which are embedded in the social contexts in which they are used.
View of language learning	People learn language through working with whole texts.
Syllabus elements	All the elements of a text-based syllabus are given unity and direction by being organised with reference to holistic models of content and methodology.
Content	The content of a text-based syllabus is based on whole texts, which are selected in relation to learner needs and the social contexts which learners wish to access.
Methodology	The methodology which supports a text-based syllabus is based on a model of teaching and learning in which the learner gradually gains increasing control of text types. Using this model, it is possible to develop sound principles for selecting and sequencing the content elements of the syllabus . . . and for determining the methodology with which to implement the syllabus.

the scaffold is the environment the teacher creates, the instructional support, and the processes and language that are lent to the student in the context of approaching a task and developing the abilities to meet it . . . . Scaffolding must begin from what is near to the student's experience and build to what is further from their experience . . . . (n.p.)

The notion of scaffolding is very relevant to an approach that starts with learner-to-learner-generated texts. Inherent in these texts is evidence of the learners' current abilities, and such texts offer the teacher the basis from which to provide help at points most meaningful for the learners. This help includes moving toward target repertoires based on the original texts, which are specifically relevant to the learners.

An approach that inherently involves the teacher and learners in scaffolding is the teaching-learning cycle, which developed through the genre-based approach to writing (Callaghan & Rothery, 1988; Hammond, Burns, Joyce, Brosnan, & Gerot, 1992; Martin, 1999). Martin's (p. 131) version of this cycle, which grew out of an earlier model developed by Callaghan and Rothery, is shown in The Teaching-Learning Cycle.

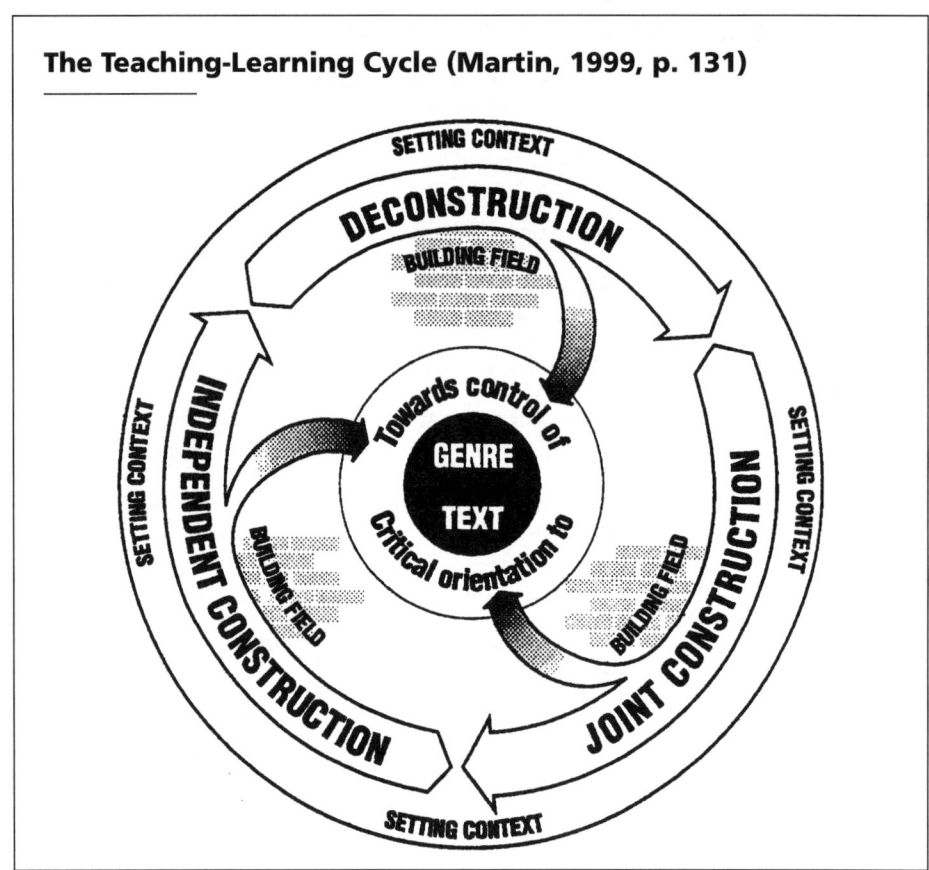

> *The teaching learning cycle is divided into 3 phases, the modelling or deconstruction phase, joint construction and individual construction. The cycle can be entered at any point according to students' needs and can be accessed at different levels in that teachers can move back and forth between phases as appropriate, focusing on different aspects of the genre. The modelling phase allows for all aspects of the genre to be made explicit from social context to lexicogrammatical features, joint construction makes the process of genre writing clear by engaging students, with the teacher as guide, in creating an example of the genre and finally, individual construction moves students on to writing a draft of their own text for peer and teacher conferencing before the final version is written. After this stage, students and teacher can engage in a more creative or critical analysis of the target genre, questioning its structure and purpose, re-writing it as a different genre etc. (Drury, 2001, pp. 16–17)*

This approach offers an overarching framework for understanding the continual process of deconstruction, joint construction, and independent learner construction of texts. It can also be seen as a continual cyclical process concentrating on improving the learners' ability to create meaningful, socially situated, and appropriate texts. What this meant for my classroom was that I could understand learner texts within the cycle of deconstruction, joint construction, and independent construction. The specific genre that the class focused on was casual conversation between peers.

COMMUNICATIVE LANGUAGE TEACHING

CLT has become an umbrella term for many classroom practices that focus on the communicative function of language. Breen and Candlin (2001) outline a communicative methodology that recognizes the socially embedded nature of language. They state that the

> *communicative curriculum defines language learning as learning how to communicate as a member of a particular socio-cultural group and the social conventions governing language form and behaviour within the group are, therefore, central to the process of language learning. (p. 10)*

They also state that methodology should exploit the communicative potential of the classroom, as "the classroom itself is a unique social environment with its own human activities and its own conventions governing these activities" (p. 16).

It seemed to me that the set textbook was not responsive enough to the particular configuration of social relationships found in a classroom and did not recognize them as a valuable resource. If the classroom was a potentially genuine context for communication, then I could develop communicative learning opportunities in the classroom that were genuine or near genuine. Given suitable tasks, learner-to-learner interaction could become more reflective of the learners' sociocultural group membership, in terms of age, gender, background, growing familiarity, power, and institutional role, and would be better suited to the social relationships between the learners. The texts that the learners produced when interacting together could be used to demonstrate their interlanguage, that is, their developing language systems, and from this I could explore both the learners' abilities and areas for improvement.

By taking an initial, problematic learner-to-learner text, produced in a genuine or near-genuine context of situation, I planned to guide the learners toward a more effective target repertoire of texts relevant to the social context. I was interested in using their initial contributions as a very specific learner-centered platform on which to build an explicit focus on discourse strategies relevant to the interaction, allowing the learners to learn new conventions of discourse relevant to the sociocultural situation.

The Curriculum Context

THE COURSE

The course took place in an EFL context in Japan, with the learners' first language being Japanese. I was teaching first-year Japanese university students in an oral English class at a prefectural university. The learners were 18–20 years old, and, in this particular class of 22 learners, 2 were male, and the remainder were female (a more even distribution was more common). The first-year, one-semester course consisted of thirteen 90-minute classes. Learners took additional one-semester oral English courses in their second and third years at the university. The classes were part of the overall English language curriculum that included writing, reading, grammar, and international relations classes. The learners were English majors, and the course was a compulsory unit of study. The learners had all been exposed to English instruction at high school and at primary school. Results from needs analysis surveys were varied, and there was little indication of functional needs outside the classroom for communication in English. As the learners were English majors, it could be assumed that their motivation was somewhat higher than that of a general English class, and my observations confirmed this.

CONSTRAINTS AND OPPORTUNITIES

The institutional constraints placed on the class and on me were largely underlying assumptions based on the way English language has historically been taught in Japan. Culturally, the position regarding teachers is similar to that in South Korea, "where teachers are supposed to know everything and always be correct" (Jin-Kyu, 1995, cited in Li, 2001, p. 154). Ideological beliefs in Japan about language learning traditionally value grammar-translation and the rote-learning activities of audiolingualism. There is also an emphasis on precise error correction, and silence is generally considered preferable to making mistakes. Economic constraints affecting my class included the close relationship between the English department and a particular supplier of textbooks, which held a monopoly.

Administratively, the main focus was on grades as the measurable outcome of courses, which traditionally meant written exams with right or wrong answers. The testing of oral English using spoken texts was still relatively uncommon. Institutionally, the traditional perspectives on language learning were in evidence. Also, most of the other teachers of spoken English in the department used the same textbook as I had been using and were expected to continue using it. As for the learners, they expected to use a textbook so they could study by themselves and maintain a record of their learning. Sociolinguistically, as evidenced by questions about the teaching texts they used, some of the Japanese teachers were nervous about their own competence and felt more comfortable with a traditional, teacher-centered approach with a defined content that could be understood through grammar-translation.

The assumptions in relation to these areas were brought to bear by various relevant key stakeholders: the head of department, fellow teachers, and the learners themselves. The approach I adopted with my class ran contrary to many of these underlying assumptions, but the innovation was able to proceed because of the affordances or opportunities that existed in the situation and because of negotiations with key stakeholders. In terms of opportunities, there was an institutionally accepted view about a lecturer's autonomy to make decisions about the syllabus and the ability of lecturers to set their own tests, and there was a perception that foreign lecturers (*gaikokujin kyoshi*) would bring methods and approaches that differed from those used by Japanese teachers of English.

Negotiations with stakeholders took the form of meetings with the head of department, at which I discussed the approach and showed examples of how learners could be assessed. The attention to texts that I presented had some compatibility with grammar-translation even though my processes for teaching the texts would be very different, and my relative autonomy as a foreign lecturer made the head sympathetic to this innovation. The head also suggested that as learners were not spending money on textbooks, then they might buy dictionaries from the university's book supplier, though I did not take up this suggestion at the time. I had formal and informal discussions with other teachers to inform them of the innovation and to invite them to observe. I was largely successful in gaining their support because they were not under pressure and could maintain their autonomy, as there was no imperative for them to adopt my approach or to discontinue using their own approaches and textbooks.

In the first session, I explained to the learners what was expected of them and why they would be learning in a different way. Learners were instructed to keep a portfolio of classroom materials consisting of teacher handouts and their own responses to activities, which would meet their need for a record of their learning. As the course progressed, the learners' abilities in the target repertoires increased noticeably, and this improvement, along with the tendency of Japanese learners to respect their teacher's decisions, meant there was no overt dissent. Additionally, a colleague who shared similar views on language and language learning was also keen to stop using the textbook and adopt the same approach. This had benefits for our professional development, as we were able to discuss teaching approaches, formatively assess how our classes were going through reflection and discussion of our own observations, and share learner texts and activities. The fact that I had control of learner assessment was a crucial element in allowing me the freedom to innovate without the pressure of the washback from an examination. Without this autonomy, the innovation would have been much more constrained.

Despite these positive aspects, as I began the course, I was aware of some of the difficulties I might encounter. In the first place, although I felt personally empowered by the lack of a textbook, I had to cope with the extra pressure of lesson preparation. I also had to be confident that language issues would arise that could be treated as content and that I would be able to develop and apply a consistent and effective teaching response to these language issues.

The Process of Designing the Course

The goal for the course was to improve the students' oral English ability in specific target repertoires. I aimed to achieve this by responding to learners' language needs and applying a combined approach based on the recognition of the context of situation, a text-based approach, scaffolding, the teaching-learning cycle, and CLT. Objectives for the class included building rapport with the learners through a supportive learning environment, encouraging learners to communicate meaningfully through personalized activities, arriving at content from the specific needs of learners, and using this content as a basis for point-of-need instruction. Further objectives were to improve learners' understanding of their own discourse and discourse needs, and, through the combined approach described above, to enable learners to develop their spoken English skills.

The goals and objectives were specific in that I knew what I wanted from the course and how I wanted it to happen, but until the course commenced, I could not know what the content would be. I would go into the classroom with a certain amount of preplanned material, but only to allow the learners to reach a point where their own specific language needs became evident through my observation of their learner-to-learner conversations. I intended to evaluate the course formatively by assessing what the learners produced, reflecting on my own observations with my colleague, and discussing learners' impressions of the course through informal interviews. Summative assessment of the course would involve judging whether the objectives for the course had been met, in combination with learner feedback.

THE CLASSES

In the first two sessions, I aimed to build fluency, increase rapport, learn the students' names, and introduce them to the ground rules of the classroom. The third session involved the learners in a casual conversation activity (free talking as friends) from which a problem text emerged. This became the content to explore and expand on in subsequent sessions. The following sessions were given over to exploring the original content and building activities that scaffolded the learners in the target repertoires derived from the original content. The end-of-semester examination was given in the final class.

If the content did not emerge in the third class, I had planned to use a poster-making task in Sessions 4, 5, and 6. I intended to use this task not so much to concentrate on the outcome of the task, the finished posters, but to pay attention to the learner-to-learner texts generated during the task, as they could potentially generate the content on which to base the remainder of the course. As the initial text for investigation actually arose in the third session, I used the poster-making activity toward the end of the course in Sessions 10, 11, and 12 as a site for learners to practice their casual conversation around the task.

CONTENT DEVELOPMENT

The following transcript is an example of the type of language the learners were using at the beginning of the course in the context of learner-to-learner casual conversations. This interaction provided the original content for the course and the impetus for activities to address what was inappropriate in this text in relation to its context of situation.

Learner Text 1

Learner A:	*Where are you from?*
Learner B:	*I'm from Fukuoka.*
Learner A:	*What sports do you like?*
Learner B:	*I like baseball.*

This example of the learners' spoken language demonstrates a stilted, decontextualized, nonnatural use of language. Here learners are repeating linguistic forms, correct at the lexicogrammatical (words and wordings) level but inappropriate in relation to the context of situation. The language choices would be fine in, for example, the context of a particular type of interview, but are not suited to informal casual conversation among peers. There is also no affective or emotional involvement, and the learners already know the answers to the questions. There was a strong need to use more interactional or interpersonal language, to use change-of-topic words, and to allow for some negotiation of meaning between the interactants. I chose this example as it typified problems that the class had as a whole.

I contrasted this use of language with its social context of use so that learners would be made more aware of appropriate use of discourse. I put the exchange on the whiteboard and then invited the class to comment on its appropriateness and how they could improve it. This meant a brief discussion of how language was related to context and how it was important in shaping social relationships. My role at this point was to guide the learners, using simple language, to bring out the features of the text I wanted the learners to pay attention to. Learners came up with suggestions to make the conversation more interesting by adding some kind of emotional response to the information (e.g., *wow, no way, great, fantastic, that's good*), and I listed them on the whiteboard. Also, to make the interaction more cohesive, I elicited and listed change-of-topic phrases and words, such as *by the way* and *well*. Learners were asked to practice the small interaction transcribed above with a partner, but to include emotive responses and change of topic. They then did this with a different partner and again with another partner. The result was something of an explosion of laughter and language as the learners tapped into this interpersonal meaning-making resource and expressed themselves appropriately, if a tad joyously, through English.

From this initial, small text, I was able to draw on work in the systemic functional tradition of discourse analysis (Burns & Joyce, 1997) to prepare the materials necessary to scaffold the learners in the target repertoires. This meant preparing a model text involving casual conversation between acquaintances and highlighting the discourse skills I wanted the learners to focus on. In relation to the context of situation variables, I wanted to maintain similar field, tenor, and mode to that of the initial text. In relation to tenor, the materials kept the social relationship of conversation between peers, and in relation to mode they reproduced a face-to-face dialogue, which by necessity was written down to enable the learners to analyze it. I wanted to maintain the field but also introduce explicitly to the learners the discourse skill of using the immediate context to make the conversation meaningful. I opted for a meeting while shopping. In relation to the teaching and learning cycle, the Model Casual Conversation Task shown on page 200 asks the learners to jointly deconstruct a target text. Learners worked in groups on the tasks required by the handout with assistance from me. The tasks involved sectioning the text into genre segments, for example,

- the initiation section
  A: Hi.
  B: Oh hi, how's it going?
  A: Good, good, fine.

- the first request for information and response
  B: Are you, er, doing some shopping?
  A: Yeah just a few things really, you know.
  B: Yeah.
  A: Yeah.

The students were also asked to highlight the key elements of the text that I wanted to foreground, that is, evaluative language, changes of topic, pauses, and modality.

As the teacher, I modeled and discussed aspects of the text with individual groups. We also spent time discussing what feelings words evoked and how they functioned, at what point in the dialogue the conversation might have stopped, and what aspects of the language indicated their social relationship.

In the next stage, the learners produced their own written texts in groups of two or three. I provided support by making clear the relationship between their choices and the model text. Learner Text 2 (page 201) is dramatically different from Learner Text 1.

In this text, the learners use many of the strategies practiced in the model conversation task:

1. the use of an appropriate genre construction and sequence, which uses the same or a similar sequence as in the model text:
   a. the initiating section
      A: Oh, hi!
      B: Hi!
      A: I haven't seen you for a long time.

Model Casual Conversation Task

Meeting a Friend While Shopping

A: Hi.
B: Oh hi, how's it going?
A: Good, good, fine.
B: Are you, er, doing some shopping?
A: Yeah just a few things really, you know.
B: Yeah.
A: Yeah . . . actually, I've been looking for a present, for Hiroko, but it's difficult to, you know . . . .
B: Yeah, umm, what kind of thing.
A: Oh, something like umm a present . . . something like, it's her birthday tomorrow actually. [laughs]
B: Tomorrow?
A: Yeah, tomorrow. So I've looked in Hamaya, like at the makeup and stuff, but it's not very exciting.
B: Tomorrow? How about Amu Plaza, they've got Tower Records and some kind of new shops.
A: Yeah, OK, great, Tower Records might be good. I might give that a go, I've got to go over to the station, anyway. So, anyway, good to see you and thanks for the tip.
B: That's fine. Say happy birthday to Hiroko from me.
A: OK I will, bye.
B: Yeah, bye.
A: Bye.

Context: A: Male, 20, English, buying a present for his girlfriend
B: Male, 18, English, window shopping

Relationship: Friends, but not very close friends

Task:

Genre:

Identify
  i. the initiating section
  ii the first request for information and response
  iii the extension of the response
  iv. the closure

- Underline feelings words.
- Circle changes of topic.
- Highlight pauses.
- Put a box around words/phrases that tell us *not 100%*.
- Put a wavy line under "you know."

Learner Text 2

A: Oh, hi!
B: Hi!
A: I haven't seen you for a long time. When did you come back?
B: Umm . . . a day before yesterday.
A: Do you enjoy your new life?
B: Umm . . . it is kind of good, you know.
A: Ah ha.
B: What's new?
A: Nothing . . . nothing.
B: Really?
A: I'm actually . . . my pet, Pochi, has been dead.
B: That's too bad. She was very fine . . .
A: Yeah. But we have new pet, Pochi. Jr. He is very cute.
B: Oh, I want to see him.
A: OK, let's go my home now.

    b. the first request for information and response
       A: When did you get back?
       B: Umm . . . a day before yesterday

      further request for information and response
       A: Do you enjoy your new life?
       B: Umm . . . it is kind of good, you know.

    c. the extension of the response
       A: I'm actually . . . my pet, Pochi, has been dead.

    d. the closure
       A: OK, let's go my home now.

2. the use of pauses
3. the negotiation of meaning—*Really?*
4. the use of feeling words—*That's too bad*
5. the use of modality, taught as *not 100%*—*kind of, you know*
6. the change of meaning in a single turn—*I'm actually . . . my pet, Pochi, has been dead*
7. the use of repetition—*Nothing . . . nothing*

The text was a substantial improvement on the original one, and, given the explicitly cyclical nature of the teaching-learning cycle, it could also be used as a source text for further exploration of the language choices made by the learners in relation to the social context and the notion of appropriateness. I now used the text for group deconstruction and further discussion. Issues that were discussed included questioning the grammaticality of *has been dead* and the situational inappropriateness of the phrases *Do you enjoy your new life?* and *Let's go my home now,* which was a sudden ending to the text and hence an inadequate closure. The analysis of the text also allowed me to elicit the learners' specific descriptions of what was successful about the conversation. For example, the use of *When did you get back?* was identified as an appropriate reference to shared knowledge of a personal kind by the two friends and therefore an appropriate stage in the unfolding of the genre.

Up to this point, the learners had been working at constructing conversations as scripts. To transfer this knowledge from the written modality to the spoken, learners were given the Situation-Based Role Plays shown here. As regards the teaching-learning cycle, learners were also engaging more in individual construction of the texts in that they were responsible for their part of the dialogue. The roles here were variable; for example, in Situation 2, Speaker A could be a very careful shopper, wanting the best price, and Speaker B could be friendly or unfriendly to customers.

Situation-Based Role Plays

Situation 1
    A: You are you, on vacation in London. You meet an English student for the first time. Try and make friends.
    B: You are an English student. You live in London. You are meeting a Japanese student who is on vacation for the first time.

Situation 2
    A: You are on vacation in London. You have met an English student. Now you are going shopping.
    B: You are an English store clerk.

Situation 3
    A: You are on vacation in London. You are going to get something to eat.
    B: You are an English waiter or waitress.

Situation 4
    A: You are on vacation in London. You feel ill. You are going to visit the doctor.
    B: You are an English doctor.

Situation 5
    A: You feel much better now. You meet your friend the English student for a second time. Tell her or him about your day.
    B: You are an English student. You are meeting your Japanese student friend for the second time.

For the role-play activity, the learners formed two groups, and each group formed two concentric circles. A member from the inner circle formed a pair with a member from the outer circle for the first role play. They then swapped so that both members could practice both roles. Members of the outside circle would then move clockwise, one person on, so that every learner had a new partner for the next role play. The intention was to lead the learners through these imaginary situations until they could talk about their day when they met their friend, that is, the first student again, in the final role play.

Further work included the students returning to dialogue constructions in pairs and e-mailing these dialogues to other pairs for comments on the conversations. The learners also did a poster-making activity in groups of four or five.

Though not exploited in this instance, learners' conversation skills could have been further refined by recording the pairs during the role plays and using transcripts of these as a basis for reentering the teaching-learning cycle. I did actually video record some of the conversations that arose around the poster-making task for potential further use with the class. The learners' responses to the conversations could be used in the same way. For example, following the e-mail activity the class could explore the genres of critique or giving advice, using the learners' genuinely contextualized texts as a basis.

LEARNER ASSESSMENT

Assessment of the learners was my responsibility, and I assessed them formally throughout the course by recording attendance, collecting and grading written materials, and examining portfolios. There was also an end-of-term examination task in which groups of six learners talked together in pairs. In this examination, each pair was given materials or cue cards relating to activities and content that we had covered in the class. The students were asked to use the materials as a basis for a conversation. In 20 minutes, the learners covered three or four topics, talking for about 5 minutes on each topic. I was able to focus on different pairs and different individuals within each pair, and assess their spoken English abilities by giving a grade out of 10 for each of the following criteria: grammaticality, appropriateness, intelligibility, and coherence (Breen & Candlin, 2001, p. 22).

Conclusion

This chapter has discussed an approach to responding to learners' language needs in a particular institutional context. The sequence of activities described here serves as an example of the approach I adopted to help a specific group of learners with a problem they had in producing context-appropriate discourse. The content of this sequence of activities was unknown at the beginning of the course, but the approach to deriving the content was based on theoretical ideas of text-based learning, scaffolding, the teaching-learning cycle, and CLT. With these learners, in this context, the approach was successful, and learners' language in the target repertoires improved. The innovations in the course were successful because of the particular constellation of human, institutional, social, and cultural factors in which it was embedded and the options for negotiation that this constellation allowed.

Not the Puppet Anymore: Infusing Critical Inquiry Into a Business Presentation Curriculum

MARTIN MOMODA

I was not the one speaking in front of the audience, so why did I sit with sweaty palms and a beating heart, watching my student struggle through his presentation? Because I was the TESOL instructor praying that the student would remember his lines and not draw a blank.

My reputation and job did not depend on his performance, but after 5 days of prompting, training, screening, and preening, I was hoping that the program managers, who had come to observe, would be impressed. Sitting at the back of the room, I could do nothing but watch and hope. It was too late to undo a frozen pose or unglue his gaze from a spot on the floor. He could not hear my whispered cues.

Was it fair to put so much pressure on the students, and was it productive to put so much emphasis on the final presentation? Were they learning what they really needed, or were they merely being trained as puppets? These were the questions I asked myself as I began to sense the limitations of the way I was handling the curriculum.

The Curriculum Context

The business presentation course I was teaching was part of a program run by the Overseas Vocational Training Association, a Japanese government organization responsible for providing subsidized training in international business and communication. Courses included effective meeting skills, negotiation, and cross-cultural communication. The course that I was sweating through was an intensive, 5-day, 35-hour course on business presentations (see Business Presentation Course Outline). The general purpose was to help students improve their confidence in English communication. Students were given many chances to speak in front of the class and practice a variety of presentations, including self-introductions, impromptu speeches, business briefings, product explanations, and policy proposals. Time was spent on script writing, preparing visual aids, and running through question-and-answer sessions. The week culminated in the formal and final presentation on the last day.

Motivation was never a problem, as most participants knew that English language skills would help them in their work. Many held responsible positions in major Japanese corporations. With careers in sales, management, engineering, research, and administration, they knew that English skills meant survival, success, and a big bonus. Many also expressed a desire to become better communicators and to expand their creative abilities.

Learners ranged in age from the early 20s to late 60s and came from all regions of Japan. Most were university educated, with at least 6 years of English study in a formal classroom situation. Some worked daily with native English speakers, whereas some had never spoken to a foreigner.

The students' backgrounds and experience varied, but they shared a discomfort with public speaking. There were strong signs of performance anxiety, and the formal atmosphere of the final day did nothing to help. A speaker would stumble through memorized lines; the audience would sit silently, asking no questions; and then the next speaker would stand to speak. The problem was clear. Nobody was listening, and the speakers knew it. It did not matter if the presentations were logical or even made sense. The point was only to memorize and reproduce a script. We were participating in a communicative act that had little meaning beyond the ritual of public sweating, and it reminded me of tired nights of karaoke singing. In the

Business Presentation Course Outline	
Day 1	Openings, warm-ups, introduction speeches, basic nonverbal communication exercises
Day 2	Brainstorming, feedback techniques, impromptu speeches, organization of ideas, key phrases
Day 3	Outlines, product speeches, audience feedback, script writing, visual aids
Day 4	Persuasive techniques, nonverbal communication, question-and-answer techniques, proposal speech
Day 5	Speech preparation, final presentation, discussion, video viewing, debriefing

desire for perfect performance, the speakers had become puppets, and I had to admit my complicity in pulling the strings.

AWAKENING THE PUPPET MASTER

The program managers never complained, but I was not satisfied and wanted to go beyond standard expectations. In the ESL/EFL industry of Japan, most teachers make their weary way on crowded trains to classes, and course work is assigned with little direction. Generic texts are often numbly thumbed through or discarded for more inventive activities. The idea of business presentations is included in this generic list, and low-level students spend most of their time battling pronunciation problems, memory lapses, and stage fright. The teacher knows that students are there because their companies are investing in them to make them linguistically productive, but teachers also fear a slow death from boredom. *Chemical Properties of Toxic Plastics* may be a realistic topic, but *Three Reasons Why I Love My Dog More Than My Boss* might be more entertaining.

There is also the problem of delivery. Breathing life into a scripted speech means coaching on hand movements, calculated turns of the head, and meaningful and intense gazes. Manipulating puppets is not prescribed in the texts but is the most obvious option for tired teachers. I include myself in this profile, and with the pressures of the final day approaching, repetition as a methodology easily replaced anything that a text might claim to teach.

One day, a student asked, "Are you trying to make us American?" I was shocked and instantly rejected this suggestion: "Of course not!" Or maybe I was. It was probably the best question I had been asked in a long time, and it made me think. What was my intention? Had I fallen for the pressures of delivering a product? Should I be more concerned about process? Employees need more than drills in recitation if they are to become convincing communicators. As a teacher, I needed to do more critical, reflective thinking and less string pulling. The student's question was a wake-up call.

Though I could recognize my own shortcomings, I found myself blaming the students. Memorization and recitation are familiar practices to most Japanese students who have been educated in the national public school system. I suspected that the silent audiences were the product of politely enduring formal wedding speeches and insufferable karaoke singing. Only with considerable urging would Japanese students speak out and ask questions, and they would not dare to point out faulty logic in a presentation. But what were my conclusions based on?

As I questioned my own intentions and assumptions, I began to understand the importance of critical questioning. Claims should be substantiated, assumptions questioned, and logic tested. Employees who handle toxic chemicals and six-figure accounts cannot operate on assumptions. Critical inquiry means digging under the surface of accepted facts, figures, and ideas, and questioning standard answers. How could I encourage critical inquiry in my students? How could we move beyond the mechanical reruns of scripted speeches?

CULTURAL PERCEPTIONS

Attitudes, beliefs, and habits do not change easily, especially when they are rooted in culture. Putting aside my own biases when trying to understand Japanese culture was even harder. Nonetheless, I felt I needed to try to understand how cultural factors, educational background, and protocols of public speaking were influencing behavior in the classroom.

I was aware that different methods of persuasion are used in traditional Japanese businesses. The Japanese term *nemawashi* defines a style of decision making in which negotiations take place primarily behind the scenes. Individuals are consulted in a carefully tended social network as a way to reach consensus. With *nemawashi,* direct rhetorical and persuasive techniques are not so important in a formal presentation, because an agreement may have already been reached.

I could see how the idea of a presentation itself could be culturally based. I could also understand how other factors could determine behavior. The hesitation to speak out, ask questions, question authority, and push ideas could be an expression of deference to superiors in a hierarchical social system. In a traditional Japanese meeting, it is the person of higher rank who speaks. Direct questioning could be read as a violation of face. In the classroom, where hierarchical relations are not as rigid, students might be displaying reserve as a sign of respect to the speaker.

I often pointed out what I felt was weak logic in a script, and many students would respond, "Yes, Japanese are not logical." My expectations of a logically constructed outline could have been culturally dependent, as shown in different patterns of written discourse.

The Process of Designing Activities

Understanding cultural differences was essential for me when trying to decode behavior and encourage change, but I found that overemphasizing cultural differences often backfired. Many students found conceptual understanding of culture to be an insufficient motive to change behavior. Cultural comparisons could also bring about feelings of inferiority or defensiveness, and some students would resist what felt like a compromise to their culture, as the student had implied when he asked, "Are you trying to make us American?" Active questioning and critical inquiry are not unique to my own culture. What I came to understand was simply that cultural conditioning in Japan could discourage certain kinds of behavior in certain contexts, and my job was to change the context.

My strategy was to design activities that would create incentives for behavioral change, create contexts in which students could more easily accept new behavioral norms, and introduce students to effective communication techniques. I organized these strategies into three principles and used them as a guide when improving the curriculum.

1. incentive: A good activity should have sufficient incentive to promote changes in behavior.
2. context: A good activity should provide a context in which the changed behavior is natural.
3. technique: A good activity should make necessary techniques clear and accessible.

I used a cycle of extensive observation, reflection, and revision to ensure that activities adhered to these three principles, as the following descriptions of two activities illustrate. These activities were added to the curriculum to meet the goals of active questioning and critical inquiry.

ACTIVITIES TO PROMOTE ACTIVE QUESTIONING

Observation and Reflection

If I was to promote active questioning, I first needed to observe student behavior carefully. I could see that students often waited for others to speak first or waited for a cue from the instructor. I also noticed that students would sometimes follow a certain order of speaking, with a clockwise rotation being the preferred order. Even when questions were asked more randomly, students appeared to keep track of who had spoken and who had not, allowing for everyone to speak once before anyone spoke for the second time. Interruptions and overlapping were rare, and if they occurred, students would quickly defer to each other. Students used reflective pauses, hesitations, and moments of silence when taking turns to speak.

I interviewed students, and many said they were afraid to ask stupid questions. They felt they might be the only one who needed to ask a question and were afraid to waste the time of other students. Some students explained that they felt too aggressive asking questions and were worried that they might make the speaker lose face by asking a difficult question.

Revision

I wanted to defuse this tension and encourage more active questioning. With a strong enough incentive, students should feel free to speak out with confidence. They could also learn techniques and patterns of questioning through experience. I decided that rewarding questions would overrule feelings of hesitation and that questioning could be made into a game. I designed an activity in which students were rewarded with play money each time they asked a question. I read slowly from a foreign menu and encouraged students to ask questions each time they did not understand something. After reading the menu, students could use the play money to order food. Those who had not been active enough in asking questions would have to go hungry.

Observation and Reflection

The intention behind the game was to provide a safe condition for students to ask questions. This activity increased the level of questioning, and the game element of the money made it more enjoyable for some students, but the activity was not entirely successful. After a certain point, students seemed resigned to the fact that some students were outspoken and some were quiet. At the same time, quiet students with little money felt a loss of face. Competition was the intended motivation, but competition in this situation was too brutal.

The play money and the promise of a good meal were the simulated incentives to ask questions and verify information. Though the conditions of the activity were clear, the context may have been too unrelated to reality. Furthermore, those with strong comprehension skills may have felt it redundant to ask questions just to get play money. Fear of failure was not a sufficient incentive. Intended to be a game, the activity ended up more like a student evaluation, and the play money became grade points.

I decided that I had not given the students enough questioning techniques and that the artificial incentive had been insufficient to encourage students to explore questioning techniques on their own. Furthermore, if they were operating on set habits of turn taking, deference, and use of silence, it would have been very difficult for them to change their questioning style.

Revision

The incentive and context needed to be revised. Consequently, I scrapped the menu activity and began with a completely new activity that I call the *Vending Machine*. I focused on the three principles of incentive, context, and technique, and tried to correct the weak points in the menu activity.

The class was divided into four teams. I gave the teams 10 or so minutes to work together and come up with a new concept for a vending machine. In this activity, the concept did not have to be realistic, and some of the more creative ideas included a hair-cutting machine, a fresh-fish vending machine, a brain vending machine, a shoe repair machine, and a plastic surgery vending machine.

Using one piece of paper, each team quickly brainstormed and wrote down as much information as possible about their company's vending machine. There were no restrictions on the information they could write down. It could include the dimensions of the machine, the cost of products, and target markets. It could even include the name of the company founder, the sound that the machine made when delivering the product, or the number of seconds it took for the product to appear.

Teams regrouped and competed to ask as many questions as they could. Each team was free to direct questions to any other team. The aim of the vending-machine game was for the teams to confidently answer all questions, and the way to accumulate points was to aggressively ask questions. The students addressed their questions to a specific company by saying, "I have a question for Company X." Any question related to the vending machine or company was permitted. Every time a team asked a question, it got 1 point marked on the board for all to see. If team members could not answer because they had not prepared their data, they could bluff and make up an answer on the spot. If any other team suspected a bluff, they could ask, "Please show me your data." If there was no information written down on the data sheet, the bluffing team lost a point. If the team did indeed have the data, the team that called the bluff lost a point.

Observation and Reflection

The vending-machine game encouraged and rewarded asking questions without risking loss of face. Teams being asked questions had the option to bluff if they did not have a prepared answer. The bluff option encouraged students to be spontaneous and imaginative. It also required quick thinking and a show of confidence when answering. Even if a team was caught out, there was little loss of face as the team members had not lied or shown ignorance. There were no wrong answers in this game. Questions were intended to force other teams to lose points, but many times the questions were insightful and perceptive. This kind of thinking and questioning was valuable in later activities concerning critical inquiry.

The game broke up conventional turn taking, as participants felt compelled to speak out competitively. Teams could grab any opportunity to ask a question, and there was no need to wait for a cue. The competitive element worked better in this activity as teams were allowed to question any other team. Quick initiative gained points, and quick thinking could catch other teams off guard. Only occasionally were there problems of simultaneous speaking, but at that point, I refereed.

Being able to choose what team to target also added an interesting and entertaining element to the game. At times, questions were directed at one team, either out of interest or out of a desire to win points. In most other contexts, picking on someone would be seen as unduly aggressive, but recognition that someone was being targeted in this activity was almost consistently accompanied by playful laughter. The activity was successful in promoting teamwork and mutual support. Shy students could find ways to participate on their own terms or cooperate with more outspoken students, so pressure and fear of embarrassment were not extreme. The game did not specify any particular questioning techniques, but students often discovered them on their own. They learned about pacing, turn taking, speed of response, and control of facial expressions when answering.

After rewarding the winning team, I spent time clarifying cultural differences in questioning, contexts of use, and effective techniques. Students sometimes commented that aggressive questioning is more typically Western than Japanese, but I pointed out that, in any culture, certain situations, such as court procedures and police interrogations, require this kind of questioning. Japanese business people may also find this form of questioning useful when negotiating, settling contracts, and discussing legal issues. Students were usually satisfied with their participation in this activity, but pointing out other possible techniques sometimes surprised them. For example, few groups discovered that it was easy to gain points by quickly directing the same question to the other groups or by turning a question around by asking, "And you?"

ACTIVITIES TO PROMOTE CRITICAL INQUIRY
Observation and Reflection
Another problem that I observed in the presentations was weak logic. Any topic more complex than *Three Reasons Why I Like My Dog More Than My Boss* threatened to be too difficult.

Main points were not clear, links in logic were weak, ideas were not substantiated, and speakers would sometimes end up contradicting themselves. Audiences were often confused, and speakers were unable to explain and answer questions. Initially, I tried to point out such problems in the early stages of writing, but later I tried to avoid giving away easy answers or taking over the script writing myself. I wanted the students to think independently and to ask strategic and provocative questions that would lead the presenters to think more carefully. Unfortunately, many students hit mental dead ends, became frustrated, and ended up wasting time.

Revision
I decided that I should avoid being the primary source of feedback. Students tended to believe that I had the correct answer or tried to adjust their thinking to what they thought I expected. I decided that the students should provide the feedback, and I experimented with peer assessment. Students

worked with a number of classmates so that they could gain different perspectives. Partners were encouraged to ask questions and test the logical strength of an argument.

Observation and Reflection

This activity proved to be insufficient. Many students could assess presentation scripts and ideas intuitively, but not analytically. Although they might feel that an argument was not strong, they did not know how to identify the weak points. Some students hesitated to give criticism, whereas others had trouble receiving criticism. The incentives, context, and techniques were ill defined in this activity, and the students were at a loss on how to rework their scripts.

Revision

I needed an activity that would encourage the students to ask critical questions that would expose inconsistencies in logic. I designed an activity called *The Dictator* and tried to establish a clear incentive and context. The activity, designed to encourage critical inquiry and explore questioning strategies, had three parts. In the first part, students asked questions and experimented with strategies. In the second part, I introduced more concrete techniques, and in the final part, students planned and tested strategies, followed by a debriefing. I usually spent around 3 hours on the entire activity.

In the first part, I took the role of a dictator, and the class became the citizens. The dictator announced a radical proposal for a new law, and the citizens were given 30 minutes during which they were free to ask questions. Their goal was to expose weaknesses in the proposal by asking questions. If they could expose contradictions or force the dictator into a position where the dictator could not answer, they succeeded in defeating the proposal, but if they were not successful, the new law was considered valid. If a citizen expressed an opinion, the dictator was not obligated to respond and could simply say, "Thank you for your opinion." Practice helped me remain in control and answer all questions without exposing weak links in logic.

The activity began with an intuitively illogical idea. The dictator proposed that all children be taken from their biological parents at birth and raised separately in a central child-care center. The idea was repugnant enough for many students to try hard to defeat the idea (see Simulated Scenario on page 214 for sample questions and answers). They soon found, however, that the dictator had an answer to every question. Searching for a weak point in the argument was like trying to solve a puzzle. Though a game of logic is usually disconnected from personal opinion or emotion, the provocative subject of this simulation created a stronger incentive for students to solve the puzzle.

Simulated Scenario

(Q = student question; A = dictator's answer)

Q: Why do you want to establish a central child-care home?
A: To make the country strong.
Q: What do you mean by strong?
A: Economically strong.
Q: Why would this home make the country economically strong?
A: Because this system will improve the level of education.
Q: Why would it improve education?
A: Because we can provide a more supportive educational environment.
Q: Why do you think the present system isn't good enough?
A: Because it is based on standardization and can't respond to individual strengths.
Q: What do you mean?
A: Children may have special talents that the present system cannot recognize.
Q: At what age will children be sent to the home?
A: At birth.
Q: When can they visit their parents?
A: They will never know their parents.
Q: Don't children need love from their parents?
A: Yes, of course.
Q: So you mean your system doesn't give children parental love?
A: The new system gives professional parental love.
Q: What do you mean?
A: The homes provide 24-hour parental care.
Q: Don't you think the real parents give better love?
A: No.
Q: Why?
A: Sometimes they don't have a choice and they're too busy.
Q: What do you mean by choice?
A: In the new system, children can choose parents they like.
Q: Who are the parents?
A: They are professionals.
Q: Who pays for them?
A: Taxes pay for their salaries, but many are volunteers.

In the second part, we discussed which questioning strategies worked and which did not work. Then I introduced more concrete strategies and used the material in Examples and Activities for Critical Questioning Techniques to help students understand critical questioning techniques. These included clarifying definitions, asking hypothetical questions, and exposing contradictions and assumptions.

Examples and Activities for Critical Questioning Techniques

1. **Asking for a Definition**

   Many times we use words but do not make clear how we are using them. Definitions go beyond what is explained in a dictionary. Push the speaker to explain how they are using a term.

   Key question: What do you mean by . . . ?

   Examples

Statement:	I think that it's good for employees to have more power.
Question:	What do you mean by *power*?
Statement:	I think that it's a positive thing for companies to change.
Question:	What do you mean by *change*? What do you mean by *positive*?

2. **Hypothetical Questions**

   Another powerful kind of question is the hypothetical question. Basically, any question that begins with an *if* is a hypothetical question. They are useful in pushing the speaker to give more information.

   Key question: If . . . , how/why/what . . . ?

   Examples

Statement:	It is good to cut workers' wages.
Questions:	If your wages were cut, how would you react?
	If wages are cut, how do you think the workers will feel?
	If we cut wages, why would workers would want to continue working?
	If we cut wages, why would the workers accept it?
	If you cut wages, how will it help the company?
	If this doesn't increase profits, what will you do?
	If it violates the workers' contracts, what will you do?

3. **Looking for Contradictions**

   Contradictions occur when someone says one thing and then says something else that contradicts it. Contradictions are the weakest link. If you find a contradiction, especially in the main point, it means the speaker's ideas are faulty and need more careful thought.

   Key question: Excuse me. You said . . . and then you said . . . Isn't that a contradiction?

   Exercise: Find the contradiction in these groups of statements. Complete the question. One has been done for you.

Statements:	I love summer./I hate cold food./I love hot weather./I love swimming in the summer./I love eating ice cream.
Question:	Excuse me. You said you hate cold food, and then you said you love eating ice cream. Isn't that a contradiction?

   continued on p. 216

Examples and Activities for
Critical Questioning Techniques (cont.)

Statements: Education is changing./Child-centered education is good for a child's development./It is important to see that this new system works./Teachers should guide and encourage students./Teachers should control what the students learn.

Question: Excuse me. You said . . . , and then you said . . . . Isn't that a contradiction?

Statements: War is bad./Attacking other countries is bad./People should defend their own countries./People should defend their own countries in any way possible./Peace is good.

Question: Excuse me. You said . . . , and then you said . . . . Isn't that a contradiction?

Statements: We respect all life, so we tested this drug carefully./This medicine is completely safe./We did not use humans to test the drug./It has been tested on animals./We tested it because we want to protect human life.

Question: Excuse me. You said . . . , and then you said . . . . Isn't that a contradiction?

Statements: People want to have a good life./Democracy is good because it means equality for everyone./Democracy gives people more chances. / Democracy needs wise people to make good decisions. / People with special power should make the decisions.

Question: Excuse me. You said . . . , and then you said . . . . Isn't that a contradiction?

4. **Assumption or Fact?**
Many faulty ideas are based on assumptions. Assumptions are different from facts. Assumptions are ideas that we think are factual but have no concrete logic to support them.

Exercise: What assumptions are being made in the following statements?

Statements: Gay marriage is bad because marriage should only be between a man and a woman.
Preemptive strikes are necessary.
Education is good.
God is great.

Phrases to challenge assumptions:
I think that's an assumption because . . . .
I think that's a fact because . . . .
Can you prove that?
Why do you think that's a fact?
What is that idea based on?

continued on p. 217

**Examples and Activities for
Critical Questioning Techniques (cont.)**

5. **Logic Inspection**
   When you see statements made that are based on test results, you need to ask, "Can you always depend on test results?"
   When you see statements made that are said to be based on fact, you need to ask, "Is a fact always a fact?"
   When you see statements made that are based on ideas, you need to ask, "Is an idea a good basis for drawing a logical conclusion?"

   Exercise: Look at the following statements and the information that they are based on. Find where the logic is weak.

Statement:	Most Japanese experience culture shock when they travel overseas.
Based on:	The results of questionnaires given to 50 Japanese male students
Statement:	Genetically modified (GM) food is safe for human consumption.
Based on:	Test results from complete health checks on 20,000 people who ate only GM food for 3 years
Statement:	Cigarette smoking should be banned from all public places.
Based on:	Research shows that secondhand smoke can cause cancer.
Statement:	All Japanese should study English.
Based on:	The fact that English is the international language
Statement:	These beauty products are 100% safe.
Based on:	The fact that all products have been tested on animals
Statement:	Death sentence executions should be shown on TV.
Based on:	The idea that the death sentence will make people afraid to commit a crime.
Statement:	War is sometimes necessary.
Based on:	Without war, Nazism may have taken over the world.

In the final part, students experienced the roles of both defender and questioner. I divided the class into two large groups and assigned each group a ludicrous proposal to defend, using the same set of rules as in the dictator activity. These two proposals have worked consistently over the years:

- No more kanji. (Chinese characters should be eliminated from written Japanese script.)
- Pachinko should be illegal. (Pachinko is a popular pinball game that is a marginal form of gambling.)

The students were free to interpret the language of these proposals in their own way, and the teams had 10 minutes to prepare their defense and 10 minutes to prepare their offense. The two teams faced each other, and a time limit was set for one team to question the other. The roles were then switched, and the other team asked questions.

In a final debriefing, I gave feedback on the questioning strategies students used and pointed out how and why some worked. By this stage, the incentives and goals of questioning to reveal problems with logic were clear to the students. After this activity, students applied this process of critical inquiry to their own presentation scripts and tested the logic of their ideas with each other. By the time students gave their final presentations, they had critically analyzed their presentation scripts several times. The audience was familiar with the topics and the techniques of critical inquiry, so the question-and-answer sessions were animated and stimulating, with many perceptive questions asked.

Observation and Reflection

I have conducted this activity over many years with consistent results. Though the pace of questioning is usually slower than in the vending-machine activity, this activity encourages students to think deeply and seriously. This is apparent from the nature of their questions, the concentrated expressions on their faces, and their refusal to give up.

What the students learn experientially is that intuitive reactions must be followed with logical reasoning in order to eliminate inconsistencies in an argument. Expressing disagreement or personal opinions is not enough to deconstruct a faulty argument. Skillful questioning must force the dictator to relinquish information, and the questioner then checks to see if all the pieces fit. Clever questioning can expose inconsistencies and contradictions, but clever dictators can raise the bar. Frustration impels students to try harder. Few are willing to admit defeat. Ultimately, however, the new decree is usually signed.

The purpose of this activity is to increase a sense of critical inquiry. Students learn to sniff out faulty logic, point out rusty cogs, and identify missing parts. Critical inquiry, through active questioning, is a form of quality control. After this activity, students return to analyze the scripts that they are preparing for the final day more critically.

The activities do not necessarily fit a particular time slot within the weekly program, but I usually include them on the second and third day of a 5-day course, as shown in Incorporating Critical Approaches to Questioning Into the Syllabus.

My intention is to infuse the curriculum with active and critical approaches to questioning. I want students to absorb this spirit and apply

	Incorporating Critical Approaches to Questioning Into the Syllabus
Day 1	Openings, warm-ups, introduction speeches, basic nonverbal communication exercises
Day 2	Brainstorming, feedback techniques, impromptu speeches, **Vending Machine**, organization of ideas, key phrases
Day 3	Outlines, product speeches, audience feedback, **The Dictator**, script writing, visual aids
Day 4	Persuasive techniques, nonverbal communication, question-and-answer techniques, proposal speech
Day 5	Speech preparation, final presentation, discussion, video viewing, debriefing

it to their learning. The two activities are designed to work as large-scale icebreakers and to activate a paradigm shift in classroom learning. Effects of Activities on the Curriculum shows how the activities resonate throughout the curriculum. Students can change their behavior in the time remaining as well as reevaluate their behavior in the preceding days. In order to prepare fertile ground for this experience to take root, throughout the week I emphasize the importance of interactive communication, primarily the technique of asking questions, as a way to generate and test ideas.

Evaluating the Curriculum Change

The cycles of observation, reflection, and revision will continue with this curriculum development, but the positive changes I have observed include more frequent questions, less hesitation to challenge each other, more time and enthusiasm spent on script preparation, more receptivity to criticism, and no students sleeping during presentations. These

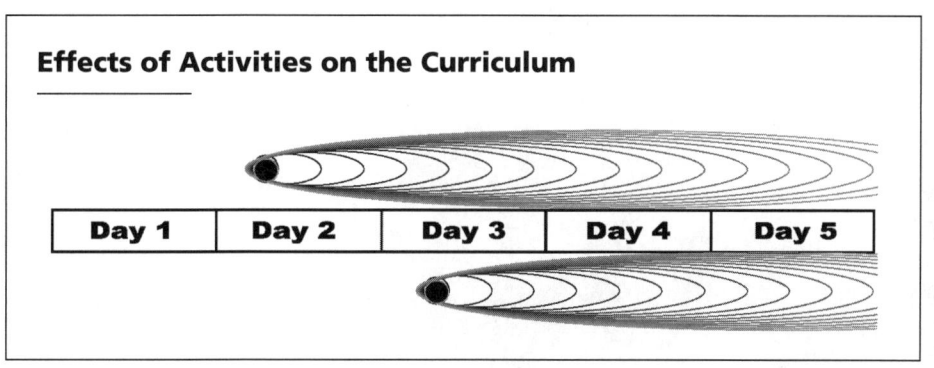

Effects of Activities on the Curriculum

changes open enormous possibilities for empirical research. The effects of uninhibited questioning may even be related to an increase in fluency and improved body language. The most definitive change, however, is the final presentation.

The final day has come. The seats have been arranged, and the first speaker faces the audience. Lower level students may have chosen topics such as *Three Reasons Why I Like My Dog More Than My Boss,* but even if the student has limited English ability, a lively debate often ensues. "Why is loyalty so important for you?" "Does it make sense to compare your boss with an animal?" "Is it necessary to like a boss?" The students are enthusiastically engaged, and I can sit in the back of the room, relaxed and free of sweaty palms.

Critical inquiry and active questioning are not easily taught through formulaic textbooks, nor can a curriculum be based on unquestioned assumptions. The process of observation, reflection, and revision was instrumental in designing these two activities, and the result was a classroom of enthusiastic and engaged students, with no strings attached.

Surviving a Crash Course in EAP Writing: A Cambodian Experience

12

STEPHEN H. MOORE

This chapter describes how I, as a relatively inexperienced English for academic purposes (EAP) teacher, survived the writing component of an intensive EAP course. It also describes the pathway to survival for the learners, none of whom had ever previously studied EAP. *Survival* seems to me the most fitting description of our situation, as we were all under intense pressure from the principal stakeholders—the people funding the program and my teaching institution—to perform well and, indeed, to aim high and actually overachieve. In the end, the surviving cohort of learners attained a reasonable level of proficiency in writing academic English, and I lived to teach another day.

The Motivation for the Adaptation and Innovation

The curriculum constraints under which I operated were related to goals, objectives, and outcomes. The goals were concerned with the broad aim of familiarizing learners with the range of academic skills expected of postgraduate students studying at an English-medium institution. These goals included being able to write in an appropriate academic style. The objectives set out performance indicator targets to be achieved in the four macroskills of listening, speaking, reading, and writing; for example, *to be able to persuade through reasoned argument*. The outcomes specified the acceptable levels of performance in the four macroskills; for example, *to be able to draft a suitable outline for an essay*. Content and assessment were not prescribed but were the means by which the goals, objectives, and outcomes would be achieved. The EAP course consisted of an integrated program of study designed to equip learners with the minimum skills needed to function adequately in a postgraduate degree taught in English. The cohort of learners was streamed into two groups. My colleague taught the higher level group, and I taught the lower level one. This chapter focuses on the writing component for the lower level group in this EAP program.

Within the first week of classes, it became quite apparent to me that no writing course book would address the writing problems of my group of learners. Therefore, I was going to have to develop some writing materials of my own, tailored to this group and its needs. In addition, I was going to have to cover a lot of ground in just 6 months, as most of the learners in the lower level group did not have even basic rhetorical skills for expressing themselves in academic written English. How to begin the process?

I spent several weeks dipping into various books, such as those by Tribble (1996), Swales and Feak (1994), and Jordan (1997), and attempting improvements by modifying some of their writing tasks. After about a month of this rather haphazard approach, a better way began to crystallize in my mind. I felt that the learners would benefit from having a map of the basic genres or text types in English and learning where and how academic texts were placed within this map. (I make no distinction between the terms *genre* and *text type* and henceforth use the term *genre*.) My plan was to cover any genres that formed part of expository academic writing, the academic essay. I was familiar with the basic theory of systemic functional linguistics (SFL; see Halliday, 1994) and possessed several introductory textbooks that explained how to apply this theory to text and discourse analysis (Butt, Fahey, Spinks, & Yallop, 1995; Gerot, 1995; Gerot & Wignell, 1994). My basic assumption was that an SFL-genre approach would both simplify and speed up the learning process. An additional assumption was that learners would have to be able to identify genres in terms of their own reading repertoires before being able to use them effectively as models for their own writing. I saw my situation as a classic example of a teacher drawing on available resources to adapt creatively and innovate in order to deliver a course the particular cohort of students needed, rather than using a standard, more easily available teaching package.

The Curriculum Context

In June 1999, I was hired as an English language instructor at the Cambodia Development Resource Institute (CDRI) in Phnom Penh, principally to teach 30 Cambodian government-employed teachers in a 6-month intensive EAP program. The participants had been selected to undertake a master's degree in education, funded by Ateneo de Manila University of the Philippines. This university is fully accredited in the Philippines, and its generous offer of funding was made available through its Cambodia Graduate Offshore Program in Education Project.

Acceptance into the master's program was conditional on attaining a sufficient level of proficiency in English. The degree course was to be taught in Phnom Penh in early 2000 as a follow-on to the EAP preparatory program. Visiting lecturers from the Philippines were to teach in intensive blocks, followed by a period of self-study and formal assessment. The attrition rates on the EAP course meant that only a dozen learners completed the course in December 1999. This was partly due to our releasing the poorest performers at various cutoff points during the course. Ateneo then decided that it would be better to integrate the remaining cohort into their on-campus program in the Philippines rather than teach the group in Cambodia as a separate class, as originally planned.

THE PARTICIPANTS

The course participants were all Cambodian nationals and teachers of various subjects in the state school sector. Their ages ranged from mid-20s to 40 years of age, with only a few females in the group. Some teachers taught primary school, and others secondary school. These participants had responded to advertisements placed in local media outlets by the Ministry of Education inviting teachers to attend a placement test and interview at CDRI several months before the commencement of the EAP program. The screening process involved candidates taking an in-house English proficiency exam that was loosely modeled on the International English Language Testing System (IELTS) examination, developed and administered by Cambridge University, the British Council, and IDP Australia. It assesses the macroskills of reading, writing, speaking, and listening. Approximately 100 candidates had come forward for this screening process, and, subject to meeting all other eligibility requirements, the top third was selected to participate in the program. The initial class consisted of 30 learners.

As a certificated IELTS examiner, I surmised that this group of learners was well below the Band 6 score, which is widely accepted as a minimum level for tertiary-level studies in English-speaking countries. The weakest learners in the group performed two full bands below where they needed to be. Conventional wisdom in EAP programs suggests that raising an IELTS score by half a band requires approximately 200 hours of EAP instruction. Two hundred hours of instruction represents about 10 weeks of full-time instruction at 4 hours per day. The Ateneo cohort would receive only 500 hours of instruction over a 6-month period. Simple arithmetic suggested that many learners could not possibly improve their level of English proficiency to the standard required, and this was a substantial burden that I carried from the outset. In spite of my protests that Ateneo's goals were unrealistic, I was, in effect, expected to perform a miracle.

THE COURSE

I have alluded to my relative inexperience as an EAP teacher when I took on this teaching position. However, I had been teaching general English and English for specific purposes in a number of countries since 1990, with 3 years in Japan, 6 months in Thailand, 6 months in Vietnam, and 3 years in Cambodia. I had also taught Cambodians in an academic setting (Moore, 1997) and had completed a master of applied linguistics degree in Australia in 1997. I was "all dressed up with somewhere to go" when I was invited to join CDRI as an EAP teacher. My immediate supervisor was a British national and CDRI's English language teaching coordinator, whom I will call Rose. As previously noted, Ateneo set the overall goals, objectives, and outcomes of the EAP program, and these formed the framework within which my supervisor and I decided on course content and assessment. The two of us spent the 2 weeks before the EAP program mapping out a rough draft of its components, as shown in Overview of the EAP Program. We developed the content, teaching methodologies, and assessment options.

The EAP course was taught from mid-June to mid-December 1999. There were approximately 500 hours of classroom instruction, as classes were conducted from Monday to Friday, every morning from 7:30 to 11:30. In addition, learners had 2–3 hours of homework assignments every day.

	Overview of the EAP Program		
	Curriculum	**Teacher**	
Weeks	**Content**	**Group A**	**Group B**
1–6	EAP skills Pronunciation Listening/speaking Reading/writing	Rose Stephen Rose Rose	Rose Stephen Stephen Stephen
7	Break		
8–19	Listening/speaking Reading/writing	Rose Rose	Stephen Stephen
20	Break		
21–26	Listening/speaking Reading/writing	Stephen	

Rose and I spent our afternoons preparing the lesson plans and materials for the following day.

The premises in which the course was conducted were excellent, with bright, quiet, air-conditioned classrooms. We had movable tables and chairs for flexible seating arrangements and the use of a conventional language laboratory for pronunciation practice and, when necessary, test administration. Learner attendance was mixed, with a core of learners attending regularly and others drifting in and out due to work commitments, family matters, and ill health.

Rose and I shared the EAP teaching load. She taught the higher level group of 10 learners, and I taught the lower level group of 20. Rose initially concentrated on developing generic academic skills, such as dictionary skills, library skills, and note-taking skills, for both groups. I focused on developing pronunciation skills. After 6 weeks, we released 5 of the weakest learners and invited the others to return for the next phase beginning in Week 8. For approximately 3 months, from Week 8 to Week 19, I implemented the genre-based approach to writing through scaffolded activities to help my group of lower level learners develop basic rhetorical skills in written academic English. After Week 19, we again released the 5 weakest learners and invited the others to return for the final phase beginning in Week 21. The initial cohort of 30 learners was thus reduced to 12 through releases and other factors.

Releasing any learners at this final stage of the course was traumatic for both the students and the teachers. The learners felt a humiliating loss of face and begged to be reinstated, and the teachers felt resentment toward the funding body for creating the false expectation that all learners who tried their best would automatically succeed. In the final 6 weeks of the program, we combined the higher and lower level groups into what would be the final cohort. At this point, Rose passed the full teaching load to me, and I was charged with creating a cohesive group that would be ready to undertake postgraduate studies in a few months. The writing program for this final stage involved further practice and consolidation of academic writing.

The EAP course itself aligned with CDRI's mandate to provide high-quality, in-house English language instruction to Cambodians working at the institution as well as on a commercial basis to outside parties, such as Ateneo. CDRI won the Ateneo contract through competitive bidding, and this success placed predictable pressure on the teaching context. Rose was under pressure from both the director of CDRI and the Ateneo representative to present progress reports confirming the delivery of the program as contracted. She in turn pressured me to deliver positive results that she could report. I passed the burden on to the learners to learn academic English quickly and to reflect their learning through assessment.

The Process of Designing and Adapting the Course

Even relatively well-educated Cambodians do not generally possess a wide repertoire of writing skills in their mother tongue. This is the result of a cultural preference for oracy over literacy and the destruction of the education system by the Khmer Rouge in the late 1970s. Early in the course, it became apparent that none of the lower level group of learners had an appropriate repertoire of academic writing skills and that most had serious difficulties in communicating coherently through the written word. They were unlikely to have first language (L1) writing skills that they could transfer to a second language (L2) to speed up the acquisition of English academic writing skills. In fact, the learners would have to develop writing skills in English that were well beyond what they practiced in Khmer. The question was, how to go about achieving this?

USING THE GENRE APPROACH

My teaching instincts drew me in the direction of the genre approach to writing as the most promising way to proceed. I was familiar with several taxonomies of English writing based on genres (Butt et al., 1995; Gerot & Wignell, 1994). I also had the good fortune to know another SFL practitioner in Cambodia, an Australian teacher and former colleague who lent me Knapp and Watkins' (1994) *Context—Text—Grammar: Teaching the Genres and Grammar of School Writing in Infants and Primary Classrooms*, a book that was to prove invaluable in conceptualizing the EAP writing course. I was wary of a book developed to assist teachers of primary school L1 learners in New South Wales, Australia, but I soon came to see how it could be adapted to suit the needs of my adult, tertiary-level L2 learners. What this book offered was a simple but strong framework on which to build a tailored course for my Cambodian learners.

Knapp and Watkins (1994) follow a functional approach to language and suggest that English discourse is arranged in genres according to three basic formal categories: order, sequence, and expansion. These formal categories, however, cannot tell much about how language is used for communicative purposes. To understand this, one needs to consider functional categories such as description, narration, explanation, instruction, and argumentation. Knapp and Watkins (p. 19) describe the simplified relationship between form and function shown opposite, and this was a very useful basic framework for my L2 learners.

Knapp and Watkins (1994, p. 22) expand this generalized relationship through a more detailed taxonomy of genres based on five functional categorizations. Their taxonomy relates processes to written products as follows:

> **Relationship Between Form and Function**
> **(Knapp & Watkins, 1994, p. 19)**
>
> | Form | | Function |
> |---|---|---|
> | Order | → | Describe |
> | Sequence | → | Narrate, explain, instruct |
> | Expansion | → | Argue |

1. describe → personal descriptions, commonsense descriptions, technical descriptions, information reports, scientific reports, definitions
2. narrate → personal recounts, historical recounts, stories, fairy tales, myths, fables, narratives
3. explain → explanations of how, explanations of why, elaborations, illustrations, accounts, explanation essays
4. instruct → procedures, instructions, manuals, science experiments, recipes, directions
5. argue → essays, expositions, discussions, debates, reviews, interpretations, evaluations

Given the enormity of the learning task within the time constraints of a 3-month course, I decided to focus on three main genres: description, explanation, and argument. A fourth genre, discussion, was tacked onto the argument genre as a derivation. I felt that if learners had a good command of these four genres, then they would at least have the essential building blocks for academic writing and would be able to develop their discursive skills from a sound foundation. This judgment was easier to make, given the purposes of this small subset of genres, which can be defined as follows:

- description: to present factual information about something by first classifying it and then describing its characteristics (Butt et al., 1995, p. 17)
- explanation: to explain why things are as they are, or how things work (Butt et al., 1995, p. 17)
- argument: to expand a proposition to persuade readers to accept a point of view (Knapp & Watkins, 1994, p. 22)
- discussion: to present information and opinions about more than one side of an issue, and possibly make a recommendation (Butt et al., 1995, p. 17)

These purposes are the essential strands of academic writing in English, but this is not to say that an ability to write these four genres will ensure an ability to write academic English. Rather, academic writing is generally a distillation of these four genres, and an ability to write them is excellent preparation for the macrogenre of academic writing. We did not spend very much time on practicing the integration of citations and referencing into academic writing, one of its defining characteristics. Given my priorities, this aspect was addressed more passively through reading skills development work, but it was taken up in the final portion of the course, in Weeks 21–26.

PROVIDING A SCAFFOLD FOR ACADEMIC WRITING

Scaffolding is the process of systematically providing teacher support and guidance to learners and strategically reducing and eventually withdrawing it when learners have internalized the routines and procedures being taught, as outlined by Hammond and Gibbons (2001):

> *Teachers need to provide temporary supporting structures that will assist learners to develop new understandings, new concepts, and new abilities. As the learner develops control of these, so teachers need to withdraw that support, only to provide further support for extended or new tasks, understandings and concepts. (p. 2)*

The idea of using some form of scaffolding had not occurred to me as I began this journey into the unknown. However, it was triggered by learner feedback indicating that most students felt completely lost when faced with a topic to write about and a blank sheet of paper. Knapp and Watkins (1994) helpfully provided scaffolding models in their descriptions of various genres.

Having determined the four genres that would be the core of the writing course, I had to make them accessible to the learners. After considerable weighing of the pros and cons of various approaches, I decided to start with a combination product-and-process approach. The product aspect was to focus initially on recognizing different genres through reading various texts. In the first stage, I taught and discussed the grammatical features of different genres, after which the learners read text samples and identified relevant grammatical elements. In the second stage, the *moves* of each genre (stretches of discourse that function as a semantic unit in its own right and, in combination with other such units, help define the genre) were discussed and confirmed, and the same texts were analyzed for them. At this point, the learners were suitably primed to begin the process of writing their own texts. However, like young children riding a two-wheeled bicycle for the first time, the learners needed the equivalent of training wheels to keep them on course. This additional support came in the form of simple but carefully calibrated scaffolding.

My processes for teaching descriptions, outlined below, show the role of scaffolding. I followed a similar procedure to teach explanations, arguments, and discussions, but with each new genre, I used less scaffolding.

Teaching Descriptions

Knapp and Watkins (1994, p. 61) note the following grammatical features of the descriptive genre:

- There is a predominant use of present tense.
- Relational verbs (*is/are* and *has/have*) are used when describing appearance/qualities and parts/functions of phenomena.
- Action verbs are used when describing behaviors/uses.
- Sentences and paragraphs are thematically linked to the topic of description, for example, through anaphoric pronominal referencing.

The learners analyzed descriptive texts, such as the one shown here, for these features in order to see that texts bearing these features were in fact descriptions and not some other genre. By extension, if learners did not use these grammatical resources in their own descriptions, then readers would not recognize the writing as description.

Sample Descriptive Text (Dunkel & Lim, 1986, p. 47)

News Media

News media are the means, or methods, by which people learn what is happening in their city, in their country, and in the world. The news media can be classified into two general categories. The categories are print media and electronic media. Print media use written material to communicate news to readers. Electronic media use air waves to send news into homes, offices, and public places.

Print media are usually divided into magazines and newspapers. Most newspapers print news daily. For example, the newspaper *The New York Times* is published every day of the year. Most news magazines are published weekly. For instance, *Newsweek* and *Time* magazines are published once a week.

The electronic media are generally divided into radio and television. Radio news is news that you listen to. In the United States, many radio stations broadcast 5 minutes of news every hour on the hour. Television news is news that you not only listen to but also watch. In Canada and the United States, for example, many people watch an hour of news on TV at 6 o'clock in the evening.

In the future, new categories of news media will develop. Even today computers are beginning to influence the transmission and reception of news.

The following three moves occur in descriptive writing, with an optional fourth marked in parentheses (Butt et al., 1995; Knapp & Watkins, 1994):

1. classification/identification
2. orientation
3. characteristics/attributes
4. (conclusion/summary)

Much academic writing relates to abstract concepts, and this dimension can add further difficulty in learning how to write. The teacher therefore needs to scaffold the phases of learning so that the learners' knowledge and language shift gradually from more concrete, or everyday, concepts to more abstract, or specialized. This is termed by some writers (e.g., Burns & de Silva Joyce, 1999; Burns & Joyce, 1997; Gerot & Wignell, 1994; Halliday, 1985; Hammond et al., 1992) as the movement from language as action, which is more typical of spoken interaction, to language as reflection, which is more typical of written texts. Therefore, it seemed worthwhile to provide access to written genres, initially through the concrete world and then, once the appropriate skills had been developed, through more abstract topics.

Scaffolded Task 1

This task focused on the first move, setting up a topic sentence involving classification or identification. Learners were given the handout Writing Topic Sentences for Descriptions, which lists concrete nouns and gives a

---

Writing Topic Sentences for Descriptions

Write sentences that classify the following words. Your sentences should be able to function as the opening sentence of descriptive paragraphs. Look at the example before you begin.

banana	bicycle	apartment	fan	watch
fire	soccer	language lab	desert	river
tomato	camera	kitchen	mountain	

Example: **lake**—A **lake** is a large body of fresh water.

1. _____
2. _____
3. _____
4. _____
5. _____
6. _____

model classificatory sentence. Learners had to write similar sentences for the other nouns in the list. For example, for the concrete noun *kitchen*, a learner might write *A kitchen is a place to cook food.*

Scaffolded Task 2
This task required the learners to complete the description pro formas in Scaffolding the Writing of Description in Three Phases, which identifies the first three moves, includes question prompts for each, and provides bullet points to assist learners in listing the content of their descriptions.

Scaffolded Task 3
For Task 3, the learners wrote about a different topic using the handout Three Basic Moves for Description (page 232), which marks off the three basic moves but does not provide question prompts or bullet points. For this task, the learners had to connect their writing through appropriate use of cohesive devices within the boundaries of each move.

Scaffolded Task 4
In this final task, the learners wrote about a new topic on lined paper without any scaffolding. To write appropriate descriptions at this stage, the learners had to draw on the grammatical and move structures of the various

---

Scaffolding the Writing of Description in Three Phases

DESCRIPTION

Classification (what it is)
- _____
- _____

Orientation (where it is)
- _____
- _____

Characteristics (what it is like)
- _____
- _____
- _____
- _____
- _____
- _____

Three Basic Moves for Description

Classification/Identification

```
_____
_____
_____
```

Orientation

```
_____
_____
_____
```

Characteristics/Attributes

```
_____
_____
_____
```

preceding practice tasks, which I hoped they had internalized. Among the concrete topics the learners described were a city, a library, and a school. They then moved on to the abstract, for example, describing a good school.

Teaching Explanations

As previously noted, the purpose of explanations is to show why things are as they are or how things work. Knapp and Watkins (1994, p. 81) highlight the grammatical features of explanation as follows:

- Explanations often use general rather than specific nouns.
- Explanations about classes of things use verbs in present tense.
- Explanations that deal with particular events or concepts can be in past, present, or future tense.
- The description stage of an explanation uses the grammar of describing.
- Explanatory sequences are basically concerned with linking verbs in such a way that a logical sequence is produced (e.g., temporally).
- Explanatory sequences cannot work without conjunctions.
- Pronominal reference is also an important feature of explanations.

- Modality is used in explanations, usually when interpretation and opinion are given.

The following two moves are required in the explanation genre, with an optional third marked below in parentheses (Butt et al., 1995; Knapp & Watkins, 1994):

1. description—classification/identification
2. explanatory sequence
3. (evaluation)

As in the unit on descriptions, the learners analyzed model explanations, such as the one shown in Model of the Explanation Genre, to identify features and were taught the basic grammar and moves in relation to concrete topics, such as *How to Shave* and *How to Fly a Kite,* before attempting abstract topics, such as *The British School System* and *How to Survive in Cambodia on a Teacher's Salary.* I followed the same scaffolding steps in teaching explanation, but, because of earlier learning, less time and explanation were needed for each phase.

Teaching Arguments

The genre of argument is one of the most important genres in academic English. It is found in spoken English in the form of debates and in written English in the form of essays, expositions, discussions, reviews, and evaluations. Knapp and Watkins (1994, p. 124) note the following features of argument writing:

- Mental verbs (e.g., *think, believe*) are used in expressing opinions.
- Conjunctions, including temporal, causal, and comparative conjunctions, are used to maintain logical relations and to link ideas.

**Model of the Explanation Genre
(Knapp & Watkins, 1994, p. 90)**

The Water Cycle

The water cycle, sometimes referred to as the hydrologic cycle, is a process that provides the earth with a continuous supply of water. Heat from the sun and gravity are key forces in the water cycle. The sun's heat constantly evaporates water from rivers, lakes, seas and oceans. Evaporation turns the water to vapour which mixes with the air and rises into the atmosphere. When this vapour laden air rises it expands and cools due to the falling temperature. Then as the temperature continues to fall the air loses its capacity to hold the water vapour because it reaches saturation point, or dew point. At this point the water vapour condenses and forms tiny water droplets or ice crystals which form clouds. Finally the cycle enters the precipitation stage where the water droplets fall back to earth as rain, hail or snow.

- Movement is from personal to impersonal voice.
- Modality is used to position the reader in relation to the arguments.
- Nominalizations, where verbal processes are expressed as nouns, are used to condense information and to deal with abstract issues.

Descriptions order meaning through classification and attributes, and explanations order meaning through temporal and cause-and-effect sequences. Arguments order their meanings based on expansion. Description and explanation tend to take an objective writing stance, whereas argument involves more subjective reasoning, evaluation, and persuasion. The purpose of argument is to persuade readers to accept a point of view through the process of expanding a proposition—a statement or idea—that people can consider or discuss. The grammatical features of argument can be mapped onto a structure consisting of at least three moves (Butt et al., 1995; Knapp & Watkins, 1994):

1. thesis, which is the major proposition or opinion
2. point followed by elaboration
3. conclusion or reiteration of the proposition

Usually, the second move is repeated several times, with each additional point and its elaboration adding further evidence and weight to the argument.

I felt that this genre required a different form of scaffolding, initially involving more teacher support. The first topic given to the learners was one they could readily relate to: *Why I Like Khmer Food*. By writing about a memorable subject, I felt, the learners would be able to think back to the process of how we had developed an argument for this topic and simply apply the same principles to later topics. Under the assumption that I could build on the scaffolding process of writing descriptions and explanations, the first step in this scaffolding process involved the brainstorming of points on which to build the argument. The class came up with the following ideas about why they liked Khmer food:

- Khmer food is cheap.
- Khmer food has a great tradition.
- Khmer food is tasty.
- Khmer food is easy to cook.
- Khmer food is not hot like Thai food or fatty like Chinese food.
- Khmer food smells good.
- Cambodians are used to Khmer food.
- Khmer food is healthy.
- There are many soup dishes in Khmer cuisine.

The next step involved elaborating or providing evidence for these ideas. To ensure that the learners could clearly see the relationship between points and elaborations, I provided elaborations to match brainstormed points, for example,

- Khmer food represents an aspect of Cambodian culture in which I take great pride.
- Fresh ingredients are always used in Khmer cooking, such as fresh fish, meats, and vegetables.
- A great variety of ingredients is used in Khmer cooking, and together the result is delicious food.
- Khmer cooking has developed over generations as parents teach their children how to cook Khmer style.
- It is easy to prepare a good Khmer meal for just 2,000 riels (US$0.50).
- When someone is cooking Khmer food, people nearby want to eat.
- Khmer cooking does not cause stomach problems or contribute to heart disease.
- Cambodian people eat Khmer cooking all their lives, for almost every meal.
- *Prahoc* and *corco* soups are especially popular in Khmer cooking.
- In Khmer cooking, meats are usually grilled, and vegetables are often stir-fried.

After matching the elaborations with the established points, the learners organized and ranked the points in order of importance according to their own reasoning. They wrote about them, starting with the most important point and its elaboration first. After this stage, the learners exchanged written drafts and read the work of their classmates. Here individual differences emerged and caused great interest and debate. This feedback sometimes resulted in learners rearranging the flow of their arguments. Once this stage was completed, learners had to write an appropriate introduction and conclusion for their written arguments, linked to the rhetorical thrust of their claims and evidence. The final written drafts were impressive in terms of coherence, and this gave the learners considerable confidence that they did in fact understand how to write an argument genre, such as the model shown on page 236, which I wrote. We were then able to apply the same principles to other concrete topics, such as the problems of traffic and pollution in Phnom Penh, and then to more abstract topics, such as the problems of state education in Cambodia.

> ## Model of the Argument Genre
>
> **Why Khmer Food Is One of the Best Cuisines in the World**
> I think Khmer food is one of the best cuisines anywhere. Although Thai and Vietnamese foods are well known throughout many parts of the world, few foreigners have discovered the delights of Khmer food. There are a number of reasons for stating that Khmer cuisine is exceptionally good.
>
> First and foremost, the food is very tasty. This is because only fresh ingredients are used, and they are mixed together in unique ways in Khmer cooking. The result is a wonderful blend of mouthwatering tastes that are undeniably delicious. Khmer food is also very healthy, and this is an important feature for modern, health-conscious families. The fresh fish, meats and vegetables used in Khmer cooking are rich in protein and vitamins. Khmer food is easy to cook since most dishes are grilled, fried or stir-fried. Thus even an inexperienced chef can usually manage to prepare simple Khmer dishes. If on the other hand, you prefer to eat out, then you will be pleased to find that Khmer food is also very cheap. A good, well-balanced meal can be enjoyed for less than one dollar.
>
> Anyone who is unfamiliar with Khmer food is missing out on a real Asian treat. They should rush out to the nearest Asian restaurant and demand a traditional Khmer meal. I am sure that they will be glad they did.

Teaching Discussions

Discussion was the final genre I taught to these learners. This genre is also based on expansion and is essentially an argument with more than one perspective, as can be seen in Model of the Discussion Genre.

The grammatical features of discussions are basically the same as arguments. However, the structure of discussion involves the following five moves, rather than three, with the first and last moves optional (Butt et al., 1995; Knapp & Watkins, 1994):

1. (statement of issue that provides an optional preview of the discussion)
2. arguments for the proposition presented through points and elaborations
3. arguments against the proposition presented through points and elaborations
4. conclusion
5. (recommendation or considered opinion)

Having acquired the basic rhetorical skills of the argument genre, the learners had little difficulty perceiving the different orientation of discussions. Accordingly, they needed less time to practice writing. In fact, we skipped over concrete topics and focused directly on writing discussions

> **Model of the Discussion Genre
> (Adapted from Oshima & Hogue, 1983, p. 31,
> as cited in Gerot & Wignell, 1994, p. 216)**
>
> **Controlling Genetic Research**
> Genetic research has produced both exciting and frightening possibilities. Scientists are now able to create new forms of life in the laboratory due to the development of gene splicing.
>
> On the one hand, the ability to create life in the laboratory could greatly benefit mankind. For example, because it is very expensive to obtain insulin from natural sources, scientists have developed a method to manufacture it inexpensively in the laboratory. Another beneficial application of gene splicing is in agriculture. Scientists foresee the day when new plants will be developed using nitrogen from the air instead of from fertilizer. Therefore food production could be increased. In addition, entirely new plants could be developed to feed the world's hungry people.
>
> Not everyone is excited about gene splicing, however. Some people feel that it could have terrible consequences. A laboratory accident, for example, might cause an epidemic of an unknown disease that could wipe out humanity.
>
> As a result of this controversy, the government has made rules to control genetic experiments. While some members of the scientific community feel that these rules are too strict, many other people feel that they are still not strict enough.

about abstract topics, such as the strengths and weaknesses of the British primary school system and whether or not English was a difficult language for Cambodians to learn.

In summary, the genre approach to developing basic rhetorical skills in academic writing allowed these learners to grasp the essential qualities of each genre. The order in which they learned the genres enabled them to transfer learning from the earlier, simpler texts to the later, more complex ones. The shift from concrete to abstract topics helped build the learners' confidence in their own understanding of different genres. Scaffolding played an essential role in supporting the learners in the initial stages of tackling each genre. With the introduction of each subsequent genre, less scaffolding was necessary. The learners also came to see the value of systematically planning and organizing their writing before writing a first draft as a useful technique for improving their written expression.

The Process of Evaluating the Course

The contrast between the learners' academic writing before and after instruction was striking, and their texts showed phenomenal improvement in overall comprehensibility. In spite of other, sometimes intrusive errors, such as in spelling and lexical selection, compositions written in the appropriate genre communicated meaning well and were relatively easy to read. This major achievement showed that giving the learners appropriate tools enabled them to express their ideas in a manner that was generally appropriate and comprehensible. Unfortunately, I have no before-and-after samples of student writing to include in the chapter. However, to observe a similar effect, I encourage the interested reader to take a small descriptive text and randomly manipulate spelling and lexis while maintaining the integrity of the move structure and the grammatical features common to descriptions. The resulting discourse should be pleasingly comprehensible.

Throughout the course, I collected samples of students' writing to make formative judgments on how well they were progressing. In particular, I focused on the move structure and associated grammatical features that I had taught, without penalizing other errors, and the learners found this to be a very fair basis on which to judge their writing. This formative assessment also enabled the pacing of the course to be fine-tuned, allowing the class to spend slightly more or less time on any particular genre or grammatical feature. Formative assessment provided some evidence that learners were confusing generic moves and associated grammatical features. The learners themselves usually corrected these errors quickly when I showed them which parts of their writing were causing problems for the reader. The wisdom of teaching only four genres was also apparent at this stage, as the learners' difficulties might have been hopelessly compounded if they had had to keep track of more genres.

At the end of the course, summative assessment provided strong evidence of the learners' ability to express themselves appropriately in academic English discourse, a result that was especially important in the eyes of the other stakeholders. Indeed, the reasonable quality of the learners' writing was a benchmark for the success of the EAP program in achieving its goals and enabling Ateneo to proceed with the follow-up postgraduate training.

The success of the writing course owed a great deal to the role that creativity played throughout the teaching process, in terms of adapting materials to the Cambodian context and being responsive to learners' feedback about their writing needs. The curriculum constraints, though forbidding at the outset, proved less inhibiting as the learners and I found ways to adapt and make progress toward the curriculum goals.

Chifa: Freewriting Within a Required Curriculum for Adults

13

SPENCER SALAS AND KYRA GARSON

Chinese food arrived on the shores of Lima, Peru, with a wave of Asian immigration in the first part of the last century. South American flavors slowly infused themselves into the ancient recipes, and the Peruvian version of *chifa*—Chinese food with a Peruvian twist—emerged. These days, the smell of *chifa* wafts deep into the Amazonian jungle, up and down the Pacific coast, and into the Andes. Natives swear that, with a liter of Inca Cola, it is the best Chinese food on the planet.

Planning and teaching creatively within a required curriculum for adults is like *chifa*. Small but creative modifications in teaching can infuse an adult language program with local energy and flavor.

The Motivation for the Adaptation and Innovation

Strangely enough, even in advanced-level courses, many adult students remain reluctant to write and even more reluctant to share their writing with their peers. This reluctance perhaps results from a view of writing as either right or wrong, a belief that imperfect writing has no value. Consequently, many students fall out of the habit of writing and seldom engage in sustained writing in any language. Perhaps students need their teachers to think longer and harder about how to engage them in a required curriculum. In this context, we argue that freewriting is an unobtrusive but powerful way of infusing a curriculum with individuality and open communication.

WHERE DOES FREEWRITING COME FROM?

Freewriting, as its name implies, surfaced as a liberatory practice that brought to the fore the right to generate and develop one's own ideas through written language. It has been championed in the work of many authors, including Elbow (1998a, 1998b, 2000), Fulwiler (1986n 1987), Goldberg (1986), Heard (1995), and Macrorie (1980, 1984). Goldberg describes freewriting as "writing down the bones—the essential, awake speech" (p. 4). For Belanoff, Elbow, and Fontaine (1991), freewriting is what happens "when you remove almost all the normal constraints involved in writing" (p. xii). For Macrorie (1991), freewriting is digging: "Often we dig in it, we find surprise, and a voice. Then we can revise it: sort the dross from the gold, arrange those chunks in different order" (p. 188).

Freewriting is a series of short, exploratory exercises with pen, pencil, or keyboard in which students create unbroken language in constant motion, without stopping, without thinking too much, and without editing (Elbow, 1998a, 1998b, 2000). For Elbow (2000), freewriting means

> *not showing your words to anyone (unless you later change your mind); not having to stay on topic—that is freely digressing; not thinking too much about spelling, grammar, and mechanics; not worrying about how good the writing is—even whether it makes sense or is understandable (even to oneself). (p. 85)*

Freewriting is sometimes full of ideas and sometimes void of them, but it has one elemental rule: Do not stop moving your pen or pencil across the page, even if that means writing a word repeatedly or making nothing but circular motions. A sprinkling of freewriting in the classroom becomes a pedagogical *chifa,* something very close to and even better than the original curriculum.

The Curriculum Context

El Instituto Cultural Peruano-Norteamerico del Cusco (ICPNA Cusco) is a contemporary Peruvian version of the binational center. It is an autonomous, not-for-profit cultural institution characterized by the high quality of its English language programs. Hundreds of adult students enroll in English classes that they attend on their way to work, on their way home, or on Saturday and Sunday. Most classes meet daily for 1–2 hours. The center has a well-thought-out, established program within the framework of a popular commercial EFL textbook series. The series provides an excellent framework through which adult students can work with a variety of interactive communicative strategies.

For us, freewriting has been a way of integrating student perceptions about spoken and written texts into this required curriculum. Although time constraints and administrative directives often prevent teachers from teaching creatively within a tight curriculum framework, a 3-minute freewriting session can be a tactical break from the routine of instruction. Freewriting gives a high degree of ownership and authenticity to adult students working within a compulsory syllabus. Within the nonthreatening, low-pressure format of freewriting, we have found that even reticent students have a lot to say.

In our classrooms, we write and we *dig* (Macrorie, 1991) a little every day as we encourage focused freewriting using prompts and unfocused freewriting without prompts. However, we have found that focused freewriting tends to yield more penetrating and thoughtful exploration.

During freewriting sessions, students can write about anything, ranging from a simple, evocative word they encounter in the textbook to thematic concepts contained in a unit of work. Frequently, their writing is a reaction to a reading, a more formal writing activity, a video, a discussion, or a listening activity. The aim of freewriting is to encourage students to negotiate the curriculum constantly and actively through expressive writing. Our specific emphasis is on the communicative process rather than the product, although both have been equally inspiring.

We use freewriting strategically across the curriculum. Sometimes freewriting becomes the prelude to a lesson, and, as the students arrive, with their minds full of daily trivialities or more serious concerns, a quick freewriting session creates a space for reflection and settling in. Students begin freewriting without waiting for their peers, and, as the other students arrive, they, too, begin freewriting. This session establishes reflection and expression as part of the daily routine and sets the stage for inquiry, with writers delving into consciousness and personal expression. At other times, we use freewriting to conclude a lesson, enabling the students to depart in a reflective, meditative frame of mind. Before they return to the world outside the class, the students typically have a final minute or two to engage with the content of the lesson and to clarify or struggle with their reactions. They leave the classroom thinking about their writing and the questions their writing generates. We sometimes incorporate freewriting into the flow of the lesson as part of a teachable moment.

By doing freewriting in small increments of 2–5 minutes, the students become less intimidated by the blank page and begin to write for longer periods. We avoid freewriting sessions of more than 5 minutes, as it loses its spontaneity and students are tempted to begin revising, editing, and correcting. We prefer multiple, short freewriting sessions of 2–3 minutes during a 2-hour lesson.

Connecting Freewriting to a Required Curriculum

We incorporated freewriting into the content of the curriculum in a number of ways, as shown in the activities described below that one of us (Kyra) used in her classrooms for intermediate-level and advanced-level English learners. The aim of the first two activities was to prepare students for what was to come by activating prior knowledge and creating an easy segue into new material.

ACTIVITY 1: PREPARING FOR A UNIT OF WORK

As a prelude to a unit on descriptive writing, we gave the students the noun group *The Feeling of a Place* as a prompt for writing and asked them to freewrite for 3 minutes. One advanced-level student responded in this way:

> *Strong wind blowing through me. Sand is in my pockets and my eyes. I can hear only one whispering sound of wind, and no more. Time is endless as well as the place is unknown and far from anything else in my life. Death is walking around since water and thirst are my friend and enemy always around whispering cheerful words one talking about sadness and death the other. Life is a lively feeling never before I was more aware of my own body than now. Some insects come across me. They ignore me and my thoughts, they look for their own needs. (Angel)*

ACTIVITY 2: PREPARING FOR A GRAMMAR STRUCTURE

As a prelude to a grammar focus on the third conditional, we asked the students to write using a word prompt, *Regrets*.

ACTIVITY 3: CONCLUDING A TOPIC

We concluded a unit on the environment with the prompt *How Can We Protect Our Environment?* Here is an unedited freewriting response from a student:

> *We can do many things in order to protect our country and environment. Peru and others undeveloped countries do not have laws to protect their environment that includes oceans, rivers, plants, etc. e.g.: we have a beautiful attraction in Ica city, Paracas, this place has many endangered species that could disappear because there is a new project to generate gas. It is said that they have taken an environment system security and we should not be afraid of seeing our reserve die; but I am not sure about this system. I am not an environment expert but I think we should not allow a gas company to be built, because we usually see on television 'accidents' which destroy our environment. (Nelson)*

ACTIVITY 4: RESPONDING TO DISCUSSION

When a class discussion has finished, students may still have a lot more to say, and a short freewriting session allows for individual closure to a larger group discussion. Writing helps students sort out their perceptions and to reflect on new ones introduced by their peers. It creates a space for reflecting on what has and has not been said. Freewriting encourages students to think aloud to themselves on paper. Following a discussion about a written text on the environment, two students wrote about the discussion in this way:

> *I liked several of the comments and ideas in the discussion. One about how the earth is bleeding, how it will take time to heal itself. Also, we have realized about that we don't feel the necessity of something until we don't have it anymore. (Guillermo)*

> *I got frightened the world has been . . . . We, the people who should take care of it are the ones who endanger it. Maybe we are too selfish. I had never before thought of this before yesterday we read this beautiful speech given by a red man. Let's stop thinking so irresponsible and start taking care of what we have as our support for a better life. Big industries have to assume their responsibilities of preserving nature. (Elena)*

ACTIVITY 5: WRITING PUBLICLY

Freewriting is typically an individual activity, but it can also have a collaborative format. We wrote a prompt—*Community*—on a large piece of wrapping paper and asked students to respond publicly, using magic markers. One variation of this public writing is to place several different prompts around the room and have students move from one to another, switching after 1 minute. Another variation is to pass prompts from person to person and have them write off each other on the same page by starting their writing where another's has stopped.

Working With Freewriting in the Classroom

Initially, students are reluctant to share their work, so it is helpful if the teacher models how to share and how to be an authentic, thoughtful, and interested audience member. In some cases, students simply volunteer to read something from their freewriting to the group, and it is enough to have just one or two students read aloud. At other times, students exchange notebooks with a partner or pile all the notebooks in the center of a circle and randomly select one to read and share a line or two that seems particularly relevant or poignant to them. This works well at the end of a unit or course when the class has 15 minutes to spare. When time allows, sharing can also take the form of a Quaker circle: Students only read when they are moved to share their thoughts, which requires significant self-control on the part of the teacher, who may have to deal with periods of silence. A time saver is to have students exchange writing and anonymously read something that strikes them as interesting.

We try to create an environment where really listening becomes a component of learning and where interruptions are discouraged. While others read or speak, we take mental or written notes, and many of the best questions arise from this time of uninterrupted listening. Of course, questions do not always have answers, and they often lead to more questions and more writing. We model and encourage a question or reaction to what has been written. We discourage students from correcting their peers, we emphasize the differences between response, correction, and editing. If an idea is unclear, teachers can model supportive but challenging responses (e.g., *I'm not sure I understand what you mean here. Could you give me an example, or try to say it in another way?*).

We believe that teachers who write for and with others are better teachers of writing. By freewriting with students, teachers gain a firsthand understanding of the process and the frustrations students encounter when faced with a blank piece of paper. When students see a teacher freewriting, they feel moved to write, too. Listening to teachers read their freewriting, with all its imperfections, helps students understand that the goal of the exercise is not to produce a perfect piece of prose but to engage in a process of writing as thinking aloud.

Freewriting escapes the high stakes of teacher-driven, traditional assessment. To grade freewriting would defeat its purpose in that it would no longer be free. We prefer a self-evaluation approach to freewriting that we typically include in our calculation of class participation. At the beginning of the course, we address students' questions about freewriting with the Freewriting Handout, inspired by Fulwiler (1986).

Evaluating the Curriculum Change

By the time we began freewriting in Peru, freewriting had already been established as a powerful, if controversial, force in North American composition classrooms. One of its earliest critics, Hillocks (1986), derided freewriting as "the act of doodling on paper" (p. 176). Hillocks's early critique, and others that have followed, have failed, however, to dilute the popularity of freewriting. Belanoff et al. (1991) explain that "whatever its position and however individual teachers and writers feel about it, surely freewriting is a familiar strategy to almost everyone in composition" (p. xiii). We argue that freewriting has been less explored in the EFL classroom.

> **Freewriting Handout**
>
> **What Is a Freewriting Journal?**
> A freewriting journal is a space to practice writing and thinking. It is a place where you can write without fear of correction. Write how you feel like writing. No one will read it unless you ask him or her to. From time to time, I will ask volunteers to share either a whole entry, a passage, or a line. If you share frequently, please encourage your classmates to take a turn.
>
> **What to Write**
> Use your freewriting journal to respond to the prompts we take up in class and for spontaneous freewriting. Record your responses to class discussions and readings, or reactions to other issues you may feel like writing about. Go back to your freewriting, respond to what you have written, and invite others to respond to what you have written.
>
> **When to Write**
> We will try to write in our journals every day, but you are welcome to write more whenever you want. Write at home, while you are waiting for the bus, when you are listening to music, or whenever you have a couple of minutes and the spirit moves you.
>
> **Submitting Your Journal**
> At the end of the term, write a one-page introduction to your journal, including an evaluation of its worth to you. You will not submit your journal, only your reflective introduction.

Although we recognize the need for language activities that focus on form and accuracy, freewriting has given us a way of infusing our individual and collective creativity into a required curriculum. Freewriting has transformed the apparently mundane topics we encounter in commercial textbooks into authentic, relevant, contemporary issues. Students often respond passionately and are motivated to express themselves more clearly. They are prompted to search independently for the new vocabulary and structures they need to express their emerging thoughts. Rather than simply regurgitating textual material, paraphrasing, or summarizing, our adult students vigorously interact with texts, ideas, and each other. Freewriting has created a space for ideas to emerge and take form, and the students have gained the confidence to articulate them. Two students wrote about the freewriting sessions in this way:

> *I think it's important to write whatever thought goes through your head because it's real, much more than whatever thought you think about and*

therefore censor. You should never do that. That only limits yourself, your thoughts, your feelings.

I don't know why, but it makes me feel that I can write whatever could be nice or ugly. But I can write. Also, I found that I can write about simple things, like a window . . . . It's awesome. I'm trying to write, but I don't know what. I'm passing from one subject to another, another, another thing is that I am hungry. I wish I could eat the chocolate in my bag, but I can't stop writing.

Conclusion

The National Writing Project (http://www.nwp.org/) provides a wealth of information for teachers who aspire to teach with writing. Certainly, freewriting is not the only kind of writing out there, but we have found it to be a strategic location for teachers and students to begin a dialogue with their individual and collective voices. Although we began freewriting with intermediate-level and advanced-level students, we believe that the beauty of freewriting is that it can be used at all levels. For beginning-level students, freewriting might take the form of a list of nouns, verbs, adjectives, or questions. Beginning-level students might also freewrite in their first languages.

Drawing exclusively from the imaginations of teachers and students, freewriting has no limits. In its rawest form, it has no direction. It requires nothing more than a blank page, a pencil or pen, and a few short minutes. The pen or pencil leads to thought, and across the empty space of the page, ideas emerge. Freewriting taps into the kinesthetic power of thought and locates a required curriculum in the unique and multiple perspectives and realities of students. In Peru, that's *chifa*.

References

Aebersold, J. A., & Field, M. L. (1997). *From reader to reading teacher: Issues and strategies for second language classrooms.* New York: Cambridge University Press.

Allwright, D. (1993). Integrating "research" and "pedagogy": Appropriate criteria and practical possibilities. In J. Edge & K. Richards (Eds.), *Teachers develop teachers research* (pp. 125–135). London: Heinemann.

Allwright, D., & Bailey, K. M. (1991). *Focus on the language classroom: An introduction to classroom research for language teachers.* Cambridge: Cambridge University Press.

Angelou, M. (1981). Life doesn't frighten me. In *Just give me a cool drink of water before I die, oh pray my wings are gonna fit me well, and still I rise* (p. 158). New York: Bantam Books.

Angier, J. (Producer). (1998). *Nova: Lost at sea: The search for longitude* [Videotape]. Boston: WBGH.

Aristizabal, J. J. (2000, February 22). *Longitude: A challenging reading.* Retrieved February 25, 2000, from http://www.amazon.com/gp/product/customer-reviews/0140258795/

Baker, J., & Westrup, H. (2000). *The English language teacher's handbook.* London: Continuum.

Barber, K. S. (2002). The writing of and teaching strategies for students from the Horn of Africa. *Prospect, 17*(2), 3–17.

Belanoff, P., Elbow, P., & Fontaine, S. (1991). *Nothing begins with N: New investigations of freewriting.* Carbondale: Southern Illinois University Press.

Benson, P. (2001). *Teaching and researching autonomy in language learning.* London: Longman.

Blackboard Academic Suite [Computer software]. (2006). Washington, DC: Blackboard. Available from http://www.blackboard.com/

Breen, M., & Candlin, C. (2001). The essentials of a communicative curriculum in language teaching. In D. R. Hall & A. Hewings (Eds.), *Innovation in English language teaching: A reader* (pp. 9–26). London: Routledge.

Breen, M. P., & Littlejohn, A. (2000). The significance of negotiation. In M. P. Breen & A. Littlejohn (Eds.), *Classroom decision-making: Negotiation and process syllabus in practice* (pp. 5–43). Cambridge: Cambridge University Press.

Brindley, G. (1989). *Assessing achievement in the learner-centred curriculum.* Sydney, Australia: National Centre for English Language Teaching and Research.

Brinton, D. M., Snow, M. A., & Wesche, M. B. (1989). *Content-based second language instruction.* New York: Newbury House.

Brooke, R. E. (1991). *Writing and sense of self.* Urbana, IL: National Council of Teachers of English.

Brown, H. D. (2001). *Teaching by principles: An interactive approach to language pedagogy* (2nd ed.). New York: Addison Wesley Longman.

Bryant, F., & Bryant, B. (1958). All I have to do is dream [Recorded by the Everly Brothers]. On *The fabulous style of the Everly Brothers* [Record]. London: London Long Playing.

Burns, A. (1996). Starting all over again: From teaching adults to teaching beginners. In D. Freeman & J. C. Richards (Eds.), *Teacher learning in language teaching* (pp. 154–177). New York: Cambridge University Press.

Burns, A. (1999). *Collaborative action research for English language teachers.* Cambridge: Cambridge University Press.

Burns, A., & de Silva Joyce, H. (1999). *Focus on grammar.* Sydney, Australia: National Centre for English Language Teaching and Research.

Burns, A., & de Silva Joyce, H. (Eds.). (2001). *Teachers' voices 7: Teaching vocabulary.* Sydney, Australia: National Centre for English Language Teaching and Research.

Burns, A., & Joyce, H. (1997). *Focus on speaking.* Sydney, Australia: National Centre for English Language Teaching and Research.

Butt, D. G., Fahey, R., Spinks, S., & Yallop, C. (1995). *Using functional grammar: An explorer's guide.* Sydney, Australia: National Centre for English Language Teaching and Research.

Calkins, L. M. (1986). *The art of teaching writing.* Portsmouth, NH: Heinemann.

Callaghan, M., & Rothery, J. (1988). *Teaching factual writing—a genre based approach.* Sydney, Australia: Disadvantaged Schools Program, Metropolitan East Region.

Candlin, C. N. (1984). Syllabus design as a critical process. *Language Learning and Communication, 3*(2), 129–145.

Candlin, C. N. (1997). General editor's preface. In B. L. Gunnarsson, P. Linnel, & B. Nordberg (Eds.), *The construction of professional discourse* (pp. viii–xiv). London: Longman.

Carr, C. (1994). *The alienist.* New York: Random House.

Carson, J. G. (1993). Reading for writing: Cognitive perspectives. In J. G. Carson & I. Leki (Eds.), *Reading in the composition classroom: Second language perspectives* (pp. 85–104). Boston: Heinle & Heinle.

Choi, S. M. (2000, February 22). *How interesting to know something I have never thought!* Retrieved February 25, 2000, from http://www.amazon.com/gp/product/customer-reviews/0140258795/

Cole, M., & Wertsch, J. (n.d.). *Beyond the individual-social antimony in discussions of Piaget and Vygotsky.* Auckland, New Zealand: Massey University. Retrieved July 17, 2004, from http://www.massey.ac.nz/~alock//virtual/colevyg.htm

Coleman, H. (1987). Little tasks make large return: Task-based language teaching in large crowds. In C. N. Candlin & D. F. Murphy (Eds.), *Language learning tasks* (pp. 121–146). London: Prentice Hall.

Cranmer, D., & Laroy, C. (1992). *Musical openings: Using music in the language classroom.* Harlow, England: Longman.

cummings, e. e. (1998). Since feeling is first. In The American Poetry and Literacy Project (Ed.), *101 great American poems* (p. 74). Mineola, NY: Dover.

Daniels, H. (2002). *Literature circles: Voice and choice in book clubs and reading groups.* Portland, ME: Stenhouse.

Danoff, B., & Nivert, T. (1971). Take me home, country roads [Recorded by John Denver]. On *Poems, prayers, and promises* [Record]. New York: RCA Records.

Davis, C. (1985). *Action research: An investigative approach to personal and school development* (mimeograph). Adelaide: South Australian Education Department.

Dembo, M. H., & Eaton, M. J. (1997). School learning and motivation. In G. D. Phye (Ed.), *Handbook of academic learning: The construction of knowledge* (pp. 65–103). San Diego: Academic Press.

Dickinson, E. (1962). Hope is the thing with feathers. In O. Williams & E. Honig (Eds.), *The Mentor book of major American poets* (p. 187). New York: Mentor Books.

Do, H. T. (1999). Foreign language education policy in Vietnam: The emergence of English and its impact on higher education. In J. Shaw, D. Lubelska, & M. Noullet (Eds.), *Partnership and interaction: Proceedings of the Fourth Annual Conference on Language and Development.* Pathumthani, Thailand: Asian Institute of Technology. Retrieved May 20, 2005, from http://www.languages.ait.ac.th/hanoi_proceedings/hanoi1999.htm

Drury, H. (2001). *Teaching genres in the disciplines: Can students learn the laboratory report genre on-screen.* Retrieved March 3, 2005, from http://learning.uow.edu.au/LAS2001/selected/drury.pdf

Dunkel, P., & Lim, P. (1986). *Intermediate listening comprehension.* Rowley, MA: Newbury House.

Dylan, B. (1962, May). Blowin' in the wind. *Broadside, 6,* 1.

Elbow, P. (1998a). *Writing with power: Techniques for mastering the writing process* (2nd ed.). New York: Oxford University Press.

Elbow, P. (1998b). *Writing without teachers* (2nd ed.). New York: Oxford University Press.

Elbow, P. (2000). *Everyone can write: Essays toward a hopeful theory of writing and teaching writing.* New York: Oxford University Press.

Ellis, R. (1994). *The study of second language acquisition.* Oxford: Oxford University Press.

Feez, S. (1998). *Text-based syllabus design.* Sydney, Australia: National Centre for English Language Teaching and Research.

500 miles. (1962). [Recorded by Peter, Paul, and Mary]. On *Peter, Paul, and Mary* [Record]. Los Angeles: Warner Brothers.

Frank, A. (1993). *Anne Frank: The diary of a young girl.* New York: Bantam. (Original work published 1947)

Freeman, D., & Johnson, K. E. (1998). Reconceptualizing the knowledge-base of language teaching education. *TESOL Quarterly, 32,* 397–417.

Frey, M.V. (1939). Kumbaya [Recorded by Joan Baez]. On *Joan Baez in concert* [Record]. New York: Vanguard.

Frost, R. (1962a). The road not taken. In O. Williams & E. Honig (Eds.), *The Mentor book of major American poets* (p. 250). New York: Mentor Books.

Frost, R. (1962b). Stopping by woods on a snowy evening. In O. Williams & E. Honig (Eds.), *The Mentor book of major American poets* (p. 249). New York: Mentor Books.

Fulwiler, T. (1986). *Teaching with writing.* Upper Montclair, NJ: Boynton/Cook.

Fulwiler, T. (1987). *The journal book.* Upper Montclair, NJ: Boynton/Cook.

Gerot, L. (1995). *Making sense of text*. Gold Coast, Australia: Antipodean Educational Enterprises.

Gerot, L., & Wignell, P. (1994). *Making sense of functional grammar*. Gold Coast, Australia: Antipodean Educational Enterprises.

Goffin, G., & King, C. (1960). Will you still love me tomorrow? [Recorded by Carol King]. On *Tapestry* [Record]. Los Angeles: Ode.

Goldberg, N. (1986). *Writing down the bones: Freeing the writer within*. Boston: Shambhala.

Graves, K. (1996). *Teachers as course developers*. Cambridge: Cambridge University Press.

Gray, J. (1998). The language learner as teacher: The use of interactive diaries in teacher education. *ELT Journal, 52*, 29–37.

Green, A. (1989). *Academic literacy*. Portsmouth, NH: Boynton/Cook Heinemann.

Guglielmino, L. M. (1986). The affective edge: Using songs and music in ESL instruction. *Adult Literacy and Basic Education, 10*(1), 19–26.

Guthrie, W. (1947). This land is your land [Recorded by Pete Seeger]. On *Children's concert at Town Hall* [Record]. New York: Columbia Records.

Hadfield, J. (1998). *Classroom dynamics*. Oxford: Oxford University Press.

Hall, D. R. (2001). Materials production: Theory and practice. In D. R. Hall & A. Hewings (Eds.), *Innovation in English language teaching: A reader* (pp. 229–239). London: Routledge.

Hall, D. R., & Kenny, B. (1988). An approach to a truly communicative methodology: The AIT pre-sessional course. *English for Specific Purposes, 7*, 19–32.

Halliday, M. A. K. (1985). *Spoken and written English*. Geelong, Australia: Deakin University Press.

Halliday, M. A. K. (1994). *An introduction to functional grammar* (2nd ed.). London: Edward Arnold.

Halliday, M. A. K., & Hasan, R. (1985). *Language, context, and text: Aspects of language in a social-semiotic perspective*. Geelong, Australia: Deakin University Press.

Hammond, J., Burns, A., Joyce, H., Brosnan, D., & Gerot, L. (1992). *English for social purposes: A handbook for teachers of adult literacy*. Sydney, Australia: National Centre for English Language Teaching and Research.

Hammond, J., & Gibbons, P. (2001). What is scaffolding? In J. Hammond (Ed.), *Scaffolding: Teaching and learning in language and literacy education* (pp. 1–14). Sydney, Australia: Primary English Teaching Association.

Hawai'i State Department of Education. (2005). *Hawai'i content and performance standards III database.* 2005. Retrieved September 30, 2006, from http://standardstoolkit.k12.hi.us/index.html

Heard, G. (1995). *Writing toward home: Tales and lessons to find your way.* Portsmouth, NH: Heinemann.

Hillocks, G. (1986). *Research on written composition: New directions for teaching.* New York: National Conference on Research in English.

Holliday, A. (1994). *Appropriate methodology and social context.* Cambridge: Cambridge University Press.

Hughes, L. (1949). Mother to son. In L. Hughes & A. Bontemps (Eds.), *Poetry of the Negro 1746–1949* (p. 104). Garden City, NY: Doubleday.

Hughes, L. (1998). Dream deferred (Harlem). In The American Poetry and Literacy Project (Ed.), *101 great American poems* (p. 75). Mineola, NY: Dover.

Intensive English Program. 2001. *AD302 advanced reading and composition syllabus.* Unpublished syllabus, Colorado State University.

Jackson, J. (1998). Reality-based decision cases in ESP teacher education: Windows on practice. *English for Specific Purposes, 17,* 151–168.

Jacobsen, D. A., Eggen, P., & Kauchak, D. (2002). *Methods for teaching: Promoting student learning.* Columbus, OH: Merrill.

Jennings, W., & Horner, J. (1997). My heart will go on [Recorded by Celine Dion]. On *All the way: A decade of song* [CD]. New York: MSN Music.

Johns, A. M. (1993). Reading and writing tasks in English for academic purposes classes: Products, processes, and resources. In J. G. Carson & I. Leki (Eds.), *Reading in the composition classroom: Second language perspectives* (pp. 274–289). Boston: Heinle & Heinle.

Jordan, R. R. (1997). *English for academic purposes: A guide and resource book for teachers.* Cambridge: Cambridge University Press.

Jordon, D. (2002). The notion of two-ways/both ways schooling. *Ngoonjook,* no. 22, 46–47.

Kemmis, S., & McTaggart, R. (Eds.). (1988). *The action research planner.* Geelong, Australia: Deakin University Press.

Kenny, B. (1993). For more autonomy. *System, 21,* 431–442.

Kilmer, J. (1919). Trees. In L. Untermeyer (Ed.), *Modern American poetry* (p. 119). New York: Harcourt, Brace, & Howe.

Kim, Y. G. (2000, February 22). *Read and will find fun.* Retrieved February 25, 2000, from http://www.amazon.com/gp/product/customer-reviews/0140258795/

Klingner, J., & Vaughn, S. (2000). The helping behaviors of fifth graders while using collaborative strategic reading during ESL content classes. *TESOL Quarterly, 34,* 69–98.

Knapp, P., & Watkins, M. (1994). *Context-text-grammar: Teaching the genres and grammar of school writing in infants and primary classrooms.* Broadway, Australia: Text Productions.

Kral, I., & Schwab, R. G. (2003). *The realities of Aboriginal adult literacy acquisition and practice: Implications for remote community capacity building* (Research Paper No. 257). Canberra: The Australian National University, Centre for Aboriginal Economic Policy. Retrieved August 12, 2004, from http://www.anu.edu.au/caepr/Publications/DP/2003_DP257.pdf

Kramsch, C. (1994). *Context and culture in language teaching.* Oxford: Oxford University Press.

Lamb, M. (2002). Explaining successful language learning in difficult circumstances. *Prospect, 17*(2), 35–52.

Lave, J., & Wenger, E. (1990). *Situated learning: Legitimate peripheral participation.* Cambridge: Cambridge University Press.

Le, V. C. (1999). Language and Vietnamese pedagogical contexts. In J. Shaw, D. Lubelska, & M. Noullet (Eds.), *Partnership and interaction: Proceedings of the Fourth Annual Conference on Language and Development.* Pathumthani, Thailand: Asian Institute of Technology. Retrieved May 20, 2005, from http://www.languages.ait.ac.th/hanoi_proceedings/hanoi1999.htm

LeFevre, K. B. (1989). *Invention as a social act.* Urbana: University of Illinois Press.

Legutke, M., & Thomas, H. (1991). *Process and experience in the language classroom.* Harlow, England: Longman.

Leki, I. (1993). Reciprocal themes in ESL reading and writing. In J. G. Carson & I. Leki (Eds.), *Reading in the composition classroom: Second language perspectives* (pp. 9–32). Boston: Heinle & Heinle.

Leland, C., & Fitzpatrick, R. (1994). Cross-age interaction builds enthusiasm for reading and writing. *The Reading Teacher, 47,* 292–301.

Lems, K. (2001). An American poetry project for low intermediate ESL adults. *English Teaching Forum, 39*(4), 24–29.

Li, D. (2001). Teachers' perceived difficulties in introducing the communicative approach in South Korea. In D. R. Hall & A. Hewings (Eds.), *Innovation in English language teaching: A reader* (pp. 149–168). London: Routledge.

Linda, S. (1939). Mbube (Wimoweh) [Recorded by The Weavers]. On *The Weavers at Carnegie Hall* [Record]. New York: Vanguard.

Livingston, J., & Evans, R. (1955). Que sera, sera [Recorded by Doris Day]. On *Que sera, sera* [Record]. New York: Columbia Records.

Lo, R., & Fai Li, H. C. (1998). Songs enhance learner involvement. *English Teaching Forum, 36*(3), 8–11.

Longfellow, H. W. (1962). The arrow and the song. In O. Williams & E. Honig (Eds.), *The Mentor book of major American poets* (p. 83). New York: Mentor Books.

Lynch, A. (2003). The relationship between second and heritage language acquisition: Notes on research and theory building. *Heritage Language Journal, 1*(1). Retrieved August 14, 2004, from http://www.international.ucla.edu/lrc/hlj/article.asp?parentid=3615

MacGowan-Gilhooly, A. (1996). *Achieving clarity in English*. Dubuque, IA: Kendall/Hunt.

Macrorie, K. (1980). *Telling writing* (3rd ed.). Rochelle Park, NJ: Hayden.

Macrorie, K. (1984). *Writing to be read* (Rev. 3rd ed.). Upper Montclair, NJ: Boynton/Cook.

Macrorie, K. (1991). The freewriting relationship. In P. Belanoff, P. Elbow, & S. Fontaine (Eds.), *Nothing begins with N: New investigations of freewriting* (pp. 173–188). Carbondale: Southern Illinois University Press.

Markee, N. (2001). The diffusion of innovation in language teaching. In D. R. Hall & A. Hewings (Eds.), *Innovation in English language teaching: A reader* (pp. 118–126). London: Routledge.

Martin, J. R. (1999). Mentoring semogenesis: "Genre-based" literacy pedagogy. In F. Christie (Ed.), *Pedagogy and the shaping of consciousness: Linguistic and social processes* (pp. 123–155). London: Cassell.

Masefield, J. (1967). Sea fever. In B. J. Thompson (Ed.), *All the silver pennies* (p. 127). New York: Macmillan.

Mayher, J. S. (1990). *Uncommon sense: Theoretical practice in language education*. Portsmouth, NH: Boynton/Cook Heinemann.

Mayher, J. S., Lester, N., & Pradl, G. M. (1983). *Learning to write/writing to learn*. Portsmouth, NH: Boynton/Cook Heinemann.

McBroom, A. (1977). The rose [Recorded by Bette Midler]. In *The Rose* [film]. Hollywood, CA: Twentieth Century Fox.

McCarthy, M., & Carter, R. (1994). *Language as discourse: Perspectives for language teaching*. London: Longman.

McCarthy, M., & Carter, R. (2001). Designing the discourse syllabus. In D. R. Hall & A. Hewings (Eds.), *Innovation in English language teaching: A reader* (pp. 55–63). London: Routledge.

McCourt, F. (1996). *Angela's ashes*. New York: Scribner.

McCourt, F. (1999, October 7). On becoming a teacher. *The New York Times Magazine*, pp. 14–16.

McCourt, F. (2000, August). *Memoir of a memoir*. Paper presented at the Maui Writers Conference, Maui, Hawai'i.

McKay, P. (2006). Teachers introducing change in required curricula for school-age English language learners: Influences and processes. In P. McKay (Ed.), *Planning and teaching creatively within a required curriculum for school-age learners* (pp. 1–11). Alexandria, VA: TESOL.

Michael row the boat ashore [Recorded by Pete Seeger]. (1994). On *Folk music of the world* [CD]. New York: Legacy Records.

Millay, E. (1962a). Love is not all. In O. Williams & E. Honig (Eds.), *The Mentor book of major American poets* (p. 432). New York: Mentor Books.

Millay, E. (1962b). Recuerdo. In O. Williams & E. Honig (Eds.), *The Mentor book of major American poets* (p. 424). New York: Mentor Books.

Moll, L. C., & Gonzalez, N. (1994). Lessons from research with language-minority children. *Journal of Reading Behavior, 25,* 439–456.

Moore, S. H. (1997). Surveying Cambodia: How questionnaire surveys can bring diversity to EFL classrooms. In P. A. Denham (Ed.), *Higher education in Cambodia: Perspectives on an Australian aid project* (pp. 109–118). Belconnen, Australia: University of Canberra Press.

Murphey, T. (1990). *Song and music in language learning: An analysis of pop song lyrics and the use of song and music in teaching English to speakers of other languages*. Bern, Switzerland: Peter Lang.

Murphey, T. (1998). Motivating with near peer role models. In B. Visgatis (Ed.), *On JALT 97: Trends & transitions* (pp. 201–203). Tokyo: Japan Association for Language Teaching.

Murphey, T., & Jacobs, M. (2000). Encouraging critical collaborative autonomy. *JALT Journal, 22,* 228–244.

Neamon, M., & Strong, M. (1992). *Literature circles: Cooperative learning for grades 3–8*. Englewood, CO: Teacher Ideas Press.

Neel, J. (1989). *Plato, Derrida and writing*. Urbana: University of Illinois Press.

New South Wales Adult Migrant English Service. (2003). *Certificate I in spoken and written English*. Surry Hills, Australia: Author.

Nguyen, T. H. A. (2002). Cultural effects on learning and teaching English in Vietnam. *The Language Teacher, 26*(1). Retrieved May 20, 2003, from http://langue.hyper.chubu.ac.jp/jalt/pub/tlt/02/jan/an.html

Nguyen, X. T. (1993). Education in Vietnam: An overview. *Journal of Vietnamese Studies, 6,* 5–23.

Nunan, D. (1988). *The learner-centred curriculum*. Cambridge: Cambridge University Press.

Nunan, D. (Ed.). (1992a). *Collaborative language learning and teaching*. Cambridge: Cambridge University Press.

Nunan, D. (1992b). *Research methods for second language teachers.* Cambridge: Cambridge University Press.

Nunan, D. (1999). *Second language teaching and learning.* London: Heinle & Heinle.

Oldfield, J. (2002). *Building literacy and numeracy for remote-area Aboriginal communities* (Vol. 1). Batchelor, Australia: Batchelor Press.

Oshima, A., & Hogue, A. (1983). *Writing academic English.* Reading, MA: Addison-Wesley.

Pally, M. (2000). *Sustained content teaching in academic ESL/EFL.* Boston: Houghton Mifflin.

Poe, E. A. (1850). Annabel Lee. In T. Powell (Ed.), *The living writers of America* (pp. 126–127). New York: Stringer & Townsend.

Richards, J. C. (1998). *Beyond training.* Cambridge: Cambridge University Press.

Richards, J. C., & Lockhart, C. (1994). *Reflective teaching in second language classrooms.* Cambridge: Cambridge University Press.

Richardson, N. (2001). *Public schooling in the Sandover River region of Central Australia during the 20th century—a critical historical survey.* Unpublished master's thesis, Flinders University, Adelaide, South Australia.

Riis, J., & Sante, L. (1997). *How the other half lives: Studies among the tenements of New York.* New York: Penguin Classics. (Original work published 1890)

Robinson, E. A. (1922). Richard Cory. In The American Poetry and Literacy Project (Ed.), *101 great American poems* (p. 39). Mineola, NY: Dover.

Romano, T. (1995). *Writing with passion.* Portsmouth, NH: Boynton/Cook Heinemann.

Rosenblatt, L. M. (1964). The poem as event. *College English, 26,* 123–128.

Rosenblatt, L. M. (1977). *Literature as exploration.* New York: Noble & Noble. (Original work published 1938)

Rosser, C. (1995). Anne Frank: A content-based research class. *TESOL Journal, 4*(4), 4–6.

Rothery, J., & Stenglin, M. (1994). *Writing a book review: A unit of work for junior secondary English* (Write It Right Resources for Literacy and Learning). Sydney, Australia: Metropolitan East Disadvantaged Schools Programme.

Saliers, E. (1992). Galileo [Recorded by the Indigo Girls]. On *Rites of passage* [CD]. New York: Sony.

Seeger, P. (1961). Where have all the flowers gone? [Recorded by Peter, Paul, and Mary]. On *Peter, Paul, and Mary* [LP]. Los Angeles: Warner Brothers.

Sharon, S. (1980). Cooperative learning in small groups: Recent methods and effects on achievement, attitudes, and ethnic relations. *Review of Educational Research, 50,* 241–271.

Simon, P. (1970). Bridge over troubled water [Recorded by Simon and Garfunkel]. On *Bridge over troubled water* [Record]. New York: Columbia.

Simon, P. (1966). Richard Cory [Recorded by Simon and Garfunkel]. On *Sounds of silence* [Record]. New York: Columbia Records.

Slavin, R., & Cheung, A. (2003). *Effective reading programs for English language learners: A best-evidence synthesis* (Report No. 66). Baltimore, MD: Johns Hopkins University, Center for Research on Education of Students Placed at Risk. Retrieved August 2, 2004, from http://www.csos.jhu.edu/crespar/techreports/report66.pdf

Soars, J., & Soars, L. (1986). *Headway intermediate.* Oxford: Oxford University Press.

Sobel, D. (1995). *Longitude: The true story of a lone genius who solved the greatest scientific problem of his time.* New York: Penguin Books.

Spencer, C., & Arbon, B. (1997). *Foundations of writing: Developing research and academic writing skills.* Lincolnwood, IL: National Textbook Company.

Stevenson, R. L. (1989). The wind. In *A child's garden of verses* (p. 46). San Francisco: Chronicle Books.

Stott, T., & Holt, R. (1991). *First class English for tourism.* Oxford: Oxford University Press.

Summerfield, G., & Summerfield, J. (1989). *Texts and contexts.* Portsmouth, NH: Boynton/Cook.

Swain, M. (1985). Communicative competence: Some roles of comprehensible input and comprehensible output in its development. In C. M. S. Gass (Ed.), *Input in second language acquisition* (pp. 235–256). Rowley, MA: Newbury House.

Swales, J. M., & Feak, C. B. (1994). *Academic writing for graduate students: A course for nonnative speakers of English.* Ann Arbor: University of Michigan Press.

Tollefson, J. W. (Ed.). (1995). *Power and inequality in language education.* Cambridge: Cambridge University Press.

Travis, M. (1955). Sixteen tons [Recorded by T. E. Ford]. On *Sixteen tons* [CD]. Hamburg, Germany: Bear Family Records.

Tribble, C. (1996). *Writing.* Oxford: Oxford University Press.

Vale, D., Scarino, A., & McKay, P. (1993). *Pocket ALL.* Carlton, Australia: Curriculum Corporation.

van Lier, L. (1996). *Interaction in the language curriculum.* London: Longman.

Vygotsky, L. (1972). *Mind in society.* Cambridge, MA: MIT Press.

Wajnryb, R. (1990). *Grammar dictation.* Oxford: Oxford University Press.

Wallace, M. J. (1991). *Educating foreign language teachers.* Cambridge: Cambridge University Press.

Wallace, M. J. (1998). *Action research for language teachers.* Cambridge: Cambridge University Press.

Wilcox, E. W. (1998). Solitude. In The American Poetry and Literacy Project (Ed.), *101 great American poems* (p. 33). Mineola, NY: Dover.

Wilhelm, J., Baker, T., & Dube, J. (2001). *Scaffolding learning.* Retrieved February 7, 2005, from http://www.myread.org/scaffolding.htm

Woodfield, H., & Lazarus, E. (1998). Diaries: A reflective tool on an INSET language course. *ELT Journal, 52,* 315–322.

Woodward, T. (1991). *Models and metaphors in language teacher education: Loop-input and other strategies.* Cambridge: Cambridge University Press.

Wright, T. (1991). *Roles of teachers and learners.* Oxford: Oxford University Press.

Zeichner, K. M., & Liston, D. P. (1996). *Reflective teaching. An introduction.* Mahwah, NJ: Lawrence Erlbaum.

About the Editors and Contributors

Valerie Bainbridge is currently the acting head of the School of Education and Humanities at Batchelor Institute of Indigenous Education, in Australia. She is substantively a senior lecturer in the School for the Preparation for Tertiary Studies. Previously, she managed the ESL programs offered through Batchelor for students whose first language is an Australian Indigenous language. She has worked with Batchelor in program management roles and worked in the South Australian schools sector as a deputy principal, where her major focus was ESL program delivery for migrants and refugees, as well as Indigenous students. She has a particular interest in curriculum development and second language acquisition.

Martyn Brogan has taught English in migrant education settings since 1988. He has taught graduate certificate, diploma, and MA/MTESOL candidates since 1995 in Australia and Vietnam. He lived in Vietnam in 1998 and 1999, and has had positions teaching and coordinating certificate and noncertificate EFL teacher training programs in Vietnam since 1991.

Abigail Brown, an ESL instructor at TransPacific Hawai'i College, in the United States, holds an MA in ESL from the University of Hawai'i (UH). She has taught ESL for more than 13 years and served as reading curriculum coordinator at the Hawai'i English Language Program, UH. She currently serves as sociopolitical action chair for Hawai'i TESOL. Her interests include curriculum design and materials development.

Anne Burns is a professor in the Department of Linguistics and former dean of the Division of Linguistics and Psychology at Macquarie University, Sydney, in Australia. She teaches in the professional doctorate and PhD applied linguistics programs of the department both on-campus and externally. She has conducted extensive research in the Australian Adult Migrant English Program (AMEP), where she specializes in action research in collaboration with teachers of adult ESL learners. She is the editor of *Teaching English from a Global Perspective* (TESOL, 2005).

Helen de Silva Joyce is director of Community and Migrant Education with the New South Wales Department of Education and Training, in Australia. She has been involved in adult education for more than 20 years, specializing in language and literacy and workplace education. In this field, she has worked as a teacher, writer, editor, manager, and researcher. For the past 15 years, she has also been involved in teacher education at the University of Technology, Sydney; Macquarie University; the University of Western Sydney; and the University of Sydney.

Sarah Dodson-Knight teaches French in the Department of Foreign Languages and Literatures at Colorado State University (CSU), in the United States. She has also taught composition and literature to native speakers, ESL, and EFL in France. She occasionally directs plays in French starring CSU students and community members and has presented many workshops on using drama to teach foreign and second languages.

Kyra Garson, a Vancouver, Canada, native, has taught English all over the world, most recently at El Instituto Cultural Peruano-Norteamerico del Cusco, in Peru.

Kathleen Graves is on the graduate faculty at the School for International Training, in the United States. She is the editor of *Teachers as Course Developers* (Cambridge University Press) and author of *Designing Language Courses: A Guide for Teachers* (Heinle & Heinle). In addition to curriculum development, her professional interests include helping teachers create learning communities in their classrooms and collaborative professional communities with fellow teachers.

Todd Heyden holds an MA in TESOL from the School for International Training and a PhD in English education from New York University. He is an associate professor of English at Pace University, in the United States, where he teaches composition and literature.

Janet M. D. Higgins has worked in the United Kingdom, the Middle East, and the Far East as an ESOL teacher and teacher trainer. She has designed and taught study skills and English for specific purposes courses. She is a practical assessor for the British University of Cambridge Local Examination Syndicate Diploma in English Language Teaching to Adults Teacher Certification Scheme, and since 1991 she has worked in Japan.

John Knox has worked as a language teacher for more than 12 years in a variety of EFL and ESL contexts and has been an associate lecturer in the Linguistics Department at Macquarie University, in Australia, since 2000. His research interests include language education, online learning and teaching, media discourse, and intercultural communication.

Kristin Lems is coordinator of the ESL/bilingual education program in the Department of Curriculum and Instruction in National College of Education, National-Louis University, in the United States. She was a Fulbright Scholar in Algeria for 2 years and taught ESL in Iran. Her dissertation was a finalist for the 2005 Outstanding Dissertation of the Year award of the International Reading Association.

John McAndrew is a lecturer in the Department of Linguistics at Macquarie University, in Australia. He has been involved in language teaching for more than 15 years and holds a PhD from Macquarie University. His research interests include the discourse-based approach, communicative language teaching, systemic functional linguistics, critical discourse analysis, and ideology in language.

Martin Momoda has taught ESL/EFL in Japan for more than 15 years and in Thailand for 5 years. He has completed an MA in applied linguistics through Monash University and is finishing an MA in international development through the University of Melbourne. He works on self-study ESL texts for rural Laos supported by the Language Education Support Association.

Stephen H. Moore teaches applied linguistics at Macquarie University, in Australia. His research interests include discourse analysis, English for specific purposes, and testing and evaluation. He taught English in Phnom Penh, Cambodia, from 1994 to 1995 and from 1998 to 2000.

Janine Oldfield has been an ESL teacher since 1996 in Australia, the Philippines, and Cambodia. She has taught in tertiary and ESL institutions as well as nongovernment organizations. She has been an adult education lecturer at Batchelor Institute of Indigenous Education, in Australia, since

2001. She was awarded a master of adult education in 2003 from Deakin University (Victoria). She has special interests in Indigenous education, literacy and numeracy acquisition, and epistemology.

Spencer Salas freewrote with Kyra Garson during his 2-year tour as the U.S. Department of State's senior English language fellow to Peru. He is currently a doctoral candidate at the University of Georgia, in the United States.

Jennifer Wharton is an associate professor of ESL and ESL program coordinator at TransPacific Hawai'i College, in the United States. She has taught ESL for more than 15 years in Massachusetts, Taiwan, and Hawai'i. She also served as president and program chair for Hawai'i TESOL. Her interests include content-based instruction and curriculum development.

Index

Page numbers followed by an *f, t,* or *n* indicate figures, tables, or footnotes.

A

Action research. *See also* TESOL postgraduate program
    defined, 10
    introduction to, 59–60
    large/mixed-ability classes and, 90–92
    maintenance of learning and, 68–71
    method change/introduction and, 75–80
    modified loop-input techniques and, 66
    motivating students and, 71–74
    needs analysis and, 61
    postcourse, 67–68
    student interactions and, 80–89
    syllabus design and, 89
Active questioning, 209–212
Activities
    Advanced Reading and Composition and, 150–151
    business presentation course and, 208–219, 214*f,* 215–217*f,* 219*t*
    freewriting within a curriculum and, 242–243
    garden design project and, 23*t,* 24*f,* 25*f,* 26*f*
    planning and, v–vi
    student interactions and, 81–82
    TransPacific Hawai'i College (TPHC) program, 98, 116–117, 117–118

AD302. *See* Advanced Reading and Composition
Adopters, defined, 6
Advanced Reading and Composition
    conclusions, 156
    curriculum context and, 146–147
    evaluation and, 154–156
    introduction to, 143
    motivation for curriculum adaptation and, 143–145
    paraphrasing exercise and, 158–159
    reading circle handout and, 156–157
    syllabus design and, 147–154
    timeline for, 148*t*
Aebersold, J. A., 145
Airport Project. *See* English for Tourism III (EFT III)
The Alienist. *See* Freshman composition course
"All I Have to Do is Dream," 187*t*
Allwright, D., 10, 69
American poetry performance project, 180–188
Angela's Ashes, 165
Angelou, M., 182*t*
"Annabel Lee," 182*t*
Anne Frank's diary, 166
Anti-writing, 164
AR. *See* Action research
Arbon, 144
Argument genre, 227*f*, 233–236, 236*f*
Aristizabal, J. J., 152
Arithmetic, garden design project and, 23*t*, 27
"The Arrow and the Song," 182*t*
Assessment
    English for Tourism III (EFT III) and, 135–138, 136*t*
    oral EFL class and, 203
    self, 129*f*, 136*t*
Assumptions, 2, 215–217*f*
Ateneo de Manila University of the Philippines. *See* Cambodia Development Resource Institute (CDRI)

Attributes, 231*f*, 232*f*
Australia. *See* Batchelor Institute of Indigenous Tertiary Education (BIITE)

B

Bailey, K. M., 69
Bainbridge, V., 2, 5–6, 8, 12, 259. *See also* Garden design project
Barber, K. S., 32
Batchelor Institute of Indigenous Tertiary Education (BIITE)
    conclusions, 31–35
    curriculum context and, 17–20
    evaluation and, 27–31
    introduction to, 15–16
    motivation for curriculum adaptation and, 17
    outcomes of, 22*t*
    process of curriculum adaptation and, 20–26
    project activities and, 23*t*, 24*f*, 25*f*, 26*f*, 28*f*, 34*f*, 35–42, 35*f*, 36*f*, 38*f*
    Students Making Garden Feature, 16*f*, 19*f*
"The Beautiful Rainbow," 111*f*. *See also* TransPacific Hawai'i College (TPHC) program
Belanoff, P., 240, 244
Benson, P., 126
Bibliographies, freshman composition course and, 172*t*
BIITE. *See* Batchelor Institute of Indigenous Tertiary Education (BIITE)
Blackboard, 166
Bligh, D. A., 58
"Blowin' in the Wind," 187*t*
Boards, online, 166–169, 167*t*
Book reviews, Advanced Reading and Composition and, 151
Both Ways philosophy, 20
Brainstorming, business presentation course and, 206*t*
Breen, M., 5, 193, 203
"Bridge Over Troubled Water," 187*t*
Brindley, G., 126, 128
Brogan, M., 2, 259. *See also* TESOL postgraduate program
Brown, A., 2, 6, 8, 12, 259. *See also* TransPacific Hawai'i College (TPHC) program

Bryant, B., 187*t*
Bryant, F., 187*t*
Buddhism, 183
Burns, A., 1–14, 198, 259–260
Business presentation course
    activity design and, 208–219, 214*f*, 215–217*f*, 219*t*
    curriculum context and, 205–208
    evaluation and, 219–220, 219*f*
    introduction to, 205
    outline of, 206*t*
Butt, D. G., 222, 226, 234

C

CADT. *See* Certificate I in Applied Design and Technology (CADT)
Calkins, L. M., 169
Cambodia, 9. *See also* Intensive EAP writing course
Cambodia Development Resource Institute (CDRI)
    course design and, 226–237
    curriculum context and, 222–225, 224*t*
    evaluation and, 237–238
    introduction to, 221
    motivation for curriculum adaptation and, 221–222
    scaffolding and, 229*f*, 230*f*, 231*f*, 232*f*
Candlin, C., 126, 189, 193, 203
Carr, C. *See* Freshman composition course
Carson, J. G., 145
Carter, R., 122
CAT. *See* Centre for Appropriate Technology (CAT)
CDRI. *See* Cambodia Development Resource Institute (CDRI)
Center-to-periphery model, 3–5, 4*t*
Centre for Appropriate Technology (CAT)
    conclusions, 31–35
    curriculum context and, 17–20
    evaluation and, 27–31
    introduction to, 15–16
    motivation for curriculum adaptation and, 17

    outcomes of, 22*t*

    process of curriculum adaptation and, 20–26

    project activities and, 23*t*, 24*f*, 25*f*, 26*f*, 28*f*, 34*f*, 35–42, 35*f*, 36*f*, 38*f*

    Students Making Garden Feature, 16*f*, 19*f*

Certificate I in Applied Design and Technology (CADT)

    conclusions, 31–35

    curriculum context and, 17–20

    evaluation and, 27–31

    introduction to, 15–16

    motivation for curriculum adaptation and, 17

    outcomes of, 22*t*

    process of curriculum adaptation and, 20–26

    project activities and, 23*t*, 24*f*, 25*f*, 26*f*, 28*f*, 34*f*, 35–42, 35*f*, 36*f*, 38*f*

    Students Making Garden Feature, 16*f*, 19*f*

Certificates in Spoken and Written English (CSWE)

    conclusions, 31–35

    curriculum context and, 17–20

    evaluation and, 27–31

    introduction to, 15–16

    motivation for curriculum adaptation and, 17

    outcomes of, 22*t*

    process of curriculum adaptation and, 20–26

    project activities and, 23*t*, 24*f*, 25*f*, 26*f*, 28*f*, 34*f*, 35–42, 35*f*, 36*f*, 38*f*

    Students Making Garden Feature, 16*f*, 19*f*

Change, curriculum

    accounts of practice and, 12–13

    action research and, 75–80

    drive for, 5–6

    extent of, 6–9

    learning from, 9–12

    scale of, 7*f*

Change agents, defined, 6

Characteristics, 231*f*, 232*f*

Cheung, A., 33

Chifa, 239. *See also* Freewriting within a curriculum

Choi, S. M., 152

Classification, 231*f*, 232*f*

Classrooms, changes within, 7*f*, 8

Classrooms, learner-centered, 98–99

Clients, defined, 6

Cloze exercises, 30–31, 185

CLT. *See* Communication language teaching (CLT)

Cohesive devices, Advanced Reading and Composition and, 150–151

Cole, M., 18

Coleman, H., 122

Collaborative learning models, 99

College students, working with elementary students. *See* TransPacific Hawai'i College (TPHC) program

Communication language teaching (CLT), 189, 193–194. *See also* Oral EFL class

Community involvement, 96–97

Competencies, reinforcement of, 95

Components, changes within, 7*f*, 8

Computers, 30, 54–56*t*, 166–169, 167*t*

Construction, teaching-learning cycle and, 192*f*

Consumers, 123

Content, 32–33, 47–48, 197–203

Context

    Advanced Reading and Composition and, 146–147

    business presentation course and, 205–208, 209

    English for Tourism III (EFT III) and, 123–126, 124*f*

    freewriting within a curriculum and, 240–241

    freshman composition course and, 163–165

    garden design project and, 17–20

    impact of, 33

    intensive EAP writing course and, 222–225

    oral EFL class and, 190, 194–196

    study skills program and, 45–46

    study skills program (SSP) and, 45–46

    teaching-learning cycle and, 192*f*

    TESOL postgraduate program and, 60–63

    TransPacific Hawai'i College (TPHC) program and, 100–105, 101*f*

Context-Text-Grammar: Teaching the Genres and Grammar of School Writing in Infants and Primary Classrooms, 226

Contextualizing language, as a teaching strategy, 29
Continuing education. *See* TESOL postgraduate program
Contradictions, business presentation course and, 215–217*f*
Conversational English. *See* Oral EFL class
Cooper, 6
Cranmer, D., 186
Critical inquiry, 212–219, 214*f*, 215–217*f*, 219*t*
CSWE. *See* Certificates in Spoken and Written English (CSWE)
Cultural considerations
    business presentation course and, 207, 208
    curriculum change and, 6
    garden design project and, 31
    study skills program and, 54–56*t*
    TransPacific Hawai'i College (TPHC) program and, 112–113*t*, 116–117
cummings, e. e., 180, 182*t*
Curriculum. *See also specific curriculum titles*
    changes within. *See* Change, curriculum
    defined, vii
    as dynamic system, v–vi
    models of, 4*t*
    outcomes of, 21–22
    overview to making changes in, 1–3
    requirements for English language teaching in Vietnam and, 61–62
    requirements of, 3–5
    TransPacific Hawai'i College (TPHC) program and, 100–105, 101*f*, 105–109

D

Daniels, H., 149
Danoff, B., 187*t*
Darcy, S., 29
Data collection, project design and, 130*t*, 131–132
De facto model, 3–5, 4*t*
de Silva Joyce, H., 1–14, 260
Decision making, defined, 208

Deconstruction, teaching-learning cycle and, 192*f*

Definitions, asking for, 215–217*f*

Dembo, M. H., 64

Description, 227*f*, 229–232, 230*f*

Developmental considerations, 96

Devices, cohesive, Advanced Reading and Composition and, 150–151

Diaries, learner, 136*t*. See also Double-entry journals

Dickinson, E., 182*t*

The Dictator, as an activity, 213

Discussion boards, online, 166–169, 167*t*

Discussion genre, 236–237, 237*f*

Discussion skills, study skills program and, 54–56*t*

Dodson-Knight, S., 2, 6, 8, 260. See also Advanced Reading and Composition

Double-entry journals, 169–171

"Dream Deferred," 182*t*

Drury, H., 193

Dunkel, P., 229*f*

Dylan, B., 187*t*

E

EAL. See English as an additional language (EAL)

EAP. See English for academic purposes (EAP)

Eaton, M. J., 64

Educational context, vi*f*

EFL. See English as a foreign language (EFL)

EFT III. See English for Tourism III (EFT III)

Eggen, P., 64

Elbow, P., 240

Elementary students. See TransPacific Hawai'i College (TPHC) program

Ellis, R., 64

English as a foreign language (EFL), 2. See also Business presentation course; Freewriting within a curriculum; Oral EFL class; TESOL postgraduate program

English as a second language (ESL), 2. See also Advanced Reading and Composition; Freshman composition course; Garden design project;

Grammar-based adult ESL program; TransPacific Hawai'i College (TPHC) program

English as an additional language (EAL), 2

English for academic purposes (EAP), 2. *See also* Advanced Reading and Composition; Freewriting within a curriculum; Freshman composition course; Grammar-based adult ESL program; Intensive EAP writing course; Oral EFL class; Study skills program (SSP)

English for Hotel Management, 120

English for Secretarial Science, 120

English for specific purposes (ESP), 2, 79–80. *See also* Business presentation course; English for Tourism III (EFT III)

English for Tourism III (EFT III)
- assessment/evaluation and, 135–139
- classes for, 120*t*
- conclusions, 139
- course outlines and, 140–141
- curriculum context and, 123–126, 124*f*
- curriculum overview and, 130*t*
- introduction to, 119–120
- Language Analysis Assignment and, 137*f*
- motivation for curriculum adaptation and, 120–123
- needs analysis and, 127*f*
- overview of, 142*t*
- processes of, 126–128
- project design and, 128–135
- project stages and, 130*t*

English to speakers of other languages (ESOL), 2

ESL. *See* English as a second language (ESL)

ESOL. *See* English to speakers of other languages (ESOL)

ESP. *See* English for specific purposes (ESP)

Evaluation
- action research and, 66
- Advanced Reading and Composition and, 154–156
- business presentation course and, 206*t*, 219–220, 219*f*
- English for Tourism III (EFT III) and, 133*f*, 138–139, 138*f*
- freewriting within a curriculum and, 244–246
- intensive EAP writing course and, 237–238

Evaluation *(continued)*
    processes of, vi, vi*f*
    project design and, 130*t*
    study skills program and, 48–51, 52*t*, 53, 56–57
    TransPacific Hawai'i College (TPHC) program and, 109–110
Evans, R., 187*t*
Exams
    action research and, 78, 83
    assessment and, 136*t*
    grammar-based adult ESL program and, 179
    International English Language Testing System (IELTS) and, 223
Expansion, 227*f*
Experiential Cycle, 138*f*
Explanation genre, 232–233, 233*f*

F

Facility considerations, study skills program and, 48
Facts, business presentation course and, 215–217*f*
Fahey, R., 222
Feak, C. B., 222
Feedback. *See* Evaluation
Feez, S., 190
Fiction as a teaching tool. *See* Freshman composition course
Field, M. L., 145, 190, 192*f*
Fitzpatrick, R., 97, 110–111
"500 Miles," 187*t*
Fluency, 163, 297
Fontaine, S., 240
Form, function and, 227*f*
Forums, Advanced Reading and Composition and, 151
Foundations of Writing: Developing Research and Academic Writing Skills, 143–144
Freeman, 13
Freewriting within a curriculum
    conclusions, 246
        connecting freewriting to a curriculum and, 242–243

curriculum context and, 240–241
evaluation and, 244–246
freewriting handout and, 245*f*
introduction to, 239
motivation for curriculum adaptation and, 239–240
working with in a classroom and, 243–244

Freshman composition course
conclusions, 174–176
curriculum context and, 163–165
introduction to, 161
motivation for curriculum adaptation and, 161–163
process of curriculum adaptation and, 165–174
reacting to quotations from the novel and, 170*f*
rewriting a passage in a different voice and, 171*f*
sample letters and, 168*f*

Frey, M. V., 187*t*
Frost, R., 182*t*
Fulwiler, T., 240, 244
Function, form and, 227*f*

G

Galileo. *See* Advanced Reading and Composition
Garden design project
conclusions, 31–35
curriculum context and, 17–20
evaluation and, 27–31
illustrated, 16*f,* 19*f*
introduction to, 15–16
motivation for curriculum adaptation and, 17
outcomes of, 22*t*
overview of, 20–21
process of curriculum adaptation and, 20–26
project activities and, 23*t,* 24*f,* 25*f,* 26*f,* 28*f,* 34*f,* 35–42, 35*f,* 36*f*

Garson, K., 2, 5, 260. *See also* Freewriting within a curriculum
Generic model, 3–5, 4*t*
Genre, 192*f,* 222, 226–228

Gerot, L., 222, 226
Gibbons, P., 228
Goals
    Advanced Reading and Composition and, 153
    goals-objectives model and, 3–5, 4*t*
    of learning, v
Goffin, G., 187*t*
Goldberg, N., 240
Grammar, 91. *See also specific course titles*
Grammar-based adult ESL program
    American poetry performance project and, 180–188
    conclusions, 188
    curriculum context and, 178–179
    introduction to, 177
    process of curriculum adaptation and, 180
Graves, K., 9, 260
Gray, J., 66
Green, A., 165
Group work, 30, 87–88
Guglielmino, L. M., 180
Guided discussion, TransPacific Hawai'i College (TPHC) program and, 116–117
Guthrie, W., 187*t*

H

Hadfield, J., 69
Haiku, 183–185, 184*f*
Hall, D. R., 120, 122, 126, 139
Halliday, M. A. K., 190, 222
Hammond, J., 228
Hanoi University of Foreign Studies (HANU)
    conclusions, 71
    context/problems and, 60–63
    history of, 62–63
    introduction to, 59–60
    large/mixed-ability classes and, 90–92

    maintenance of learning and, 68–71
    method change/introduction and, 75–80
    motivating students and, 71–74
    participants of, 63–64
    postcourse action research and, 67–68
    program design and, 64–67
    student interactions and, 80–89
    syllabus design and, 89
HANU. *See* Hanoi University of Foreign Studies (HANU)
Hasan, R., 190
Hawai'i, 8. *See also* TransPacific Hawai'i College (TPHC) program
Hawai'i State Department of Education, 95
Heard, G., 240
Heyden, T., 2, 260. *See also* Freshman composition course
Higgins, J. M. D., 2, 8, 12, 260–261. *See also* Study skills program (SSP)
High school students, 93
Higher-level students, working with, 26
Hillocks, G., 244
Holliday, A., 61
"Hope Is the Thing With Feathers," 182*t*
Horner, J., 187*t*
Hotel Management, English for, 120
How the Other Half Lives, 173
Hughes, L., 182*t*
Hypothetical questions, business presentation course and, 215–217*f*

I

IELTS. *See* International English Language Testing System (IELTS)
Implementers, defined, 6
Impromptu speeches, business presentation course and, 206*t*
Inbound tourism. *See* English for Tourism III (EFT III)
Incentive, business presentation course and, 209
Independent construction, teaching-learning cycle and, 192*f*
Innovation. *See* Change, curriculum
Institutions
    changes within, 7*f*, 8

Institutions *(continued)*
  needs of, v
  philosophies of, 18–20
  requirements of, 3
El Instituto Cultural Peruano-Norteamerico del Cusco (ICPNA Cusco)
  conclusions, 246
  connecting freewriting to a curriculum and, 242–243
  curriculum context and, 240–241
  evaluation and, 244–246
  freewriting handout and, 245*f*
  introduction to, 239
  motivation for curriculum adaptation and, 239–240
  working with in a classroom and, 243–244
Intensive EAP writing course
  course design and, 226–237
  curriculum context and, 222–225, 224*t*
  evaluation and, 237–238
  introduction to, 221
  motivation for curriculum adaptation and, 221–222
  scaffolding and, 229*f,* 230*f,* 231*f,* 232*f*
Intensive English Program (IEP). *See* Advanced Reading and Composition; Intensive EAP writing course
Interactions, student, 80–89
International English Language Testing System (IELTS), 223
Interviewing, 133*f*
Isolation, as a challenge, 96

J

Jacobs, M., 97, 99
Jacobsen, D. A., 64
Japan, 8, 9, 183. *See also* Business presentation course; Okinawa University; Oral EFL class
Jennings, W., 187*t*
Johns, A. M., 145
Johnson, K. E., 13
Joint construction, teaching-learning cycle and, 192*f*

Jordan, R. R., 222
Jordon, D., 19
Journals. *See* Diaries, learner; Double-entry journals
Joyce, H., 198

K

Kauchak, D., 64
Kemmis, S., 10
Kenny, B., 123, 126, 139
Kilmer, J., 182*t*
Kim, Y. G., 152
King, C., 187*t*
Klingner, J., 99
Knapp, P., 226, 227*f*, 228, 229, 232, 233*f*, 234
Knox, J., 2, 8, 261. *See also* English for Tourism III (EFT III)
Kral, I., 18
"Kumbaya," 187*t*

L

Lamb, M., 33
Language, challenges of, 32–33
Language Analysis Assignment, 137*f*
Large classes, 90–92
Laroy, C., 186
Lave, J., 26
Lazarus, E., 66
Learner diaries, 136*t*
Learner-centered classrooms, 98–99, 123
Learning
    learner-centered, 98–99
    processes of, vi, vi*f*
    styles of, 69–70
LeFevre, K. B., 167
Legutke, M., 121, 122, 127, 128, 129, 130, 132, 135–136
Leki, I., 144, 145, 154

Leland, C., 97, 110–111
Lems, K., 2, 4, 8–9, 13, 182, 261. *See also* Grammar-based adult ESL program
Lester, 163
"Life Doesn't Frighten Me," 182*t*
Lim, P., 229*f*
Limitations, curriculum change and, 10, 11*f*
Linda, S., 187*t*
Listening skills, 23*t*, 73, 77, 124*f*
Liston, D. P., 13–14
Literature circles, 149
Littlejohn, A., 5
Livingston, J., 187*t*
Logic inspection, business presentation course and, 215–217*f*
Longfellow, H. W., 182*t*
Loop-input techniques, modified, 66
"Love Is Not All," 182*t*
Lynch, A., 32

M

Macdonald, 126
MacGowan-Gilhooly, A., 162, 163, 165, 176
Macrorie, K., 240, 241
Masefield, J., 182*t*
Materials, planning and, v–vi
Mathematics, garden design project and, 23*t*, 27
Maturation, as a challenge, 96
Mayher, J. S., 110–111, 163, 170
"Mbube (Wimoweh)," 187*t*
McAndrew, J., 5, 9, 13, 261. *See also* Oral EFL class
McBroom, A., 187*t*
McCarthy, M., 122
McCourt, F., 12, 93, 165
McKay, P., 3, 70
McTaggart, R., 10
Memorization, rote, 188

"Michael Row the Boat Ashore," 187*t*

"Mike and the Star," 94*f*. *See also* TransPacific Hawai'i College (TPHC) program

Millay, E., 182*t*

Mixed-ability classes, 90–92

Mixed-age reading dyads, 97–98. *See also* TransPacific Hawai'i College (TPHC) program

Mode, defined, 190

Modified loop-input techniques, 66

Momoda, M., 2, 6, 13, 261. *See also* Business presentation course

Moore, S., 2, 9, 13, 261. *See also* Intensive EAP writing course

"Mother to Son," 182*t*

Motivation
- action research and, 71–74
- curriculum change and, 6, 10
- English for Tourism III (EFT III) and, 120–123
- freewriting within a curriculum and, 239–240
- freshman composition course and, 161–163
- garden design project and, 17
- intensive EAP writing course and, 221–222
- oral EFL class and, 189–190
- study skills program and, 43–45
- TransPacific Hawai'i College (TPHC) program and, 95–97

Murphey, T., 97, 99, 186

Music, 151, 185–188, 187*t*. *See also* Grammar-based adult ESL program

"My Heart Will Go On," 187*t*

N

Narration, 227*f*

"The Naughty Ghost," 98*f*. *See also* TransPacific Hawai'i College (TPHC) program

Neamon, M., 149

Needs analysis, 61, 127*f*

Neel, J., 164

Nemawashi, defined, 208

New South Wales Adult Migrant English Service (NSW AMES), 15

Nivert, T., 187*t*

Nonfiction as a teaching tool. *See* Advanced Reading and Composition

Nonverbal communication, 49–50*t*, 206*t*

Novels as a teaching tool. *See* Freshman composition course

NSW AMES. *See* New South Wales Adult Migrant English Service (NSW AMES)

Nunan, D., 70, 126

O

Objectives, models and. *See* Goals

Observation
    action research and. *See* Action research
    business presentation course and, 209–212, 212–219

Okinawa University
    conclusions, 57–58
    content/tasks and, 49–50*t*, 54–56*t*
    curriculum context and, 45–46
    development of 2000 program and, 46–51
    development of 2001 program and, 51–53
    development of 2002 program and, 53–57
    introduction to, 43
    motivation for curriculum adaptation and, 43–45
    resources, 58

Oldfield, J., 2, 5–6, 8, 12, 28, 261–262. *See also* Garden design project

Online discussion boards, 166–169, 167*t*

Opening
    business presentation course and, 206*t*
    project design and, 128–131, 130*t*

Oral EFL class
    conclusions, 203–204
    course design and, 196–203
    curriculum context and, 194–196
    introduction to, 189
    model casual conversation task and, 200*f*, 201*f*
    motivation for curriculum adaptation and, 189–190
    role-plays and, 202*f*
    theoretical foundation for the course and, 190–194, 191*t*, 192*f*

Oral skills. *See* Speaking skills
Order, 227*f*
Organization, planning and, v
Orientation, 128–131, 130*t*, 132–134, 231*f*, 232*f*
Originality, 106–107
Outbound tourism. *See* English for Tourism III (EFT III)
Outcomes, 3–5, 4*t*, 21–22, 27–29, 102–104
Overseas Vocational Training Association. *See* Business presentation course
Ownership, defined, 19–20

P

Pally, M., 162, 165
Paraphrasing, Advanced Reading and Composition and, 151, 158–159
Pedagogical reasoning skills, 66
Peer assessment, 136*t*
Peer teaching, 99
Periphery model. *See* Center-to-periphery model
Persuasive techniques, business presentation course and, 206*t*
Peru. *See* Freewriting within a curriculum
Philosophies, institutional, 18–20
Physical involvement, as a teaching strategy, 29
Plagiarism, 106–107
Planning
    action research and. *See* Action research
    processes of, v, vi*f*
Poe, E. A., 182*t*
Poetry, 181–183, 182*t*, 183–185, 184*f*. *See also* Grammar-based adult ESL program
Practice, garden design project and, 23*t*
Pradl, G. M., 163
Prediction, Advanced Reading and Composition and, 150
Preliterate students, working with, 22–25
Presentation, 130*t*, 134–135, 186–188
Process of Change, 10, 11*f*
Process writing, 100
Producers, 123

Program, defined, vii
Project learning, English for Tourism III (EFT III) and, 121–122
Project stages, 130t
Proposals, freshman composition course and, 172t

Q

"Que Sera, Sera," 187t
Questioning, active, 209–212
Quotations, 151, 170f

R

Reading circles, 149, 156–157
Reading skills
    action research and, 79
    advanced. *See* Advanced Reading and Composition
    English for Tourism III (EFT III) and, 124f
    garden design project and, 23t, 27, 38–41, 38f
    study skills program and, 49–50t, 54–56t
    TransPacific Hawai'i College (TPHC) program and, 102–104
Real-world task, 122
Reasoning skills, 66
"Recuerdo," 182t
Reflection
    action research and. *See* Action research
    business presentation course and, 209–212, 212–219
    freshman composition course and, 172t
Registered Training Organizations (RTOs), 27
Repetition, as a teaching strategy, 30
Replanning, action research and. *See* Action research
Research, project design and, 130t, 131–132
Research papers, freshman composition course and, 171–174, 172t
Resisters, defined, 6
Reviews, book, Advanced Reading and Composition and, 151
Revision, business presentation course and, 209–212, 212–219
"Richard Cory," 182t, 183

Richards, J. C., 66
Richardson, N., 18
Riis, J., 173
"The Road Not Taken," 182*t*
Robinson, E. A., 182*t*, 183
Role-playing, 23*t*, 26*f*, 151, 202*f*
Roles, student, 149–150, 157
Romano, T., 175
"The Rose," 187*t*
Rosenblatt, L. M., 170, 180
Rosser, C., 166
Rote memorization, 188
RTOs. *See* Registered Training Organizations (RTOs)
Rubin, 32

S

Salas, S., 2, 5, 262. *See also* Freewriting within a curriculum
Sante, L., 173
Scaffolding
    intensive EAP writing course and, 228–237, 229*f*, 230*f*, 231*f*, 232*f*, 233*f*, 236*f*, 237*f*
    oral EFL class and, 191–193
    as a teaching strategy, 29–30
Scale of Change Through Curriculum Innovation, 7*f*
Scanning, Advanced Reading and Composition and, 150
Scarino, A., 70
"Scary Story," 104*f*. *See also* TransPacific Hawai'i College (TPHC) program
Schwab, R. G., 18
Script writing, business presentation course and, 206*t*
"Sea Fever," 182*t*
Seating considerations, 80–81, 91
Secretarial Science, English for, 120
Seeger, P., 187*t*
Self-assessment, 129*f*, 136*t*
Sentences, topic, 230*f*
Sequence, 227*f*

Setting, teaching-learning cycle and, 192*f*
Sharon, S., 99
Simon, P., 183, 187*t*
"Since feeling Is first," 182*t*
Singing, 186
Site visits, freshman composition course and, 172*t*
"Sixteen Tons," 187*t*
Skimming, Advanced Reading and Composition and, 150
Slavin, R., 33
Soars, J., 61
Soars, L., 61
Sobel, D. *See* Advanced Reading and Composition
Social context, vi*f*
Socioeconomic considerations, curriculum change and, 6
"Solitude," 182*t*
Speaking skills. *See also* Oral EFL class
    action research and, 74
    garden design project and, 23*t*, 27
    study skills program and, 49–50*t*, 54–56*t*
    as a teaching strategy, 30
Spelling, garden design project and, 23*t*, 36–37, 41–42
Spencer, C., 144
Spinks, S., 222
SSP. *See* Study skills program (SSP)
Stevenson, R. L., 182*t*
"Stopping by Woods on a Snowy Evening," 182*t*
Storyboarding, 117–118
Strategies
    learning, 47, 102
    teaching, 29–30, 99
Strong, M., 149
Students, interactions of, 80–89
Study methods, 47, 49–50*t*
Study skills program (SSP)
    conclusions, 57–58
    content/tasks and, 49–50*t*, 54–56*t*
    curriculum context and, 45–46

    development of 2000 program and, 46–51
    development of 2001 program and, 51–53
    development of 2002 program and, 53–57
    introduction to, 43
    motivation for curriculum adaptation and, 43–45
    resources, 58
Studying abroad, 154
Success, issues affecting, 30–31
Summarizing, Advanced Reading and Composition and, 151
Summerfield, J., 164
Sustainability, 9–10, 60, 162
Swain, M., 180
Swales, J. M., 222
Syllabus design, 89, 126–128, 147–154, 191*t*
Synthesis, freshman composition course and, 172*t*
System, v, 3

T

"Take Me Home, Country Roads," 187*t*
Target language use, 95–96
Target task, 122
Task-based communicative activities, 98
Teachers of English to Speakers of Other Languages. *See* TESOL postgraduate program
Teaching
    avoiding burnout in, 1
    continuing education and. *See* TESOL postgraduate program
    learner-centered classrooms and, 98–99
    peer teaching strategies, 99
    processes of, vi, vi*f*
    reducing teacher talk and, 80–89
    scaffolding and. *See* Scaffolding
    strategies for, 29–30
    teacher education models and, 65–67
Teaching-learning cycle, oral EFL class and, 191–193, 192*f*
Technique, business presentation course and, 209

Technology
- online discussion boards and, 166–169, 167*t*
- study skills program and, 54–56*t*
- as a teaching strategy, 30

Temple Tour Project. *See* English for Tourism III (EFT III)

Tenor, defined, 190

TESOL postgraduate program
- conclusions, 71
- context/problems and, 60–63
- history of, 62–63
- introduction to, 59–60
- large/mixed-ability classes and, 90–92
- maintenance of learning and, 68–71
- method change/introduction and, 75–80
- motivating students and, 71–74
- participants of, 63–64
- postcourse action research and, 67–68
- program design and, 64–67
- student interactions and, 80–89
- syllabus design and, 89

Test of English as a Foreign Language (TOEFL), 100

Text type, intensive EAP writing course and, 222

Text-based approach, oral EFL class and, 190–191, 191*t*

Textbooks, lack of. *See* Advanced Reading and Composition

Thailand, 8. *See also* English for Tourism III (EFT III)

"The Road Not Taken," 182*t*

Theory, curriculum change and, 5

Theory, practice and, 9–10

"This Land is Your Land," 187*t*

Thomas, H., 121, 122, 127, 128, 129, 130, 132, 135–136

Time management, study skills program and, 47, 49–50*t*

Titanic, 187

TOEFL, 100

Topic sentences, 230*f*

Tourism. *See* English for Tourism III (EFT III)

TransPacific Hawai'i College (TPHC) program
- conclusions, 110–112

curriculum adaptation and, 105–109
curriculum context and, 100–105, 101*f*
evaluation and, 109–110
introduction to, 93–95
motivation for, 95–97
overview of, 114–115
participants of, 104–105, 105*t*
pedagogical principles of, 97–100
project flowchart for, 115*f*
sample activity for, 116–117, 117–118
timeline for, 112–113*t*

Travis, M., 187*t*

"Trees," 182*t*

Tribble, C., 222

U

Utopia. *See* Batchelor Institute of Indigenous Tertiary Education (BIITE)

V

Vale, D., 70

van Lier, L., 13

Variety, as a teaching strategy, 30

Vaughn, S., 99

Vending machine, as an activity, 210

Victoria University (VU). *See* TESOL postgraduate program

Videos, business presentation course and, 206*t*

Vietnam, 8. *See also* TESOL postgraduate program

Vocabulary development
Advanced Reading and Composition and, 150
garden design project and, 23*t*, 30–31, 36–37, 36*f*, 41–42
study skills program and, 49–50*t*

Voice, freshman composition course and, 171*f*

VU. *See* Victoria University (VU)

Vygotsky, L., 169

W

Wajnryb, R., 185
Wallace, M. J., 58, 66
Warmers, 69, 206*t*. *See also* Action research
Watkins, M., 226, 228, 229, 232, 233*f*, 234
Wenger, E., 26
Wertsch, J., 18
Wharton, J., 2, 6, 8, 12, 262. *See also* TransPacific Hawai'i College (TPHC) program
"Where Have All the Flowers Gone," 187*t*
Wignell, P., 222, 226
Wilcox, E. W., 182*t*
"Will You Still Love Me Tomorrow?," 187*t*
"The Wind," 182*t*
Woodfield, H., 66
Woodward, T., 66
Wright, T., 126
Writing skills
    advanced. *See* Advanced Reading and Composition
    classroom change and, 8, 9
    English for Tourism III (EFT III) and, 124*f*
    freewriting. *See* Freewriting within a curriculum
    for freshmen. *See* Freshman composition course
    garden design project and, 23*t*
    intensive EAP writing course and. *See* Intensive EAP writing course
    process writing and, 100
    TransPacific Hawai'i College (TPHC) program and, 102–104

Y

Yallop, C., 222

Z

Zeichner, K. M., 13–14
Zen Buddhism, 183

Also Available from TESOL

Bilingual Education
Donna Christian and Fred Genesee, Editors

Bridge to the Classroom:
ESL Cases for Teacher Exploration
Joy Egbert and Gina Mikel Petrie

CALL Essentials
Joy Egbert

Communities of Supportive Professionals
Tim Murphey and Kazuyoshi Sato, Editors

Content-Based Instruction in Primary and Secondary School Settings
Dorit Kaufman and JoAnn Crandall, Editors

ESOL Tests and Testing
Stephen Stoynoff and Carol A. Chapelle

Gender and English Language Learners
Bonny Norton and Aneta Pavlenko, Editors

Language Teacher Research in Asia
Thomas S. C. Farrell, Editor

Literature in Language Teaching and Learning
Amos Paran, Editor

More Than a Native Speaker: An Introduction to Teaching English Abroad
revised edition
Don Snow

Perspectives on Community College ESL Series
Craig Machado, Series Editor
Volume 1: Pedagogy, Programs, Curricula, and Assessment
Marilynn Spaventa, Editor
Volume 2: Students, Mission, and Advocacy
Amy Blumenthal, Editor

PreK–12 English Language Proficiency Standards
Teachers of English to Speakers of Other Languages, Inc.

*Planning and Teaching Creatively within a Required Curriculum
for School-Age Learners*
Penny McKay, Editor

Professional Development of International Teaching Assistants
Dorit Kaufman and Barbara Brownworth, Editors

Teaching English as a Foreign Language in Primary School
Mary Lou McCloskey, Janet Orr, and Marlene Dolitsky, Editors

Teaching English From a Global Perspective
Anne Burns, Editor

Technology-Enhanced Learning Environments
Elizabeth Hanson-Smith, Editor

For more information, contact
Teachers of English to Speakers of Other Languages, Inc.
700 South Washington Street, Suite 200
Alexandria, Virginia 22314 USA
Toll Free: 888-547-3369   Fax on Demand: 800-329-4469
Publications Order Line: 888-891-0041
or 301-638-4427 or 4428
9 am to 5 pm, EST

ORDER ONLINE at www.tesol.org/